PRONUNCIATIOI

Articulation an

By

Jeanne VARNEY PLEASANTS

Columbia University

Translated by Esther EGERTON
Head of Department of Romance Languages
High School, Plainfield, N. J.

Eleventh Reprint

1982

Lithographed in U.S.A. by

EDWARDS
BROTHERS
INCORPORATED
2500 SOUTH STATE STREET / ANN ARBOR, MICHIGAN 48104

To my son, Bernard.

INTRODUCTION

This book, written at the request of a great number of
my American pupils at the Institute of Phonetics of the
Sorbonne, is the transcription, in condensed form, of my
teaching both there and elsewhere since 1920. In it I have
incorporated the result of my experience not only with
American students in France, but also as a student myself
at an American University of which I am a graduate, as
well as that of two additional years of residence in the
United States, during which I made a practical study of
the American theory and system of education. I believe,
therefore, that the book will prove useful to American
students of French.

Since making the first draft five years ago, I have in
turn worked on it and laid it aside, making each time that
I took it up some modification--more often than not of a
negative character, that is to say, the omission of por-
tions of the text to the end of greater simplicity. Whenever I found myself confronted by the necessity of treating a complex question such as that of intonation, I tried
to reduce it to its simplest expression by casting aside
everything that was too complicated and elaborate.

Inasmuch as there are several books which study the
question of the pronunciation of French from a historical
or scientific point of view, it seemed useless for me to
add to their number. Limiting myself therefore to the description of sounds and to the explanation of rules which
govern French articulation and intonation, I have omitted
all historical and scientific discussion of the subject
and have sought to give to this book the virtue and value
of immediate utility. For the same reason, I have avoided
as much as possible recourse to phonetic symbols and have
omitted any reference to the phonetic triangle. Here, as
in my oral teaching, I have intended to present a practi-

IV

cal, reliable and simple guide to French pronunciation.

Phonograph records are often of great practical aid to a student of phonetics, especially if he has a good ear. There are now in preparation a series of records designed to accompany the exercises and reading lessons. By their use, a student will be able to compare and check his own pronunciation with that of a French person.

In order to facilitate the use of the book, I have avoided as much as possible both footnotes and reference to material on other pages than the one on which a given subject is discussed, and thus at times I have been obliged to repeat short paragraphs. Very infrequently I have repeated a rule or list, but only when it seemed important that the student should become thoroughly familiar with it.

I have nowhere compared French sounds to English sounds for the purpose of indicating any similarity between them. Inasmuch as the fundamental principles of articulation of the two languages are so very different, it seems unprofitable to attempt to establish even the slightest connection. The only apparent exception which I have permitted myself is in the discussion of the French closed e, which with the greatest caution and from one point of view only I mention with the English short i.

I wish here to express my thanks to the following persons: Dr. WILLIAM RALEIGH PRICE, State Supervisor of Modern Languages of the University of the State of New York, and Monsieur HUBERT PERNOT, Professor at the Sorbonne for their interest in my book; Mademoiselle N. PERNOT, who read a part of the manuscript; my friend, Madame BARA de TOVAR, of the Institute of Phonetics of the Sorbonne, for her tireless patience pitilessly put to the test during the pronunciation aloud of several thousand words; my sister, Mademoiselle LINE VIDON (now Madame Maxime Barret) who formerly gave courses in phonetics at the University of Grenoble (Patronage des Etrangers, and who kindly read part of my manuscript, filling several gaps in my treatment of liaison; Mademoiselle BERTHE des COMBES FAVARD, authority in the matter of teaching pronunciation of our language to Americans, and Monsieur LOUIS CHAPARD, Instructor of French in the University of Michigan, both of whom have shown great interest in the book; my husband, CHARLES E. VARNEY, who read the completed manuscript; and although last, by no means least, my pupil and friend, Miss ESTHER EGERTON, Head of the Department of Romance Languages, Plainfield High School, Plainfield, New Jersey, not only for her translation, but also for many useful suggestions made possible by her comprehension of the needs and difficulties of American students and her practical ex-

perience in teaching. Without her encouragement and assist-
ance I should not have completed the book at this time.

JEANNE VIDON-VARNEY

New York, June, 1932.

The lines above were written in June, 1932. I should
like today, more than a year later, to speak here of my
debt to Monsieur PIERRE FOUCHÉ, Director of the Institute
of Phonetics of the Sorbonne, under whose direction I have
taught during the year just past. I wish especially to
thank him not only for his invaluable advice with regard
to my own studies but also for the privilege of attending
his lectures. As a consequence I have felt the need of
making some modifications in my two chapters on intonation,
in order to follow more closely his method which respects
the truth in all its details.

Plainfield, September, 1933.

TABLE OF CONTENTS

VIII

Classification: voiced, voiceless; plosives,
fricatives, sibilants, hushing consonants,
nasals, laterals or liquids, bi-labials, labio-
dentals, dentals, palatals, uvular.Law of an-
ticipation.Release.p, b, d, t, k, g, f, v, s,
z, ch, ∫; ʒ,ʒ; m, n, gn, ɲ; l; front lingual
rolled r; uvular r; Parisian r.Supplementary
reading exercises.

PART II.

Stress group.Breath-group.Normal stress.Inten-
sity.Musical pitch.Stress for emphasis.Declara-
tive sentences.The rising part.The falling part.
Interrogative sentences.Exclamatory sentences.

Spellings.General considerations.When completely
silent.When pronounced.In monosyllables.Special
observations.

General considerations.Obligatory.Prohibited.
Optional.Change of sound in liaison.

General rule. an, ɑ̃; on, ɔ̃; in, ɛ̃; un, œ̃.

Definition.Regressive.Progressive.

PART III.

LEXICON

X

Chapter I.
PRELIMINARY NOTES

1. PHONETICS. The noun "phonetics," as well as the corresponding adjective "phonetic," will be frequently used in this book. It seems desirable, therefore, to include at the very beginning a short discussion of these words.

For many people the term "phonetics" has an unfortunate signification, since they associate it, though incorrectly, merely with the phonetic symbols--which to them seem dry, artificial, forbidding, dead. In reality, however, the phonetic symbols form only a small portion of this subject. Indeed, from one point of view it would not be incorrect to say that they are not essential to it at all, being merely a part of its nomenclature--convenient, it is true, but not indispensable to the study of the subject in its largest aspect. It will be seen that they play only a small role in the present book.

What then is phonetics? It is the study of the sounds of a language, of the proper way to produce them, to group them, and to stress them, in order to express all our sentiments, all our ideas, our sensations, joys, sorrows, hopes. The oral use of a language is its most important expression. By means of vowels whose timbre may be infinitely varied--sometimes full and rich, sometimes thin and shrill, sometimes deep and sonorous--in turn gay or sad, intense or restrained, by means of consonants at times clearly and rapidly articulated and at others purposely retarded, by means of the ceaseless rise and fall of the voice, we may express to others a thousand shades in the color of our thought.

Is it possible then to say that the subject of phonetics is dry, artificial, dead?...What study could be more living? What, more gracious?

II. USE OF THE PHONETIC ALPHABET. The adjective "phonetic" as applied to a spoken language indicates perfect regularity of agreement between its separate sounds and the alphabet which furnishes the elements of its written expression. That French is not a phonetic language is evident from the following facts:

1. Each separate letter of the alphabet does not always represent a sound, (in the word août, for example, four letters represent only one sound).

2. The same sound may be represented by several different letters (in the words ça, ce, se and nation, the letters ç, c, s, and t are pronounced in the same way).

3. The same letter may represent different sounds (in the words ce and car, the letter c represents the sounds

s and k).

One may easily understand, therefore, in dealing with such a language, the advantage of using an alphabet in which each sound is represented by a single letter or symbol and in which each letter or symbol represents a single sound.

I assume that every advanced student of French understands the significance of the phonetic symbols; but for those who dislike to use them, I have adopted (except for the Exercises for Practice) in the cases where the phonetic symbol and the letter of the ordinary alphabet are not the same for the representation of a given sound, the following arrangement:

For each vowel, I have used (except infrequently in lists of sounds) before the proper phonetic symbol, the letter or group of letters which usually represents that vowel sound in the ordinary alphabet, together with the word closed, open, mute, nasal, posterior or anterior when necessary:

open o, ɔ

For each consonant, I have used (except infrequently in lists of sounds) before the proper phonetic symbol, the letter or group of letters which usually represents that consonant sound in the ordinary alphabet:

ch, ʃ

For this purpose I have used the symbols of the International Phonetic Alphabet, with which most Americans who have taken advanced courses in French are familiar.

Name of sound	Symbol	Example
anterior a	a	patte
posterior a	ɑ	pâte
closed o	o	rose
open o	ɔ	robe
closed e	e	été
open e	ɛ	lait
closed eu	ø	deux
open eu	œ	neuve
ou	u	loup
u	y	du
i	i	lit
mute e	ə	le
on	ɔ̃, õ	mon
an	ɑ̃	dans
in	ɛ̃	fin
un	œ̃	chacun
semi-vowel ou	w	louis
semi-vowel u	ɥ	lui
yod	j	bien, soleil, vieille

Name of sound	Symbol	Example
p	*p*	papa
b	*b*	bébé
t	*t*	ta
d	*d*	dans
k	*k*	quatre
g	*g*	gai
f	*f*	folle
v	*v*	va
s	*s*	son
z	*z*	rose
ch	*ʃ*	chat
j	*3*	juge
m	*m*	maman
n	*n*	nez
gn	*ɲ*	gagne
l	*l*	lit
r	*r*	rien

: indicates that the sound represented by the preceding symbol is long.

:: indicates that the sound represented by the preceding symbol is very long.

' indicates that the following syllable is stressed.

* indicates that the following sound receives the stress for emphasis.

‿ indicates liaison or linking; in a few cases, a nasal vowel.

⌐ indicates that liaison, linking or elision is impossible.

| indicates the end of a stress-group.

‖ indicates the end of a breath-group.

III. GOOD PRONUNCIATION. What is good pronunciation in French?

It would be false to assert that there is only one which is good. Carefully directed and supervised teaching in French schools tends more and more, it is true, to standardise pronunciation; but there still remain many variations, more or less marked, in the speech not only of different regions, but even of different individuals of the same region. That there are not two persons whose pronunciation is exactly the same is as true in France as in any other country.

However, speaking in general terms, one may say that cultivated persons native to a given region all show in their speech habits certain common characteristics. Usually the model recommended to foreigners is that of Paris. But it must be remembered that Paris is not all of France--(far from it!) and that there are several provincial pronunciations which are not only agreeable to the ear but from the

historical point of view, are as good as that of the capi-
tal.

Nevertheless it has seemed to me proper for three rea-
sons to base my discussion of French speech on the Parisian, or rather upon one of the Parisian pronunciations--
first, because this it is that "sets the style in good
pronunciation"; second, because it is beautiful, rich, and
sonorous; and third, because the majority of foreigners
who study in France pass the greater part of their time in
Paris.

But even there one is faced with the necessity of choos-
ing the pronunciation which he wishes to adopt. That of
the uneducated classes is of course out of the question.
Of the two others, one may be called the ultra-modern;
one, the classic (but classic in the French sense, "capable, because of its perfection, of serving as a model").
The former, that of some members of the very young genera-
tion, tends by the law of least resistance to reduce all
vowels to uncertain sounds (which might be called middle,
being neither open nor closed) and to identify two nasals
which are by nature as different as in and un, thus giving
to the pronunciation of our language the effect of something lacking precision, dull, impoverished. The latter
pronunciation is characterized by good taste, by sounds
enunciated clearly but without exaggeration, by sonorous
vowels, whose timbre is clearly open or closed; and it has
preserved as a precious part of its heritage a sound non-
chalantly suppressed by the younger generation--the posterior a, so rich, so deep, so vibrant, capable of suggesting by its beauty and nobility a whole world of senti-
ment, sensations, ideas.

I have chosen the latter.

Chapter II.
THE SPEECH-ORGANS

The speech-organs are divided into two groups:
    A. The movable organs
    B. The immovable organs
A. The movable organs are:
    1. The vocal chords   les cordes vocales
    2. The tongue   la langue
    3. The lips   les levres
    4. The soft palate, of which the tip is called the
        uvula la luette palais
B. The immovable organs are:
    1. The teeth   les dents
    2. The teeth-ridges   l'alvéole

3. The hard palate
4. The nasal cavity *les fosses nasales*

MOVABLE ORGANS

1. VOCAL CHORDS, (fig.1, V.C.). The vocal chords are, in reality, not chords at all, but the edges of the windpipe. They are situated in the larynx. The space between

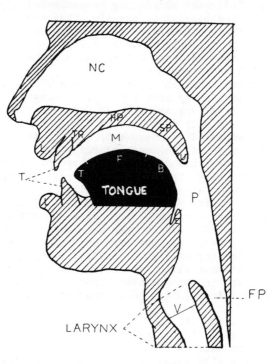

Fig.1-The Organs of Speech.
B Back of tongue. E Epiglottis. F Front of tongue. FP Food passage. HP Hard palate. L Lips. M Mouth. NC Nasal cavity. P Pharynx. SP Soft Palate. T Teeth. TR Teeth ridge. U Uvula. VC Vocal chords.

the vocal chords is called the glottis.

LARYNX, (fig.1, larynx). The larynx is the upper extremity of the passage which permits the release of the air from the lungs to the pharynx. Most people use indifferently, to indicate the same phenomenon, the terms "vibrations of the larynx" and "vibrations of the vocal chords".

PHARYNX, (fig.1, P). The pharynx is the space in the throat which is located immediately behind the mouth, and through which the air passes from the larynx to the mouth or the nose.
POSITION OF THE VOCAL CHORDS. The vocal chords may assume different positions:

    a. The vocal chords may be separated, leaving free passage to the air. They are in this position when we breathe, and also when we make the following sounds: p, t, k, f, s, ʃ. These consonants are called the breathed or voiceless consonants.

    b. The vocal chords may be brought together in such a way that the air, forcing a passage for itself, causes them to open and close with exceedingly rapid but perfectly regular movements. These movements are spoken of as vibrations of the vocal chords and produce musical notes which vary as to their pitch and intensity. They are in this position when we sound the vowels, as well as the following consonants: b, d, g, v, z, ʒ, m, n, l, ɲ, r. These consonants are called voiced consonants.

    c. The vocal chords may be almost completely brought together from one end to the other, leaving only a very narrow opening through which a slight amount of air may pass. They are in this position when we whisper.

2. TONGUE, (fig.1, C). The tongue consists of four parts:

    a. The tip (fig.1, T)
    b. The front part (fig.1, F)
    c. The back part (fig.1, B)
    d. The side-edges, parallel to the molars.

The different parts of the tongue may move with great rapidity and extreme flexibility, thus taking the most varied positions and producing an infinite number of modifications of the sound produced by the vocal chords.

3.LIPS, (fig.1, L). The lips include:

    a. The corners of the mouth
    b. The upper lip
    c. The lower lip

The corners of the mouth may be separated (as for e, i) or brought together (u, o), and the lips may take very different positions. For example, they may be opened vertically (ɑ), opened horizontally (a), completely closed (p,m), or thrust forward (ʃ,ʒ), etc. These different positions modify the sound produced by the vocal chords.

4.SOFT PALATE, (fig.1, S.P.). The soft palate includes:

a. The soft palate, as it is generally understood (fig.1, SP).

b. The uvula or tip (fig.1, U).

The soft palate may be lowered to a greater or less degree, thus leaving an opening which permits the air to pass partially or entirely through the nose ($\tilde{a}, \tilde{o}, \tilde{\epsilon}, \tilde{\infty}$,m,n, ɲ) or it may be raised, so that the entrance to the nasal cavity is completely closed, and the air is thus prevented from passing through the nose but is forced out through the mouth.

IMMOVABLE OR RIGID ORGANS

1.TEETH. The two rows of teeth (upper and lower) include each 4 incisors, 2 canines, 4 pre-molars, and 4 or 6 molars.

2.TEETH-RIDGES, (fig.1, TR). The teeth-ridges are that part of the upper and lower jaws in which are embedded the roots of the teeth.

3.HARD PALATE, (fig.1, HP). The hard palate, called also roof of the mouth, is the part of the palate which is located between the teeth-ridges and the soft palate.

The tip, the side-edges, the front and back parts of the tongue may be brought into contact, to a greater or less degree, either with the teeth, the teeth-ridges, or the hard palate, thus modifying the space in the interior of the mouth, and consequently the sound produced by the vocal chords.

4.NASAL CAVITY, (fig.1, NS). The nasal cavity is the double canal of the nose by which the sound formed by the vocal chords escapes. At the same time the soft palate is lowered sufficiently to permit the entrance of the air.

IMPORTANT REMARK. In speaking French, the soft palate, the lips, and the tongue are much more easily moved, more supple, more flexible than in speaking English. The lips may be thrust far forward or drawn far back. The tongue takes numerous positions which to Americans seem exaggerated; for example, it may be raised much higher either in the rear,(u ,o) or in the front,(e, i, y). It changes position with a rapidity and a flexibility unknown in English.

But the great difference in the articulation of the two languages consists not only in the varied positions which the organs may take, but the extreme suppleness, flexibility and rapidity with which they move. In order to acquire a clear and precise pronunciation it is necessary to do gymnastic exercises for the purpose of giving practice to the muscles of these organs, in the same way in which a violinist trains the muscles of his fingers by exercises which he repeats regularly each day.

Chapter III.
THE FRENCH SYLLABLE

Although the subject of syllabification is to be treated at length in a later chapter, the student before going further, should here understand one of the fundamental principles of division into syllables in French, for this principle has a noticeable effect on pronunciation. Where a **single** consonant separates two vowels, this consonant is sounded with the second vowel, thus forming what is called the regular French syllable: consonant plus vowel. The contrast between the English and French principle of syllable division may be seen by the comparison:

English	French
cap-able	ca-pable
amus-ing	amu-sant

A detailed discussion of the subject of Syllabification will be found in Chapter IX.

Chapter IV.
"THE FRENCH ACCENT"

It may at first thought seem strange that before beginning the study of isolated sounds I stop to consider the problem of intonation--or, as it is popularly known, "the French Accent." I do this because it is by his faults in intonation that a foreigner may be detected in France even more quickly than by his faults in pronunciation, and French people find the former far more shocking to the ear than the latter.

If the student pronounces the reading lessons which have been arranged for each sound, without having any idea of French intonation, he will run the risk of forming incorrect speech-habits from which he will later rid himself only with difficulty. For this reason I take up this subject here, although I do it in a very brief way and use for illustration only declarative sentences, reserving detailed discussion for a later chapter (X).

With the very first French word that the student speaks he may use correct intonation. In what then does it consist? It consists chiefly in two phenomena, which occur not separately but simultaneously--certain syllables are marked by special stress and at the same time by a change of the musical pitch of the voice.

The unit of French speech is not as in English, the grammatical word, but the **stress-group** (groupe rythmique, mot phonétique). This group, it is true, may contain only one grammatical word, but usually it consists of a group

of several words closely related in thought--such as a
noun subject with its modifiers, a pronoun subject with
its verb:

> Venez
> La petite fille│court
> Elle .court
> Jean│ouvre la fenêtre

It is the last pronounced syllable of each stress-group
which is the most important for correct intonation, for it
is there that occur the special stress and the change of
musical pitch mentioned above.

   a. Special stress.
      This stress is marked in two ways:
         1. always by a greater force (intensity)
            given to the whole syllable and more
            particularly to its vowel. This stress
            is called therefore a vowel-stress,
            (accent vocalique).
         2. often by a lengthening of the vowel, as
            will be explained later. (p.20).
         NOTE: Every pronounced syllable of a
            stress-group is clearly sounded with
            equal force and equal duration until
            the last is reached. Then, as has been
            said above, the last syllable receives
            greater force than the preceding one,
            and often is somewhat lengthened. It is
            sometimes said that this French stress
            on the last syllable has no counterpart
            in English. This is not quite true; for
            an approximation of it may be found in
            some English sentences or expressions
            consisting altogether of monosyllables
            or of monosyllables with the exception
            of the last word:
               Here and 'there, to ex'cess
   b. Change of musical pitch; that is, a rising of
      the musical pitch of the voice when the sent-
      ence is not finished or a falling at the end
      of the sentence:
               La petite fille│ court

When the sentence is made up of only one
stress-group there is a rising and a falling
part without any pause whatsoever:

Venez
Elle court

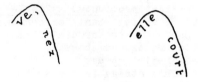

When the sentence is made up of more than two
stress-groups, all those which correspond to a
question, to the expression of expectation, to
the arousing of curiosity and interest, form a
group whose final syllables progressively rise.
This group is spoken of as the rising part of
the sentence. On the other hand, all the
stress-groups which answer the questions pro-
posed in the rising part, thus satisfying expectation, curiosity, and interest, form a
group whose final syllables progressively fall;
and this is known as the falling part. Thus,
in the sentence by A. Daudet,

Monsieur le sous-préfet,‖ grisé de parfums,‖
ivre de musique,‖ essaye vainement de résister |
au nouveau charme | qui l'envahit,‖ we have:

Question: Monsieur le sous-préfet | grisé de
parfums ‖ ivre de musique ‖

Answer: essaye vainement de résister | au
nouveau charme | qui l'envahit.

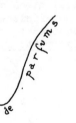

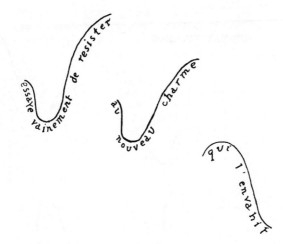

It is mainly in these two facts: <u>special stress</u> (marked
by intensity and duration) and <u>change in the musical pitch</u>
of the voice (marked by falling) that the secret of "the
French Accent" lies.

To these two general laws should be added the four following observations:

    a. the note on which the first syllable of the whole
       sentence is pronounced is rather <u>low</u>.

    b. the rising of the pitch of the vo<u>ice</u> is not ob-
       tained in a monotonously regular ascent but by
       rich internal modulations:

DO NOT SAY:

OR:

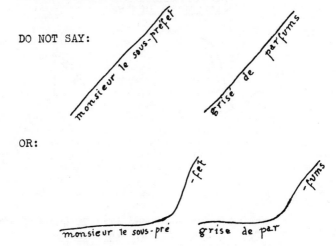

BUT SAY EITHER:

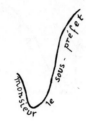

OR:

c. the note of the initial syllable of a stress-
group is always very much lower than the note of
the preceding stressed syllable. Remark in the
following instances the drop of the musical pitch
after <u>fille</u> and after <u>Jean</u>:

La petite fille| court
Jean| ouvre la fenêtre

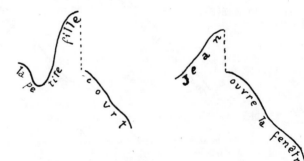

and also (in sentence already quoted) after
-<u>fet</u>, -<u>fums</u>, -<u>sique</u>, -<u>ter</u>, <u>charme</u>:

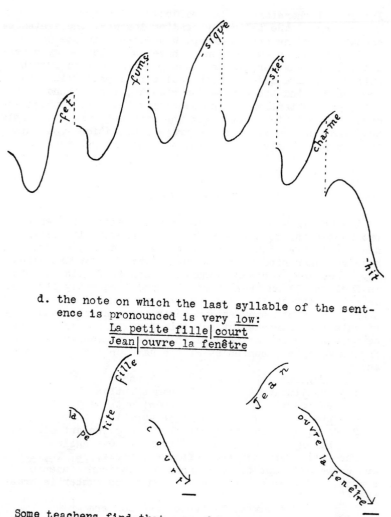

d. the note on which the last syllable of the sentence is pronounced is very <u>low</u>:
   <u>La petite fille|court</u>
   <u>Jean|ouvre la fenêtre</u>

Some teachers find that a useful method in connection
with French intonation is that of counting. It is true
that if one counts rapidly in English: "One, two, three;
one, two, three, four; one, two, three, four, five;" he
has used an approximation of the French intonation, but
only an approximation, because even though the two elements of special stress and change of pitch are present,
there are no internal modulations, these being replaced by
a monotonous rising, and a staccato movement, unusual in

14

French and therefore to be avoided.

In many of the following reading lessons, the sentences contain only one stress-group. When more than one occurs in a sentence or expression, I have so indicated by a vertical line. However, in the passages quoted from French authors, I have made no such indication; preferring that the reader find the groups for himself, for I cannot too often call attention to the necessity that the student accustom himself to determining the stress-group. It is only thus that he can acquire the proper intonation--something that in time and with practice will become habitual.

Chapter V.
THE FRENCH VOWEL

The vowels are the most important element of French pronunciation. To them are due its sonority, its distinctness, its life, its light. Each one, powerful, comprehensive, unhurried, rich, each keeping its own individuality, they are much more important than in English. Whereas in English all unstressed vowels, and frequently stressed as well, (especially i, a, and u) are slurred and indistinct, in French they retain their own qualities and distinguishing characteristics. This fact is evident if one contrasts the following English words and sentences with French words and sentences of the same or similar appearance:

English	French
1. constitution	constitution
president	président
supply	je supplie
2. Discipline is difficult	La discipline est difficile
The animal is agile	L'animal est agile

The three forms of the definite article, le, la, les, are especially apt to be slurred by American students of French, and thus a confusion of gender or number is created:

le livre, la table, les cahiers

French vowels are pure; that is, each vowel represents a single sound, and each vowel is generally pronounced on a single note.

1. EACH VOWEL REPRESENTS A SINGLE SOUND.

It should be remembered that I use here the definition of the term diphthong from the point of view of the phonetician, that is the pronunciation in the same syllable, of two vowels of which one is stronger than the other; and this phenomenon is produced by the movement of one or more of the speech-organs, (tongue, lips, jaw) during the emission of the sound. In French there are no diphthongs.

English	French
a. blow	beau
b. day	des

a. For the vowel sound of English "blow", the lips, at first open as for o are brought together as for ou, u : the tongue, at first slightly raised at the back as for o, is then lifted higher as for ou, u . These two movements take place during the emission of the sound, thus producing a diphthong.

For the vowel sound in French "beau", the lips even before the beginning of the sound, are pushed very far forward, the tongue is lifted a little at the back. The lips and tongue remain completely motionless during the emission of the vowel.

b. For the vowel sound of English "day", the tongue, at first slightly raised as for open e, ε , is raised somewhat more in the front part as for i. This movement takes place during the emission of the sound, thus producing a diphthong.

For the vowel sound in French "des", the tongue, lifted in the front part of the mouth, remains motionless during the emission of the vowel.

NOTE: In passing from one sound to another in these English diphthongs, the lips and tongue move slowly and constantly, thus producing intermediary sounds. This lingering transformation of sound, one of the greatest beauties of the English language, is unknown in modern French. When a French person pronounces two successive vowels they are never in the same syllable but always in two successive syllables, and the movements are extremely rapid.

In French the movements of the different organs are simultaneous and take place before the emission of the sound; they are not successive during the emission. It is only when the position has been taken that the vowel is pronounced, and it is only when the pronunciation has been finished that the speech-organs take either their normal position or the one preparatory to the following sound. The procedure is:

1. preparation
2. pronunciation
3. relaxation or preparation for next sound.

Of course, in ordinary speech all this takes place rapidly, but it is a useful exercise for the student to retard the process in order to study its mechanics. There will be found in connection with the study of each sound an exercise for practice which should be done slowly at the beginning and before a mirror so that the student may compel his speech-organs to remain motionless during the pronunciation of each vowel.

2. EACH VOWEL IS PRONOUNCED ON A SINGLE NOTE.

(To this statement there are only exceedingly rare exceptions). Many American students of French, when speaking to a lady some distance away for the purpose of attracting her attention, say "Madame", singing the last syllable on several notes:

ma da⌒me

In French, however long the vowel may be (and in this case it is never as long as in English), it is pronounced on a single note:

ma — da — me

NOTE: The student should not confuse the terms "different note" (change in pitch) and "different sound" (change in articulation).

Several factors combine to give the French vowel all its characteristics. The chief ones to be studied are the following:

1. the flexibility of the tongue
2. the groove formed lengthwise in the tongue
3. the flexibility of the lips
4. the movements of the jaw
5. the separation of the teeth
6. the "attack" or beginning of the vowel.

1. THE FLEXIBILITY OF THE TONGUE. The tongue is supple, active, rapid in its movements. The tongue of most Americans is almost inactive, relaxed, incapable of elasticity, loath to assume extreme positions. It must be trained, and successful training can be accomplished only by regularly repeated exercises which by daily gymnastics will make the articulation smooth.

2. THE GROOVE FORMED LENGTHWISE IN THE TONGUE. The tongue is divided through the center by an axis. For the articulation of the vowels, the tongue is lifted or depressed on both sides of this axis, and forms a groove from back to front by which the air, already set in motion by the vocal chords, may escape freely. If this groove is obstructed at any point, the vowel is indistinct and dull.

3. THE FLEXIBILITY OF THE LIPS. The lips play a very important part in the articulation. Americans find great difficulty in separating the lips from the gums and are obliged to make a real effort in order to learn to push the lips forward, to move them with suppleness and rapidity. Exercises such as:

i, u, i, y, i, u, i, y

will give to the lips this necessary flexibility. Furthermore, it is both lips which must be supple. Many Americans, while moving the lower lip sufficiently, keep the upper motionless.

4. THE MOVEMENTS OF THE JAW. Abrupt jerks of the jaw are to be avoided. The movements must be gentle. When the jaw is lowered for an open vowel, it should not be raised again immediately, as is often done by Americans, but only after the vowel has been pronounced with all the richness of timbre which characterizes it.

5. THE SEPARATION OF THE TEETH. Many students keep the jaws too close together and clench the teeth. In French the teeth are never clenched, even for the sounds during which they must be very close together, such as e, i. Otherwise the air could not pass freely.

6. THE "ATTACK" OR BEGINNING OF THE VOWEL. Contrary to the procedure in English, the "attack" or beginning of the French vowel is very gentle, --it begins by little vibrations which increase in size. One may represent in graphic form the English vowel as follows:

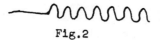

Fig.2

whereas the French vowel, so represented, is as follows:

Fig.3

In English, the vowel dies away; in French, it increases in vigor. (This increase takes place without movement of the speech-organs and without change in pitch).

If the student thoroughly understands and accepts the statements in the preceding pages and if he carefully studies the position of the speech-organs for each sound, he will discover that what is necessary is not an extraordinary effort of the muscles, but an extraordinary flexibility. If the organs are in their exact position, the muscles having been properly trained by means of the practice exercises, the effort will be scarcely noticeable. One should avoid the appearance of any effort or exaggeration and especially of any stiffness of the muscles. These, I cannot repeat too often, should be flexible and not strained.

When, in giving the position for the vowels, I use the word "tense", the student should remember that it means "not relaxed". It does not mean "strained".

It should never be forgotten that "a correct pronunciation is the result of the proper training of the muscles of the speech-organs." The American student must acquire a "new set of pronunciation-habits." (Knowles and Favard).

Chapter VI.
THE VOWELS

In this chapter, as well as in the two following, the purpose of which is to give to the pupil the clearest possible indication of the way to produce the separate sounds of French speech, I have made use not only of careful directions for the position of the speech organs, but also of various devices.

FIGURES. It has not been possible to include in this experimental edition the photographs and drawings of the original manuscript, about two hundred in number. They will, however, appear in the definitive edition. Within a few months, plates showing these figures may be obtained from the author. Similarly, many illustrative words and expressions, which have been omitted both in the text and in the lexicon, will be included in the definitive edition.

EXERCISES FOR PRACTICE. For each sound, I have arranged exercises intended to make the muscles of the tongue, lips, or the soft palate more flexible. It is only by daily repitition of these exercises that the pupil can acquire a good pronunciation. They may be compared to the finger training exercises of a student of the piano or violin; although often requiring not only an exaggeration but also a retardation of movement, they are intended to enable the student to move his speech-organs later with much greater flexibility and rapidity. They should be done before a mirror, for in no other way can the student have an accurate idea of the position of his speech-organs. No amount of theory by itself can compare in usefulness to theory reinforced by careful daily practice.

READING EXERCISES. For each sound I have composed also a reading exercise. Avoiding as much as possible long lists of isolated words, I have preferred to combine in short sentences or groups of words several examples of the sound under consideration, for thus of course it is most often found in speech. In addition, the student will find short paragraphs from our best French prose writers and poets, selections which are read in American High Schools and Colleges. In these paragraphs I have underlined the spelling of the sound studied.

VOCABULARY. By far the greater number of words employed in the reading exercises were selected from text-books for beginners; to these I have added others easy to understand because of the fact that they exist in the same or a similar form in English but with a different pronunciation, together with a considerable number of simple current expressions. It is only in rare instances that, in order to illustrate certain rules for which there are no well-known examples, I have used words which are scientific or somewhat unusual. In Part III, my lists of different spellings for each sound are complete.

MISTAKES TO BE AVOIDED. In order to combat incorrect tendencies which may have become habitual to Americans accustomed to speaking French, as well as to anticipate and make impossible the acquisition of such habits by beginners, I have inserted, at the foot of each page treating with a sound, a list of mistakes in articulation which Americans are especially prone to make. This list, arranged with the greatest care, is the result of observation through a long teaching experience.

Of course the technical explanations for the position of different organs are intended especially for students who have no "ear", or for those who, having a very delicate "ear", have never enjoyed the opportunity of studying oral French with a French person. It is hoped, too, that teachers may here find a model for their explanations of the speech phenomena, even though they may wish to simplify them in their own work.

CLASSIFICATION OF THE VOWELS

The vowels are classified as open, closed, and nasal; in addition to these three groups there are three other vowels of which one is said to be posterior and one anterior, and the mute e.

I have not followed the order generally adopted in treating the vowels. I have begun with the two a's, because when pronouncing these vowels the tongue may be said to be in a neutral position, which is very easy to take, and because they may be classed neither among the closed nor among the open. Next I have taken up the closed vowels, starting with the one for which the tongue is drawn back the farthest and proceeding to the one for which it is advanced the farthest. Then I have treated the open vowels, proceeding in the same way as for the closed, then the mute e; lastly, I have discussed the nasal vowels.

1. ANTERIOR A, a. Anterior a is so called because its point of articulation is in the <u>front</u> or <u>anterior</u> part of the mouth.

2. POSTERIOR A, ɑ. Posterior a is so called because its point of articulation is in the <u>back</u> or <u>posterior</u> part of the mouth.

3. CLOSED VOWELS. There are six closed vowels, so call-

ed because during their pronunciation the jaws are fairly close together and the contact between the tongue and the palate is very marked. These vowels, starting with the one whose point of articulation is farthest back in the mouth and proceeding to the one of which it is the farthest forward, are:

$$u,o,e,\varnothing,i,y$$

4. OPEN VOWELS. The open vowels are so called because for their pronunciation the lower jaw is dropped (the mouth is open); consequently, the contact of the tongue with the hard palate is less marked than in the case of the corresponding closed vowels. They are, starting with the one whose point of articulation is farthest back:

$$ɔ,ɛ,œ$$

5. NASAL VOWELS AND MUTE E. I shall treat nasal vowels and the mute e at a later point.

It must not be supposed that these vowels mentioned above are the only ones which exist in French, for there is really a far greater number. In the case of a French woman whose pronunciation is the most cultivated that I have ever had the privilege of hearing, I have noted no less than eight a's! And nearly as great a range is distinguishable in her other vowels. But I feel that it is sufficient to limit my teaching to two a's, two o's, two e's, two eu's, one ou, one u, one i, four nasals and the mute e. When the pupil can pronounce these vowels perfectly, according each one the timbre, the amplitude, the richness that combine to give it beauty, he may feel that he has accomplished a great deal.

DURATION

Stressed vowels are long when they are placed before the following sounds or groups of sounds: r, ʒ, z, v, vr.

Posterior a, ɑ, is long when it is placed before one or more sounded consonants.

In other positions, the vowels are short.

In order to facilitate the handling of the book I have
adopted a somewhat unusual arrangement. The student will
find on each even page the description of the position tak-
en by the various speech-organs in the production of a giv-
en sound, together with a warning against certain mistakes
which an American is especially prone to make. On the opposite page, the odd, he will find exercises for practice,
and reading lessons. Additional exercises will be found at
the end of the chapter. The student should of course make
an effort to master one sound before attempting another.

ANTERIOR A, *a*

TONGUE {
TIP: touching and even protruding beyond lower teeth.
BACK AND FRONT: fairly free, flat. Whole tongue placed higher in mouth than for posterior a, *ɑ*.
MUSCLES: relaxed.

LIPS {
CORNERS OF MOUTH: in normal position.
OPENING: horizontal.
MUSCLES: not very tense.

TEETH   Space between upper and lower teeth: 3/4 inch.

AVOID

1. Raising front part of tongue too high: (whence sound resembling open e, *ɛ*).
2. Separating jaws too widely.
3. Slurring of _a_ in the article _la_, and in unstressed syllables.
4. Giving nasal quality, when placed before m, n, or gn, *ɲ*

POSTERIOR A, *ɑ*

TONGUE {
TIP: flattened, behind lower teeth, touching them.
BACK: slightly raised. {Whole tongue placed lower
FRONT: flat.   {in mouth than for anterior a.
MUSCLES: fairly tense.

LIPS {
CORNERS OF MOUTH: in same place as in normal position.
OPENING: vertical.
MUSCLES: relaxed.

TEETH   Space between upper and lower teeth: 3/4 inch.

AVOID

1. Raising back of tongue too high.
2. Relaxing muscles of tongue too much.
3. Separating lips too little.
4. Pronouncing with nasal quality when before m, n, or gn, *ɲ*.

FOR PRACTICE. Before mirror.

TO TRAIN TONGUE, LIPS, AND JAW TO REMAIN MOTIONLESS:
Pronounce a as long as possible, taking care to have mouth
wide open. Repeat several times.

a
à

READING LESSON

SHORT. La, ma, sa, là, tabac.
chat. J'ai mal à l'estomac.
J'ai du tabac| dans ma taba-
tière. La femme| et le chat.
Le Carnaval de Venise. A bon
chat,| bon rat. Elle a du
tact. La table| de la salle.
Evidemment. Prudemment. Solennel. (solanɛl)
LONG. La part| du barbare. Il
est tard. C'est rare. J'a-
chète| du lard. C'est dom-
mage. Elle a mis du fard.
SHORT AND LONG. Papa| a à al-
ler dans le Var. A la| barre,
l'avocat parle. Le tabac| lui
fait mal à l'estomac. Il va
à la gare.

Elle lava la vaisselle,
usant ses ongles roses sur
les poteries grasses et le
fond des casseroles. Elle
savonna le linge sale, les
chemises et les torchons
qu'elle faisait sécher sur
une corde; elle descendit
à la rue chaque matin, les
ordures, et monta l'eau,
s'arrêtant à chaque étage
pour souffler. (Maupassant)

"Oui! mais s'il est sage,
Sur son doux visage
La Vierge se penchera,
Et longtemps lui parlera."
(Desbordes-Valmore)

avoir à + infinitive
J'ai à vous parler.

FOR PRACTICE. Before mirror.

TO TRAIN LIPS AND TONGUE: a, a, a, a, a, a
Do not pronounce while moving tongue or lips. Pronounce
only when they are in position.

â, a+s

READING LESSON

SHORT. Bas, las, trois, ah!
cas. En tous cas. Il est las.
Ils sont trois. Le roi| donne
la croix. Il croît.
LONG. Pâte, câble, vase,
fable, phrase. Le gros câble.
La flamme jaunâtre. Une belle
âme. La fable de l'âne. Il se
fâche. Elle est lâche.
SHORT AND LONG. Il a trois
ânes. Le bas du cadre. Jac-
ques| habite un château| à
Blois. Le roi| est las et pâle.
POSTERIOR AND ANTERIOR A.
Mât, ma. Mâtin, matin.
Châsse, chasse. Mâle, malle.
Pâte, patte. Grâce, trace.
Madame| est pâle. Jacques|
passe par là.

Nous mangeons dans la première salle, au milieu de
gens très râpés, très af-
famés, qui raclent leurs as-
siettes silencieusement.-Ce
sont presque tous des hommes
de lettres, me dit Jacques
à voix basse. (Daudet).
Il faisait un froid à fendre
les dolmens, un de ces
froids déchirants qui cas-
sent la peau...(Maupassant)

Elle brame
Comme une âme
Qu'une flamme
Toujours suit.

(Victor-Hugo)

la vase = la boue
le vase = pour les fleurs

OU, *u*

TONGUE { TIP: behind ridge of lower incisors.
BACK: raised in direction of junction of hard and soft palate.
MUSCLES: tense.

LIPS { LIPS: very rounded, pushed forward.
CORNERS OF MOUTH: brought forward, held tense.
OPENING: horizontal rather than vertical.
MUSCLES: tense.

TEETH   Space between upper and lower teeth: 1/10 inch.

AVOID

1. Raising tongue too much in front of mouth and not enough in back.
2. Relaxing muscles too much.
3. Moving lips or tongue while pronouncing vowel.
4. Throwing lips forward insufficiently.
5. Changing tone while pronouncing vowel.

CLOSED O, *o*

TONGUE { TIP: brought back farther than for ou, *u*; consequently, not touching ridge of lower incisors.
BACK: raised in rear of mouth, not as much as for ou, *u*, and touching hard palate on both sides in region of last molars.
MUSCLES: tense.

LIPS { LIPS: pushed very far forward.
CORNERS OF MOUTH: brought forward, held very tense.
OPENING: slight, horizontal.
MUSCLES: tense.

TEETH   Space between upper and lower teeth: 1/4 inch.

AVOID

1. Moving tongue while pronouncing: (whence diphthong:o-*u*).
2. Relaxing muscles too much.
3. Moving lips and lower jaw.
4. Changing tone while pronouncing.

FOR PRACTICE. Before mirror. *ou*
TO TRAIN TONGUE, LIPS, AND JAW TO REMAIN MOTIONLESS.
Pronounce *u* as long as possible without stopping. Repeat
several times.

READING LESSON

SHORT. Sou, doux, loup, bout, fou. J'ai un sou. Elle coud. Tu joues. La roue de l'auto. Le Doubs| est une rivière. Il est jaloux. Tout d'un coup. Le clown du cirque. LONG. Bouge, rouge, Louvre, douze. La robe| est rouge. Elle est jalouse. Ils sont douze. Je vais à Tours. Il ferme| la porte du Louvre. Il lit toujours. Elle bouge. SHORT AND LONG. La nounou| la trouve| sur la pelouse. |Tout d'un coup,| elle l'ouvre.

hanny

D'heure en heure on se disait: "Maintenant, ils sont à Eyguières, maintenant, au Paradou". Puis, tout à coup, vers le soir, un grand cri: "Les voilà!" et là-bas, au lointain nous voyons le troupeau s'avancer dans une gloire de poussière. Toute la route semble marcher avec lui. (Daudet)

  Comme un bruit de foule,
Qui tonne et qui roule,
Et tantôt s'écoule
Et tantôt grandit.
    (Victor Hugo)

FOR PRACTICE. Before mirror. *O+S*
TO TRAIN TONGUE: *u, o, u, o, u, o* *^*
Do not move lips. Do not pronounce while moving tongue. *O*
Pronounce only when in position. *eau*
READING LESSON
au

SHORT. Eau, pot, pôle, sauce, trop. Il est tôt. Il est sot. Il fait beau. Le chat| fait le gros dos. Le pain chaud. Il lui faut de l'eau. "Allô!.| Allô!..." LONG. Sauge, rose, pause, mauve, chose. La sauge| est une plante. J'ai quelque chose. C'est une rose. Sa veste est mauve. Elle pause. Le pauvre. SHORT AND LONG. L'eau chaude| est dans le pot rose. Voici un pauvre.| Toto ôte son chapeau| et lui fait l'aumône. CLOSED O AND OU, *u*. Dos, doux, sot, sou, rôt, roux, tôt, tout. L'eau bout.

...et quand il était là-haut, assis au bon soleil, sa mule près de lui, ses cardinaux tout autour, étendus aux pieds des souches, il faisait déboucher un flacon de vin de son cru, --ce beau vin, couleur de rubis qui s'est appelé depuis le Chateau-Neuf des Papes, -et il le dégustait par petits coups, en regardant sa vigne d'un air attendri. (Daudet)

  La voix plus haute
Semble un grelot, *bell (small)*
D'un nain qui saute
C'est le galop;
    (Victor-Hugo)

ʃ
e
-er
-ez

CLOSED E, e

TONGUE
- TIP: behind lower incisors, touching them.
- SIDE-EDGES: raised behind upper incisors and canines, touching pre-molars.
- MUSCLES: tense.

LIPS
- LIPS: showing front teeth.
- CORNERS OF MOUTH: in normal position.
- MUSCLES: tense.

TEETH — Space between upper and lower teeth: 1/4 inch.

AVOID

1. Moving tongue while pronouncing.(whence diphthong: e-i).
2. Raising side-edges of tongue insufficiently.
3. Relaxing or stiffening muscles too much.
4. Uncovering front teeth too little.
5. Drawing corners of mouth too far apart.
6. Changing tone while pronouncing.
7. Exaggerating movements or tension.
8. Inserting the sound of yod, *j*,between a closed e and a following vowel in the same word, unless yod is written in the word;

créer	*kreje*	for	*kree*
océan	*osejã*	"	*oseã*
Européen	*œropejɛ̃*	"	*œropeɛ̃*

CLOSED EU, ø

TONGUE
- TIP: as for closed e:behind lower incisors, touching them.
- SIDE-EDGES: as for closed e:raised behind upper incisors and canines, touching pre-molars.
- MUSCLES: as for closed e: tense.

LIPS
- LIPS: as for ou, *u*: very rounded, pushed forward.
- CORNERS OF MOUTH: brought forward, held tense.
- OPENING: slight, horizontal.
- MUSCLES: tense.

TEETH — Space between upper and lower teeth: 1/4 inch.

AVOID

1. Raising side-edges of tongue insufficiently.
2. Placing tip too far back, not touching lower incisors.
3. Relaxing muscles.
4. Separating lips too much without pushing them forward sufficiently.
5. Placing resonance in throat. Pronouncing on too low a note.

NOTE: In order to pronounce a clear closed eu, ø, try to pronounce a French closed e but with lips pushed forward and rounded.

ꞋeꞋ
-er
-ez

FOR PRACTICE. Before mirror.

TO TRAIN LIPS AND TONGUE: e, o, e, o, e, o
Do not move jaw. Do not pronounce while moving lips and
tongue. Pronounce only when in position. (The position of
the speech-organs in French closed e and English short i,
as well as the sound, is approximately the same.)

READING LESSON

[vɛty]

Tes, mes, les, ces, nez,
bébé, thé. Les bébés|sont
gais. J'ai du thé. Le nez|de
la poupée. Nous avons deux
pieds. Je vais les donner.
J'irai chez l'épicier. L'hé-
rédité. Vous aimez les pou-
pées. Ces bébés|sont nés|
l'été passé. L'hérésie|a été
condamnée. La bonté et la
beauté|sont deux qualités.
J'ai des rosiers. Les
cerisiers et les pommiers|
sont des arbres fruitiers.

Et, vêtue comme une femme
du peuple, elle alla chez
le fruitier, chez l'épicier,
chez le boucher, le panier
au bras, marchandant, inju-
riée, défendant sou à sou
son misérable argent. Il
fallait chaque mois, payer
des billets, en renouveler
d'autres, obtenir du temps.

factures (Maupassant)

FOR PRACTICE. Before mirror.
I. TO TRAIN LIPS: e, ø, e, ø, e, ø
Do not move tongue or jaw. Do not pronounce while moving
lips. Pronounce only in position.
II. TO TRAIN TONGUE: ø, u, ø, u, ø, u
Do not move lips or jaw. Do not pronounce while moving
tongue. Pronounce only when in position.

READING LESSON

SHORT. Deux, peu, veut, jeu,
ceux, oeufs. Je veux deux
oeufs. Elle veut le cahier
bleu. Eugène jeûne. Les mal-
heureux|sont très nombreux.
Il est veule. Il beugle. bellow/low
coward
LONG. Je suis malheureuse.
Elle est affreuse. Tu es heureuse. Il va à Maubeuge.
SHORT AND LONG. Je veux
qu'Eugénie|soit heureuse. Il
a deux boeufs|dans la Meuse.
CLOSED E, e AND CLOSED EU, ø.
Nez, noeud, des, deux, mes,
meus, ces, ceux, fée, feu.

J'ai charge d'âmes, et je
veux, je veux vous sauver
de l'abîme où vous êtes
tous en train de rouler
tête première...Demain lun-
di, je confesserai les
vieux et les vieilles. Ce
n'est rien...Jeudi, les
hommes. Nous couperons
court...Samedi, le meunier!
...Et si dimanche nous avons
fini, nous serons bien heureux.

(Daudet)

I, *i*

TONGUE	TIP: as for closed e: behind lower incisors, touching them. SIDE-EDGES: raised behind upper incisors a little more than for closed e and touching canines and part of incisors. MUSCLES: as for closed e: tense.
LIPS	LIPS: as for closed e: showing front teeth. CORNERS OF MOUTH: as for closed e: drawn apart. MUSCLES: as for closed e: tense.
TEETH	Space between upper and lower teeth: 1/4 inch.

AVOID

1. Relaxing tongue too much.
2. Raising side-edges of tongue insufficiently.
3. Uncovering front teeth insufficiently.
4. Drawing corners of mouth too far apart.
5. Stiffening muscles.

U, *y*

TONGUE	TIP: as for i: behind lower incisors, touching them. SIDE-EDGES: as for i: raised behind upper incisors, touching canines and part of incisors. MUSCLES: as for i: tense.
LIPS	LIPS: very rounded, pushed forward. CORNERS OF MOUTH: brought forward; tense. OPENING: slight, horizontal. MUSCLES: tense.
TEETH	Space between upper and lower teeth: 1/4 inch.

AVOID

1. Moving tongue while pronouncing (whence two sounds: $j+y$)
2. Raising side-edges insufficiently.
3. Relaxing muscles.
4. Opening lips too wide; pushing them insufficiently forward.

NOTE: In order to pronounce a clear u, y, try to pronounce a French i, but with lips pushed forward and rounded.

FOR PRACTICE. Before mirror.
TO TRAIN TONGUE: e, i, e, i, e, i
Do not move lips. Do not pronounce while moving tongue.
Pronounce only when in position.

READING LESSON

ivre

SHORT. Dis, y, si, ni, ami, ceci, lit. Je dis merci|à Marie. Ni lui ni elle|n'a fini. Il lui dicte|une lettre. Il est triste. Prix unique. Six vitres. Dix pipes. La petite fille.
LONG. Il ouvre le livre. Il faut vivre. La lyre|qu'il a prise. Le rire|de l'homme ivre. Sur la rive. La frise grise.
SHORT AND LONG. La discipline| est difficile. La petite *shutter* fille. Il tire le brise-bise. *draught-protector* Il lit|dans le livre. Ils lui disent| de finir.

Tout le petit bois conspire pour l'empêcher de composer son discours...Monsieur le sous-préfet, grisé de parfums, ivre de musique, essaye vainement de résister au nouveau charme qui l'en- *leans on elbows* vahit. Il s'accoude sur *unhooks* l'herbe, dégrafe son bel *stammers* habit, balbutie encore deux ou trois fois: -Messieurs et chers administrés...Messieurs et chers admi...

(Daudet)

FOR PRACTICE. Before mirror.
I. TO TRAIN LIPS: i, y, i, y, i, y
Do not move tongue or jaw; for y push lips forward as rapidly as possible. Do not pronounce while moving lips. Pronounce only when in position.
II. TO TRAIN TONGUE: u, y, u, y, u, y
Do not move lips or jaw; for y raise front part of tongue very quickly forward. Do not pronounce while moving tongue.

READING LESSON

SHORT. Une, vue, du, rue, plus, tube. La tulipe|que j'ai vue. La musique russe. Tu sculptes une statue. Il a vendu|une plume. J'ai eu|une urne.
LONG. Juge, use, sur, pur, mur, cure. Le juge l'accuse. La robe s'use. La ruse du juge. Sur le mur. Tu es sûre.
SHORT AND LONG. Il accuse le rustre. La statue|est près du mur. Une rue du Vaucluse. Tu uses la plume.

Plus de dix fois, je ne mens pas, Gringoire, elle força le loup à reculer pour reprendre haleine. Pendant ces trèves d'une minute, la gourmande cueillait en hâte encore un brin de sa chère herbe; puis elle retournait au combat, la bouche pleine...-Oh! pourvu que je tienne jusqu'à l'aube...L'une après l'autre, les étoiles s'éteignirent. (Daudet)

user - to use up/wear out

OPEN O, ɔ

TONGUE {
TIP: flattened; touching lower teeth.
BACK: raised less than for closed o; but slightly more raised than for posterior a, ɑ.
FRONT: depressed.
MUSCLES: tense.
}

LIPS {
CORNERS OF MOUTH: drawn slightly forward.
OPENING: vertical.
MUSCLES: relaxed.
}

TEETH   Space between upper and lower teeth: 5/8 inch.

AVOID

1. Raising front part of tongue too high (whence sound of open eu, œ).
2. Flattening back of tongue (whence sound of posterior a, ɑ).
3. Rounding lips insufficiently.
4. Giving nasal quality, when placed before m, n, or gn, ɲ.

OPEN E, ɛ

TONGUE {
TIP: behind lower incisors, touching them.
SIDE-EDGES: raised behind pre-molars, touching them.
MUSCLES: not very tense.
}

LIPS {
CORNERS OF MOUTH: drawn fairly far apart.
OPENING: horizontal rather than vertical.
MUSCLES: relaxed.
}

TEETH   Space between upper and lower teeth: 1/2 inch.

AVOID

1. Raising front part of tongue insufficiently.
2. Moving tongue forward (whence diphthong: e-i).
3. Separating jaws insufficiently.
4. Stiffening muscles.

FOR PRACTICE. Before mirror.

I. TO TRAIN JAW, LIPS, AND TONGUE: o, ɔ, o, ɔ, o, ɔ
For open o, ɔ, lower jaw and open lips as rapidly as pos-
sible. Do not pronounce while moving jaw, lips, and tongue.
Pronounce only when in position.

II. TO TRAIN TONGUE AND LIPS: a, o, a, o, a, o
Do not change position of lower jaw. Do not pronounce
while moving tongue and lips. Pronounce only when in position.

III. TO TRAIN TONGUE: o, a, o, a, o, a
Do not move lips or jaw. Do not pronounce while moving
tongue. Pronounce only when in position.

READING LESSON

SHORT. Robe, globe, ode, sol, Il était une fois un homme
code. La robe|est à la mode. qui avait une cervelle d'or;
La somme|est sur la note. oui, madame, une cervelle
L'homme|donne une pomme. toute en or. Lorsqu'il vint
LONG. Il a tort. Il est mort. au monde, les médecins
Tu dors. Laure sort. Le doge pensaient que cet enfant ne
a une toge. La loge. box "at opera vivrait pas...Il vécut ce-
SHORT AND LONG. Paul|ouvre la pendant et grandit au so-
porte de la loge. Paul| dort‖ leil comme un beau plant
et Laure|s'endort. d'olivier. (Daudet)

FOR PRACTICE. Before mirror.

I. TO TRAIN TONGUE: a, ɛ, a, ɛ, a, ɛ
Do not move lips or jaw. Do not pronounce while moving
tongue. Pronounce only when in position.

II. TO TRAIN JAW AND MUSCLES OF TONGUE: e, ɛ, e, ɛ, e, ɛ
For open e, ɛ, drop lower jaw as rapidly as possible and
relax muscles of tongue. Do not pronounce while moving
jaw. Pronounce only when in position.

READING LESSON

SHORT. Mais, c'est laid, Madame Loisel semblait
fait, belle. Il se tait. Vous vieille maintenant. Elle
faites une lettre. Le geste| était devenue la femme
est ferme. forte et dure et rude, des
LONG. Terre, seize, neige. ménages pauvres. Mal
J'ai vu son père. C'est le il neige peignée, avec les jupes de
seize. Il tombe de la neige. travers et les mains rouges
Son frère|est sur la chaise. elle parlait haut, lavait à
SHORT AND LONG. Pierre|pas- grande eau les planchers.
sait près de la scène. Esther| Mais, parfois...elle s'as-
est avec Madeleine. Le père seyait auprès de la fenêtre,
d'Esther|viendra le seize. et elle songeait à ce bal
ANTERIOR A AND OPEN E. Mal, où elle avait été si belle
mêle. Balle, belle. et si fêtée. (Maupassant)

OPEN EU, œ

TONGUE
{ TIP: behind lower teeth, touching them.
SIDE-EDGES: as for open e, ɛ: raised behind upper
pre-molars, touching them.
MUSCLES: rather tense.

LIPS
{ CORNERS OF MOUTH: drawn forward more than for
open e, ɛ.
OPENING: vertical, lower lip covering lower teeth.
MUSCLES: relaxed.

TEETH   Space between upper and lower teeth: 5/8 inch.

AVOID
1. Flattening tongue (whence sound resembling mute e).
2. Rounding lips insufficiently.
3. Separating jaws insufficiently.
4. Pronouncing in a colorless manner, because of the fact
   that muscles are too relaxed.
5. Placing resonance in throat.

MUTE E, ə

TONGUE
{ TONGUE: completely flat.
TIP: rounded, behind lower teeth.
MUSCLES: absolutely relaxed.

LIPS
{ CORNERS OF MOUTH: in normal position.
OPENING: slight.
MUSCLES: absolutely relaxed.

TEETH   Space between upper and lower teeth: 1/3 inch.

AVOID

1. Placing tongue too high (whence sound resembling u in
   English word but).
2. Opening mouth too much or too little.
3. Placing resonance in throat.
4. Slurring of e especially in le, article.

(The subject of retaining or omitting mute e,
ə , under different circumstances, is fully
discussed in Chapter XI).

FOR PRACTICE. Before mirror.

I. TO TRAIN LIPS: ε, œ, ε, œ, ε, œ

Do not move jaw or tongue. Do not pronounce while moving lips. Pronounce only when in position.

II. TO TRAIN LIPS AND LOWER JAW: ø, œ, ø, œ, ø, œ

Separate lips and drop jaw as rapidly as possible. Do not pronounce while moving lips and jaw. Pronounce only when in position.

READING LESSON

SHORT. Seul, neuf, jeune, boeuf, peuple. Il est seul. Le jeune peuple. La feuille de papier. La jeune fille. Le petit oeuf. LONG. Coeur, heure, neuve, soeur, fleuve. Elle pleure. C'est le bonheur. Sa soeur a peur. Elle a des malheurs. SHORT AND LONG. La jeune fil-le|cueille une fleur. Ma soeur|a grand'peur.

...L'éducation du coeur se fait par les mères et tu connais la mienne...Elle a fait de moi un piocheur, un savant. La science a rempli ma vie. Tu en as été le seul repos, le seul sourire, la seule jeunesse (Pailleron). Un coeur neuf, c'est comme une maison neuve, ce ne sont pas les vrais loca-taires qui essuient les plâtres... (Pailleron)

FOR PRACTICE. Before mirror.

TO TRAIN TONGUE AND LIPS: 1. ø, ə, ø, ə, ø, ə

Do not pronounce while moving tongue or lips. Pronounce only when in position.

2. œ, ə, œ, ə, œ, ə

Do not pronounce while moving tongue, lips, and jaw. Pronounce only when in position.

READING LESSON

STRESSED. Dis-le. Prends-le.. ...et que, sur ce, et ce. Ces poèmes sont de...? Ne viens pas. Redis-lui. Debout les morts. Le|est masculin. Ce,| adjectif démonstratif. De,| préposition. Me,| te,| se,| sont des pronoms.
UNSTRESSED, (but clearly pro-nounced). Il me l'a dit. Il te voit. Il me parle. Brusque-ment. Librement. Justement. Proprement. Semblablement. Terriblement. Parlement. Humblement. Noblement. Vous aimeriez. La chaise de mon frère.

Je te dis encore toi parce que nous sommes seuls, mais tout à l'heure, devant le monde, ce sera: vous, tout le temps: vous. La comtesse de Céran m'a fait l'honneur de m'inviter à lui présenter ma jeune femme et à passer quelques jours à son châ-teau de Saint-Germain. Or, le salon de Madame de Céran est un des trois ou quatre salons les plus influents de Paris...Tout dépend d'el-le, de nous, de toi!

(Pailleron)

minimal pairs

SUPPLEMENTARY READING EXERCISES

I. OU AND CLOSED O.
u, o

Dos, doux, sot, sou, rôt,
roux, tôt, tout. L'eau bout.
Le gros pot| est lourd. Les
roues de l'auto| roulent sur
la route. La nounou| ôte le
chapeau| et la blouse de Toto.
Au mois d'août| il fait chaud.
Les douze apôtres. Le toutou
et Toto| sautent sur la pe-
louse. La choucroute| est sur
le fourneau. Le nouveau cou-
teau. Les rouleaux de jour-
naux| sont de l'autre côté.

II. CLOSED E AND I.
e, i

Fée, fit; des, dis; ces, si;
nez, ni; les, lis; ré, ri;
bée, bis, mes, mis. Félicité
et Lili| y ont été. Discipli-
nez-les. J'ai fini| de répéter
les poésies. Emilie| les a
imités. Renée| a pris ses
livres. Il y a dix cerisiers|
chez Amélie. Emile| a été chez
l'épicier. L'iniquité. Il a
imité| le rire d'Andrée. Dis-
ciplinez-les. La petite fille|
est intimidée. Il a pris| les
poupées de Josée| et il les a
cassées. Ridé, édile, plaisir,
miné, érigé, intimer, je fi-
nirai, épicier, j'irai, fri-
sé, livré, délivré.

III. CLOSED E AND CLOSED EU.
e, ø

mouvoir —

Nez, noeud, des, deux, mes,
meus, ces, ceux, fée, feu,
bée, boeufs. Deux nez, des
noeuds, les deux, ces oeufs,
tes deux oeufs, ces jeux.
J'ai deux dés. Les deux aînés|
sont ces deux-là. Ces deux
malheureux bébés| ont été

trouvés| abandonnés. Eugénie|
veut un peu de papier. Des
yeux bleus,| des cheveux
dorés,| et un nez retroussé.

IV. I AND U.
i, y

Dire, dure; dîne, dune;
sire, sur; bise, buse;
mise, muse; ride, rude.
L'inutile sublimité. L'il-
lustre ministre. L'usine|
est minuscule. La cupidité
du public. Une pilule.

V. OU AND U.
u, y

Moulu, pourvu, Mulhouse,
moussu, couture, humour,
fourrure, sous, su, mou,
mû, bouche, bûche, rousse,
russe, pouce, puce. La cou-
turière| a voulu une four-
fure de loutre. Jules| a
couru tout le jour| sur la
mousse. Pourvu que la nour-
riture de Jules| ne soit pas
une nourriture trop lourde.

VI. OU, I AND U.
u, i, y

Doux, dis, du; sou, si, su;
loup, lis, lu; joue, j'y,
jus. Le tissu| d'une blouse
russe. Le supplice du loup.
Dis-tu doux? Sur six sous.

VII. CLOSED EU AND U.
ø, y

Jeu, jus; peu, pu; deux,
du; noeud, nu; boeufs, bu;
meus, mu. Le jeu du gueux.
Ceux du duc. Jules et
Hugues| jeûnent. Les deux
oeufs de Luc. Scrupuleux,
tuberculeux, tu veux, bru-
meux, nu, noeud. Tu as vu

le tuberculeux. Tu es peu
scrupuleux. Les deux oeufs|
sont sur le feu. Jules |veut
du feu.

VIII.CLOSED O AND OPEN O.
o,ɔ

Bône, bonne; hôte, hotte;
côte, cote; l'hôte, Loth;
saute, sotte; taupe, tope;
saule, sole; pôle, Paul;
môle, molle. Comme j'aurai
chaud. Laure et Paule|coupent
les roseaux. Auto|pour auto-
mobile, *oto| pur otomobil*.
Photo|pour photographie,
foto|pur fɔtɔgrafi. Paul|
fait l'aumône au pauvre.

IX.ANTERIOR A AND OPEN O.
a,ɔ

Malle, molle. Bal, bol.
Salle, sol. Dague, dogue.
Cale, colle. Dard, dort.
Tard, tort. Mort, mare. Sort,
sarre. Baobab, catalogue, patronage, paradoxal, odorat,
apostolat, apostrophe, philo-
sophe. Laure|part avec sa mal-
le. Jeanne a tort|de parler
si fort. Jeanne raccommode|la
sacoche d'Adolphe. La ca-
tastrophe de Carcassonne.
Marc a tort|d'apostropher le
soldat.   *parler avec*

X.ANTERIOR A AND OPEN E.
a,ɛ

Mal, mêle. Balle, belle. Sa,
c'est. Salle, celle. Germaine|
parlait à Isabelle. Elle ap-
paraît avec sa mère. Esther
a fait la quête|avec Madame.
La fenêtre|est ouverte. Ger-
maine partait|hier|quand Ma-
deleine arrivait. La mallette
de Jeannette|est pleine de
lettres.

XI. CLOSED E AND OPEN E.
e,ɛ

Et, est; ces, c'est; mes,
mais; des, dais; ré, raie;
les, lait; nez, n'est; fée,
fais; tes, tait. L'été|
avait été très sec. Les
poupées d'Esther| étaient de
vraies beautés. Les prés et
les prairies| avaient été
plantés d'arbres fruitiers|
et d'herbes vertes.

XII.OPEN O AND OPEN EU.
ɔ,œ

Mort, meurs, port, peur,
sort, soeur; corps, coeur,
sole, seule; noble, meuble.
Le cor|sonne à neuf heures.
Ta soeur sort seule. Le
jeune veuf| porte un monocle.
Laure fait bon accueil|à sa
soeur. Elle raccommode| la
seule culotte de Paul.

XIII.ANTERIOR A, OPEN O
AND OPEN EU.
a,ɔ,œ

Sole, seule, sale; d'or,
d'heure, d'art; corps,
coeur, car; mords, meurs,
mare. A la bonne heure. *Fine* dandy!
Malheur à la bonne. La robe
neuve de Madame. Ma soeur|
part à la Havane.

XIV.OPEN E AND OPEN EU.
ɛ,œ

Jeune, gêne; soeur, sert;
peur, père; meurs, mère;
seul, sel. Elle cueille|la
feuille de lierre. La jeune
Hélène|sert le beurre et
l'oeuf| à sa soeur. La jeune   klab
veuve|allait au club. Elle   Kl œb
gêne sa soeur. Leur mère
meurt. Elle a peur|de son
père.

XV. CLOSED E, CLOSED EU,
OPEN E AND OPEN EU.

θ, ø, ε, œ

Mes, mais, meus, meurt. Epée
paix, peu, peur. Ces, sait,
ceux, soeur. Nez, n'est,
noeud, neuf. Sa mère se
meurt. Elle plaît à sa soeur.
Jeannette| cueille de belles
fleurs. Seule,| elle est demeu-
rée au prieuré. Heureusement
pour ceux-ci,| elle n'est de-
meurée que deux heures;| après |
elle s'est échappée.

XVI. CLOSED EU, OPEN E
AND MUTE E.

ø, ε, θ

De, deux, d'heure; ne, noeud,
bonheur; ce, ceux, soeur; me,
meus, meurt; que, queue,

coeur. Je veux que ta soeur|
me cueille deux fleurs.
L'heureuse Renée |veut re-
venir à Montreuil. La mal-
heureuse |est en deuil.

XVII. CLOSED E, CLOSED EU,
OPEN EU AND MUTE E.

θ, ø, œ, θ

Me, mes, meus, meurt; de,
des, deux, d'heure; que,
quai, queue, coeur; ce,
ces, ceux, soeur. Les deux
dés de ma soeur. Le bleu|
est la couleur de Renée. |
Vous danseriez de bon
coeur. Le feu| est dans la
cheminée. La soeur d'Eugé-
nie| part demain. Je veux
deux fleurs. Les deux
soeurs pleurent.

(The following passage contains examples of
every vowel studied so far, eleven in number).

M. Seguin n'avait jamais eu de bonheur avec ses chèvres.
Il les perdait toutes de la même façon: un beau matin,
elles cassaient leur corde, s'en allaient dans la montagne,
et là-haut le loup les mangeait. Ni les caresses de leur
maître, ni la peur du loup, rien ne les retenait. C'était,
paraît-il, des chèvres indépendantes, voulant à tout prix
le grand air et la liberté.
Le brave M. Seguin, que ne comprenait rien au caractère
de ses bêtes, était consterné. Il disait:
--C'est fini; les chèvres s'ennuient chez moi, je n'en
garderai pas une.
Cependant il ne se découragea pas, et, après avoir
perdu six chèvres de la même manière, il en acheta une
septième; seulement, cette fois, il eut soin de la prendre
toute jeune, pour qu'elle s'habituât mieux à demeurer chez
lui.
Ah! Gringoire, qu'elle était jolie la petite chèvre de
M. Seguin! qu'elle était jolie avec ses yeux doux, sa bar-
biche de sous-officier, ses sabots noirs et luisants, ses
cornes zébrées et ses longs poils blancs qui lui faisaient
une houppelande! C'était presque aussi charmant que le ca-
bri d'Esmeralda, tu te rappelles, Gringoire?--et puis, do-
cile, caressante, se laissant traire sans bouger, sans
mettre son pied dans l'écuelle. (Daudet)

THE NASAL VOWELS

SPELLING: in general, any vowel followed by a single n or m in the same syllable. (Double n or m, with few exceptions, denasalizes a preceding vowel):

in-tro-duc-tion	but	i-nu-tile
a-ban-don	"	do-nner
fen-te	"	fe-nêtre

There are four nasal vowels, each one corresponding to an ordinary vowel. In the articulation of the ordinary vowels, the soft palate is raised so as to touch the back of the pharynx (fig. 1,P, p.5) thus preventing exhalation of air through the nose. In the articulation of the nasal vowels, the soft palate is lowered (fig.1,SP, p.5) thus allowing exhalation of air through the nose as well as through the mouth.

There is no sound completely nasal in French, that is to say, there is no sound for which all the air passes through the nose; part of it, a considerable part, always passes through the mouth; hence, the nasal vowels are only partly nasal. Students should bear this fact in mind and, when practicing, they should always take care that part of the air passes through the mouth.

Since the written n or m found in the spelling of a nasal vowel is only the mark of nasalization, it has no pronunciation of its own; it is completely silent. Many students have a strong tendency to pronounce these letters and only with difficulty rid themselves of this habit. It is especially for the benefit of such students, that the last exercise of the practice drill for each nasal vowel has been arranged.

DURATION

Stressed nasal vowels are long when they are placed before one or more sounded consonants.

In other positions, nasal vowels are short.

MISTAKES TO BE AVOIDED

The following mistakes, frequently made by foreigners in the articulation of the four nasal vowels, should be avoided:

1. Jerking jaw at beginning.
2. Lowering soft palate insufficiently (whence vowel insufficiently nasal) or on contrary, lowering it too much (whence indeterminate sound).
3. Moving back of tongue toward palate, during pronunciation of vowels (whence sound of ng in English word sing).
4. Closing lips during pronunciation of vowel (whence n or m).

ON, $\tilde{o}$ or $\tilde{\eth}$

TONGUE as for o	TIP: flattened, touching lower teeth. BACK: raised less than for closed o, but slightly more than for posterior a, a. MUSCLES: tense.
LIPS as for o	LIPS: pushed very far forward. CORNERS OF MOUTH: brought forward, held tense. OPENING: horizontal. MUSCLES: fairly tense.
TEETH	Space between upper and lower teeth: 1/4 inch.
MECHANISM	As larynx begins to vibrate, tongue, lips and jaw are being brought into position and soft palate is lowered to allow part of breath to pass through nose.

AVOID

1. Closing lips during pronunciation (whence sound of m).
2. Rounding lips insufficiently.
3. Nasalizing open o, $ɔ$, when placed before nn, mm, or gn, $ɲ$.
4. Confusing on, $\tilde{o}$, with an, $\tilde{a}$.

AN, $\tilde{a}$
CORRESPONDS TO POSTERIOR A, a

TONGUE	TIP: flattened, behind ridge of lower incisors, touching it. BACK: slightly raised. MUSCLES: fairly tense.
LIPS	CORNERS OF MOUTH: in normal position. OPENING: vertical rather than horizontal. MUSCLES: relaxed.
TEETH	Space between upper and lower teeth: 3/4 inch.
MECHANISM	As larynx begins to vibrate, tongue, lips and jaw are being brought into position, and soft palate is lowered to allow part of air to pass out through nose.

AVOID

1. Raising front part of tongue too high.
2. Opening lips insufficiently.
3. Nasalizing anterior a, a, rather than posterior a, a, when placed before nn, mm, or gn, $ɲ$.
4. Confusing an, $\tilde{a}$, with on, $\tilde{o}$.

FOR PRACTICE. Before mirror.
Do not pronounce while moving tongue, lips, or jaw. Pro-
nounce only when in position.
I. TO TRAIN SOFT PALATE: $a, \tilde{a}, a, \tilde{a}, a, \tilde{a}$
Do not move lips, tongue, or jaw during whole drill.
II. TO TRAIN TONGUE, LIPS, AND JAW TO REMAIN MOTIONLESS:
Pronounce an, $\tilde{a}$, for half a minute uninterruptedly.

READING LESSON

SHORT. Banc, sans, lent,
maman. Le banc du marchand.
Tous les ans. Quel temps
fait-il? Il fait du vent.
LONG. Chante, lente, range.
Elle est lente. Elle est
blanche. Blanche danse. Les
marchandes| vendent de la
viande. Le chantre |va au-
temple.   *cantor*
SHORT AND LONG. En entendant
le chant,| l'enfant danse. La
marchande|vend le banc à
Jean.

Elle franchissait d'un saut
de grands torrents qui
l'éclaboussaient au pas-
sage de poussière humide et
d'écume. Alors, toute ruis-
selante, elle allait s'é-
tendre sur quelque roche
plate et se faisait sécher
par le soleil. (Daudet)
Il fuit, s'élance,
Puis en cadence
Sur un pied danse
Au bout d'un flot.
(Victor-Hugo)

FOR PRACTICE. Before mirror.
Do not pronounce while moving tongue, lips, or jaw. Pro-
nounce only when in position.
I. TO TRAIN SOFT PALATE AND LIPS: $ɔ, \tilde{ɔ}, ɔ, \tilde{ɔ}, ɔ, \tilde{ɔ}$
Do not move tongue or jaw during whole drill.
II. TO TRAIN TONGUE, LIPS, AND JAW TO REMAIN MOTIONLESS:
Pronounce on, $\tilde{ɔ}$, for half a minute uninterruptedly.
III. TO TRAIN EAR, AS WELL AS LIPS, TONGUE, AND JAW:
$\tilde{a}, \tilde{ɔ}, \tilde{a}, \tilde{ɔ}, \tilde{a}, \tilde{ɔ}$

READING LESSON

SHORT. Bon, on, son, long.
Ils sont longs. Nous partons.
Ils vont sur le pont. L'a-t-
on fait promptement?
LONG. Monde, longue, oncle,
ongle. Tout le monde. Il la
gronde. Il a honte. Elle est
longue. Il y en a onze. Elle
est prompte.
SHORT AND LONG. Les bonbons
de l'oncle. On lui fait honte.
Le lion,| on le dompte. Léon
Je gronde.   *to tame*

Non, non, va! c'est bien
ici que se font, défont et
surfont les réputations,
les situations et les é-
lections, où, sous couleur
de littérature et beaux-
arts, les malins font leur
affaire...(Pailleron)
Leur essaim gronde:
Ainsi, profonde,
Murmure une onde
Qu'on ne voit pas.
(Victor-Hugo)

IN, $\tilde{\varepsilon}$

TONGUE
- TIP: behind lower incisors, touching them.
- SIDE-EDGES: raised behind pre-molars, touching them; not, however, as for open e, ε.
- MUSCLES: not very tense.

LIPS
- CORNERS OF MOUTH: fairly far apart.
- OPENING: horizontal.
- MUSCLES: relaxed.

TEETH   Space between upper and lower teeth: 1/2 inch.

MECHANISM
- As larynx begins to vibrate, tongue, lips, and jaw are being brought into position, and soft palate is lowered to allow part of air to pass out through nose.

AVOID

1. Permitting side-edges of tongue to occupy too much room in mouth, thus preventing air from passing out freely.
2. Separating corners of mouth too much.
3. Nasalization of i when placed before one n vowel:

		for	
Inutile	$\tilde{\varepsilon}nytil$	"	$inytil$
Inepte	$\tilde{\varepsilon}n\varepsilon pt$		$in\varepsilon pt$

UN, $\tilde{\oe}$

TONGUE
- TIP: behind lower teeth, touching them.
- SIDE-EDGES: raised behind upper pre-molars, touching them.
- MUSCLES: rather tense.

LIPS
- CORNERS OF MOUTH: drawn forward a little more than for in, $\tilde{\varepsilon}$.
- OPENING: horizontal.
- MUSCLES: relaxed.

TEETH   Space between upper and lower teeth: 5/8 inch.

MECHANISM
- As larynx begins to vibrate, tongue, lips, and jaw are being brought into position, and soft palate is lowered to allow part of air to pass out through nose.

AVOID

1. Raising front part of tongue insufficiently behind upper teeth.
2. Rounding lips insufficiently (whence the sound of $\tilde{\varepsilon}$).
3. Slurring un, article.
4. Placing resonance in the throat.

FOR PRACTICE. Before mirror.
Do not pronounce while moving tongue, lips or jaw. Pronounce only when in position.

I. TO TRAIN TONGUE AND SOFT PALATE: ɛ, ɛ̃, ɛ, ɛ̃, ɛ, ɛ̃
Do not move lips, or jaw during whole drill.

II. TO TRAIN TONGUE, LIPS, AND JAW TO REMAIN MOTIONLESS:
Pronounce in, ɛ̃, for half a minute uninterruptedly.

III. TO TRAIN EAR, AS WELL AS TONGUE, LIPS, AND JAW:
ã, ɛ̃, ã, ɛ̃, ã, ɛ̃

READING LESSON

SHORT. Pain, vin, mien, faim.
J'ai du pain et du vin. Il
peint la salle de bains. Il
craint le chien. Le chien
Rintintin.
LONG. Prince, dinde, sainte,
sphinx. La sainte. Elle est
peinte. Les belles teintes.
Elle porte le linge. *tint shade*
SHORT AND LONG. J'ai quatre-
vingts timbres. Elle a peint|
le sphinx.
AN, ã, and IN, ɛ̃. Mente,
mainte. Fente, feinte.

Au même moment une trompe
sonna bien loin dans la
vallée. C'était ce bon monsieur Seguin qui tentait un
dernier effort.
-Hou! hou!...faisait le
loup. -Reviens! reviens...
criait la trompe. (Daudet)

C'est la plainte
Presque éteinte
D'une sainte
Pour un mort.
(Victor-Hugo)

FOR PRACTICE. Before mirror.
Do not pronounce while moving tongue, lips or jaw. Pronounce only when in position.

I. TO TRAIN SOFT PALATE: œ, œ̃, œ, œ̃, œ, œ̃
II. TO TRAIN TONGUE, LIPS, AND JAW TO REMAIN MOTIONLESS:
Pronounce un, œ̃, for half a minute uninterruptedly.

III. TO TRAIN MUSCLES OF TONGUE, AND LIPS, AS WELL AS EAR:
ɛ̃, œ̃, ɛ̃, œ̃, ɛ̃, œ̃

READING LESSON

SHORT. Un, quelqu'un, chacun,
l'un, aucun. Il a vu quel-
qu'un. Les uns|vont à Verdun,
les autres|à Melun. Le parfum.
Il est à jeun. Il est importun.
LONG. Humble, défunte, emprunte. Il emprunte. La dé-
funte|était une humble person-
ne.
SHORT AND LONG. L'importun|
emprunte à chacun. La défunte
de Melun. Un humble.
IN, ɛ̃, AND UN, œ̃. Daim, d'un.
In, un. Quint, qu'un.

NOTE: In the following passage the sounds ɛ̃ and œ̃
are underlined.
"-Moi, Je n'entre pas. Je
suis un ami de Dieu.
"-Tu es un ami de Dieu...
Eh! b...de teigneux! Que
viens-tu faire ici?..."-Je
viens...Ah! ne m'en parlez
pas, que je ne puis plus me
tenir sur mes jambes...Je
viens, je viens de loin...
humblement vous demander...
(Daudet)

42

I.AN AND ON.

Banc, bon; pan, pont; dans,
dont; ambre, ombre; pente,
ponte; bande, bonde. Men-
tant, montons, menton, mon-
tant; pensant, ponçons, pensons, ponçant; lançant, long
son, lançons, l'on sent.
Nous pensons au bon temps.
On entend|l'oncle de la mar-
chande. Blanche a honte|de-
vant tant de monde. Le bal-
lon de l'enfant| est rond.
Sans son enfant| la maman est
dolente. Les enfants|sont
dans le fond de la chambre.
Mon oncle| vient en chantant.
Ils vont au temple|le di-
manche.

II.AN AND IN.

Lent, lin; vent, vin; dans,
daim; pense, pince; rance,
rince. Du pain, de la viande
et du vin. Le marchand| vend
vingt timbres|à l'enfant. Le
temps est incertain|ce matin,
prends garde au vent. Le
prince|pense à la sainte. Le
temple| est peint en blanc.
Jean|boit de l'absinthe.
Jean| joue avec le singe.

III.AN, ON, IN AND UN.

Ment, Moeung; lent, l'un;
quand, qu'un; dans, d'un;
dont, daim: quand, Quint,
qu'on, qu'un. On en a vu un|
en endosser un. Un bon pain
blanc. L'enfant| a un fin
parfum. Chacun|prend son
pain et son vin. Le pinson|
chante un refrain charmant.
En entendant et en grondant
l'enfant,| l'oncle songe|à un
mensonge de son enfance|et
cette pensée|le rend indul-
gent. Jean prend du pain.
Son enfant est brun. Ils ont
envahis| la Saintonge. Les
pins et les sapins| sentent
bon.

(The following passage contains examples of the
four nasal vowels, all of which are underlined).

Pour aller au village, en descendant de mon moulin, on
passe devant un mas bâti près de la route au fond d'une
grande cour plantée de micocouliers. C'est la vraie maison
du ménager de Provence, avec ses tuiles rouges, sa large
façade brune irrégulièrement percée, puis tout en haut la
girouette du grenier, la poulie pour hisser les meules, et
quelques touffes de foin brun qui dépassent...
Pourquoi cette maison m'avait-elle frappé? Pourquoi ce
portail fermé me serrait-il le coeur? Je n'aurais pas pu
le dire, et pourtant ce logis me faisait froid. Il y avait
trop de silence autour...Quand on passait, les chiens
n'aboyaient pas, les pintades s'enfuyaient sans crier...A
l'intérieur, pas une voix! Rien, pas même un grelot de
mule...Sans les rideaux blancs des fenêtres et la fumée

qui montait des toits, on aurait cru l'endroit inhabité.
Hier, sur le coup de midi, je revenais du village, et,
pour éviter le soleil, je longeais les murs de la ferme,
dans l'ombre des micocouliers...Sur la route, devant le
mas, des valets silencieux achevaient de charger une char-
rette de foin...Le portail était resté ouvert. Je jetai un
regard en passant, et je vis, au fond de la cour, accoudé,
--la tête dans ses mains,--sur une large table de pierre,
un grand vieux tout blanc, avec une veste trop courte et
des culottes en lambeaux...(Daudet)

Chapter VII.
THE SEMI-VOWELS OR SEMI-CONSONANTS

There are three semi-vowels or semi-consonants in
French. They are called by either of these two names, because in their articulation they are just half way between
the vowels and the consonants.

The main difference between a vowel and a consonant is
that for the vowel there is always a free passage, a
"groove" in the mouth from the back to the front, which al-
lows the air to pass out easily without obstacle; whereas
for the consonant, there is either a complete obstacle (p,
b, t, d, k, g, m, n, ɲ), or a narrowing of the passage (f,
v, s, z, ʃ, ʒ, l, r).

For the pronunciation of the semi-vowels, the passage
is neither as large as for the vowels nor as closed and
narrow as for the consonants. The three semi-vowels correspond to three ordinary vowels but with a narrower space
for the passage of the air.

Moreover, while French vowels are very sonorous and
very clear, the semi-vowels are less sonorous and less
clear and all very short as compared with vowels, even the
very short ones.

In the articulation of semi-vowels, the student should
take care to give to the speech-organs the same position
as when forming the corresponding vowels (with a narrower
passage for the air). As soon as the position is taken,
instead of pronouncing that vowel he should immediately
displace the speech-organs (lips and tongue) for the next
sound; it is the displacement of the speech-organs which
produces the semi-vowel.

Furthermore, although the "attack" or beginning of the
vowels in French is very smooth and soft, increasing in
volume afterward, the "attack" of the semi-vowels is
rather abrupt.

SEMI-VOWEL OU, *w*
CORRESPONDING TO THE VOWEL OU, *u*

TONGUE
- TIP: behind ridge of lower incisors.
- BACK: raised as high as possible in direction of hard palate, so that space between tongue and hard palate is very narrow.
- MUSCLES: very tense.

LIPS
- CORNERS OF MOUTH: Brought forward, held very tense.
- OPENING: horizontal.
- MUSCLES: very tense.

TEETH Space between upper and lower teeth: 1/10 inch.

MECHANISM

Cause larynx to vibrate from very beginning and start sound with much more force than for corresponding vowel. As soon as tongue, lips, jaw, and larynx are in position, instead of pronouncing the vowel ou, *w*, immediately displace speech-organs and pronounce next sound: it is the displacement of speech-organs which produces the semi-vowel.

AVOID

1. Raising tongue too much in front.
2. Permitting tongue to occupy too much room in mouth.
3. Pushing lips forward insufficiently.

SEMI-VOWEL U, *ɥ*
CORRESPONDING TO THE VOWEL U, *y*

TONGUE
- TIP: behind lower incisors, touching them.
- SIDE-EDGES: raised behind upper incisors, touching canines and part of incisors.
- BACK: lowered.
- MUSCLES: fairly tense.

LIPS
- LIPS: very rounded, pushed forward.
- CORNERS OF MOUTH: brought forward, held tense.
- OPENING: small, horizontal.
- MUSCLES: fairly tense.

TEETH Space between upper and lower teeth: 1/4 inch.

MECHANISM

Cause larynx to vibrate from beginning and start sound with much more force than for corresponding vowel. As soon as tongue, lips, jaw, and larynx are in position, instead of pronouncing the vowel u, *y*, immediately displace speech-organs and pronounce next sound: it is this displacement which produces the semi-vowel.

AVOID

1. Raising front part of tongue insufficiently.
2. Relaxing muscles.
3. Pushing lips forward insufficiently.

FOR PRACTICE. Before mirror.

<u>TO TRAIN TONGUE, LIPS</u>: u, i, u, i, u, i, wi
Pronounce each vowel distinctly and separately. Then,
after placing lips, jaw and tongue in position for u, instead of pronouncing u, pronounce i: it is this <u>displace-</u>
<u>ment</u> of speech-organs which produces the semi-vowel

READING LESSON

Je dis oui. Il est couard.
La loyauté du citoyen.
L'Equateur. C'est quadrangulaire. Elle voit au
loin, le casque qui pointe.
Louis a moins de points
que toi. Louise a joué
avec la girouette. Je vis
dans le lointain une alouette. Edouard est loyal en-
vers ses concitoyens. Il
faut avoir soin d'entrete-
nir le foyer.

Je n'avais plus le coeur à
jouer, vous pensez...oh! non...
J'allais m'asseoir dans tous
les coins et, regardant les
objets autour de moi, je leur
parlais comme à des personnes;
je disais aux platanes:"Adieu,
mes chers amis!" et aux bas-
sins:"C'est fini, nous ne nous
verrons plus!" Il y avait dans
le fond du jardin un grand
grenadier dont les belles
fleurs rouges s'épanouissaient
au soleil. (Daudet)

FOR PRACTICE. Before mirror.

I. <u>TO TRAIN LIPS</u>: $y, i, y, i, y, i, \psi i$
Pronounce each vowel distinctly and separately. Then,
after placing lips, jaw, and tongue in position for y, instead of pronouncing y, pronounce i: it is this <u>displace-</u>
<u>ment</u> of speech-organs which produces the semi-vowel.
II. <u>TO TRAIN TONGUE AND LIPS</u>:
1. $wi, \psi i, wi, \psi i, wi, \psi i$
2. $lwi, l\psi i, lwi, l\psi i, lwi, l\psi i$

READING LESSON

Je suis ruiné. Aujourd'hui
c'est le huit juin. Lui,
il la fuit. L'écuyer a es-
suyé le tuyau. La questure.
C'est équilatéral. Le
bruit de la pluie, sur la
tuile. C'est lui qui l'a
tué. Puis, j'enfile une
aiguille. La cuisinière a
fait cuire aujourd'hui
huit plats à l'huile sur
la cuisinière de la cuisine.

...Je ne suis pas un élève du
tout, je viens ici comme maître d'étude; conduisez-moi
chez le principal.
...Bamban s'était assis par
terre à cause de ses jambes
qui lui faisaient mal. Je
m'assis près de lui. Je lui
parlai...Je lui achetai une
orange...J'aurais voulu lui
laver les pieds. (Daudet)

SEMI-VOWEL YOD, *j*
CORRESPONDING TO THE VOWEL I, *i*

TONGUE
{
TIP: behind lower incisors, touching them.
SIDE-EDGES: raised behind upper incisors more than
for i.
BACK: somewhat raised toward hard palate, leaving
only narrow canal for passage of air.
MUSCLES: more tense than for i.
}

LIPS { Inactive for yod, *j*, but in position of accompanying vowel.

MECHANISM

Cause larynx to vibrate at beginning and start sound with much more force than for corresponding vowel. At beginning of word or between vowels, as soon as tongue is in position, instead of pronouncing i , *i*, immediately displace speech-organs and place them in position for next sound: it is this <u>displacement</u> of speech-organs which produces the semi-vowel. At end of word, keep larynx, lower jaw, and lips in position required for preceding vowel, place tongue in proper position for yod, *j*, and articulate it very clearly.

AVOID

1. Raising tongue insufficiently toward front.
2. Raising tongue insufficiently toward rear.
3. Relaxing muscles.
4. Making yod, *j*, partly or completely voiceless, that is to say, without vibrations of larynx.
5. Except under certain circumstances (p.   ), pronouncing yod, *j*, when placed before vowel, separately instead of together with vowel (bi-$\tilde{\varepsilon}$, instead of bj$\tilde{\varepsilon}$).
6. Articulating insufficiently when at end of word. (At first, students should add a mute e, ϑ, to pronunciation of final yod, *j*).
7. Inserting the sound of yod, *j*, between a closed e and the following vowel in the same word unless it is written in the word:

créer	*kreje*	for	*kree*
océan	*osejã*	"	*oseã*
européen	*œropej $\tilde{\varepsilon}$*	"	*œrope$\tilde{\varepsilon}$*
néant	*nejã*	"	*neã*
et on	*ej$\tilde{\mathfrak{z}}$*	"	*e$\tilde{\mathfrak{z}}$*
nazaréen	*nazarej$\tilde{\varepsilon}$*	"	*nazare$\tilde{\varepsilon}$*

FOR PRACTICE. Before mirror.

I. TO TRAIN TONGUE: *bi-ɛ̃, bi-ɛ̃, bi-ɛ̃, bjɛ̃*
Pronounce each vowel distinctly and separately three
times; then, in last word, after placing tongue in position for yod, *j*, immediately pronounce anterior a: it is
the displacement of tongue which produces the semi-vowel
yod.
II. TO TRAIN LIPS AND TONGUE:
1. *jᵃ, jo, jᵃ, jo, jᵃ, jo*
2. *aja, ojo, aja, ojo, aja, ojo*
3. *aj, oj, aj, oj, aj, oj*

READING LESSON

Souiller, soulier; vouliez, voudriez; rien.
Hier, elle ne voyait rien, mais ses yeux
vont mieux. Dès son réveil, elle commence
à travailler. Le soleil brille dans le
ciel. L'ouvrier est fier. La vieille a un
beau tablier. Le soulier de la petite
fille. Soyez sérieux. Une vieille fille.
Un vieillard. La veille de la fête. Elles
voyagent sur un yacht. Vous ne voudriez
pas. Ayant voyagé hier dans l'Ohio. La
grenouille. Couleur de rouille. Les
brouillards de Lyon.   [ruj]

On partit enfin. Je vois cela comme si
c'était d'hier: le vapeur chauffait contre le quai de Granville; mon père effaré,
surveillant l'embarquement de nos trois
colis; ma mère inquiète ayant pris le bras
de ma soeur non mariée, qui semblait perdue
depuis le départ de l'autre, comme un pou-
let resté seul de sa couvée; et derrière
nous, les nouveaux époux qui restaient toujours en arrière, ce qui me faisait souvent
tourner la tête....Nous regardions les côtes
s'enfuir, heureux et fiers comme tous ceux
qui voyagent peu. (Maupassant)

Dormeuse.
Si l'enfant sommeille,
Il verra l'abeille,
Quand elle aura fait son miel,
Danser entre terre et ciel.
(Desbordes-Valmore)

SUPPLEMENTARY READING EXERCISES

(The following passages contain examples of the
three semi-vowels, all of which are underlined).

A minuit, le gardien se levait, jetait un dernier coup
d'oeil à ses mèches, et nous descendions. Dans l'escalier
on rencontrait le camarade du second quart qui montait en
se frottant les yeux; on lui passait la gourde, le Plu-
tarque...Puis, avant de gagner nos lits, nous entrions un
moment dans la chambre du fond, tout encombrée de chaînes,
de gros poids, de réservoirs d'étain, de cordages, et là,
à la lueur de sa petite lampe, le gardien écrivait sur le
grand livre du phare, toujours ouvert:
Minuit. Grosse mer. Tempête. Navire au large.

Je courais la mer de Sardaigne en compagnie de sept ou
huit matelots douaniers. Rude voyage pour un novice! De
tout le mois de mars, nous n'eûmes pas un jour de bon. Le
vent d'est s'était acharné après nous, et la mer ne déco-
lérait pas.
Un soir que nous fuyions devant la tempête, notre bateau vint se réfugier à l'entrée du détroit de Bonifacio,
au milieu d'un massif de petites îles...Leur aspect n'a-
vait rien d'engageant: grands rocs pelés, couverts d'oiseaux, quelques touffes d'absinthe, des maquis de lentis-
ques, et, çà et là, dans la vase, des pièces de bois en
train de pourrir; mais, ma foi, pour passer la nuit, ces
roches sinistres valaient encore mieux que le rouf d'une
vieille barque à demi pontée, où la lame entrait comme
chez elle, et nous nous en contentâmes.

Personne! Le bruit s'est tu...Du milieu des lambrusques
mouillées, deux ou trois courlis s'envolent en secouant
leurs ailes...Un peu de brise chante dans les arbres...
Vers l'orient, sur la crête fine des Alpilles, s'entasse
une poussière d'or d'où le soleil sort lentement...Un premier rayon frise déjà le toit du moulin. Au même moment,
le tambour, invisible, se met à battre aux champs sous le
couvert...Ran...plan...plan, plan, plan!
Le diable soit de la peau d'âne! Je l'avais oubliée.
Mais enfin, quel est donc le sauvage qui vient saluer
l'aurore au fond des bois avec un tambour?...J'ai beau re-
garder, je ne vois rien...rien que les touffes de lavande,
et les pins qui dégringolent jusqu'en bas sur la route...
Il y a peut-être par là, dans le fourré, quelque lutin
caché en train de se moquer de moi...C'est Ariel, sans
doute, ou maître Puck.

(Daudet)

Chapter VIII.
THE CONSONANTS

A consonant is a sound, whether or not accompanied by vibrations of the larynx, in the production of which the air, as it passes through the mouth, meets a complete or nearly complete obstruction. This obstruction may be caused by the lips or by the tongue.

A voiced consonant (Fr. sonore) is a consonant accompanied by vibrations of the larynx. The voiced consonant is gentle (Fr. douce): the air, having already been stopped a first time by the vocal chords or larynx, has less force when it reaches the obstacle formed by the lips or tongue.

A voiceless consonant (Fr. sourde) is a consonant not accompanied by vibrations of the larynx. The voiceless consonant is strong (Fr. forte): the air, not having been stopped by the vocal chords, since these are open and offer a free passage, has more force when it meets the obstacle formed by the speech-organs. It will later be seen that every voiceless consonant has its corresponding voiced consonant.

There are seventeen consonants in French.

I prefer to teach the formation and pronunciation of the consonants with very little reference to technical terms. However, as the student may find these terms in other books and wish to associate them with the material from two different points of view: manner in which they are articulated, and place where they are articulated.

A. According to the manner in which they are articulated, the consonants are classified as:
1. plosive
2. fricative
3. sibilant
4. hushing
5. nasal
6. lateral or liquid.

B. According to the place in which they are articulated, the consonants are classified as:
1. bi-labial
2. labio-dental
3. dental
4. palatal
5. uvular.

A. CLASSIFICATION ACCORDING TO THE MANNER IN WHICH THE CONSONANTS ARE ARTICULATED.

I. PLOSIVES

VOICELESS	VOICED
p, t, k.	b, d, g.

These consonants are called plosive because they are
the result of an <u>explosion</u>; the air forces the obstacle
formed by the speech-organs to give way in order that it
may pass out.

The plosives are also called <u>instantaneous</u> or <u>momentary</u>
(Fr. <u>momentanées</u>) because, being the result of an explosion, their sound cannot be prolonged. We shall later see,
however, that their silent part may be prolonged.

Contrary to what happens in pronouncing English plosives, the volume of air used in the pronunciation of the
French plosives is very limited.

The articulation of such consonants includes three
phases:

1. IMPLOSION: that phase when speech-organs are
placed in position to close mouth at
some point.
2. OCCLUSION: that phase when speech-organs remain
in position.
3. EXPLOSION: (Fr. détente) that phase when speech-
organs separate.

In French, the occlusion is always complete. It is
during this phase that the muscles are most tense. (It is
this part of the plosive consonant which, in case emphasis
is desired, may be lengthened, continued. The speech-organs completely close the air passage and offer a resistance to the air, which is thus stopped in its rush. Then
suddenly and rapidly, these organs separate and permit the
air to escape, thus producing a <u>clear-cut</u> sound. (In English, the separation of the speech-organs is rather lax
and slow, and the air is very abundant).

2.FRICATIVES

VOICELESS	VOICED
f.	v.

These consonants are called fricative (Lat. fricatus,
rubbed), because they are produced by a light <u>rubbing</u> of
the air against the upper and lower lip.

3.SIBILANTS

VOICELESS	VOICED
s	z

These consonants are called sibilant (Lat. sibilo:hiss),
because they are <u>hissing</u> sounds.

4.HUSHING CONSONANTS

VOICELESS	VOICED
ch, ʃ	ʒ, ʒ

These consonants are so called because they are the
sounds which one uses in suggesting silence (<u>Hush!</u> <u>shshsh</u>).

5.NASALS

VOICED

m, n, gn, ɲ

These consonants are called nasal because part of the air necessary for their pronunciation escapes through the nose. (The student should bear in mind, however, that they are not completely nasal and that part of the air escapes through the mouth).

These three consonants are usually voiced. They may, however, become voiceless through the process of a phenomenon called assimilation of which I shall speak later.

Gn, ɲ, is also called "mouillée" (English literal translation: wet), because the contact of a large part of the moistened tongue against the hard palate gives an impression of something wet.

6.LATERALS OR LIQUIDS
VOICED
l, r. (rolled).

These consonants are called lateral (Lat. latus, -eris, side) because they are produced by the escape of the air between an obstacle in the middle of the mouth and the sides. They are also called liquid (Lat. liquidus, fluid), because they are pronounced with a smoothly flowing sound and may easily be linked to other consonants. (Do not confuse, then, a "consonne mouillée" with a "consonne liquide").

These two consonants are usually voiced. They may, however become voiceless through the process of a phenomenon called assimilation of which I shall speak later.

Fricative, sibilant, hushing, nasal, and lateral or liquid consonants are also called continuant because they may be continued, prolonged.

The articulation of all these continuants includes three phases, as for the articulation of the plosive or instantaneous (momentary):

1. PREPARATION: that phase when speech-organs are placed in position.
2. PAUSE: (Fr. tenue) that phase when speech-organs remain momentarily motionless but do not relax.
3. RELEASE: (Fr. détente), that phase when speech-organs separate.

When the consonant is placed at the end of the word the student should take great care not to overlook the third phase which is essential in order to make the word clear to a listener.

There are three r's in French:
1. Rolled (Fr. r roulé).
2. Uvular (Fr. r uvulaire).
3. Parisian (Fr. r parisien ou grasseyé).

The r preferred by most cultured French people is the Parisian, but if a student is unable to acquire this r, either of the two others is acceptable.

B. CLASSIFICATION ACCORDING TO THE <u>PLACE</u> IN WHICH THE CONSONANTS ARE ARTICULATED.

1.BI-LABIALS

p, b, and m are called bi-labial because they are articulated by the <u>two lips</u>, one against the other (Lat. labia, lip:).

2.LABIO-DENTALS

f and v are called labio-dental because they are articulated by the lower <u>lip</u> against the upper <u>teeth</u> (Lat. dens, -tis: tooth).

3.DENTALS

d, t, l, n, s, z, rolled r, are called dental because they are articulated against the <u>teeth</u> or <u>teeth-ridge</u>.

4.PALATALS

k, g, ʃ, ʒ, Parisian r, are called palatal because they are articulated against hard <u>palate.</u>

5.UVULAR

Uvular r is so called because it is articulated by the tip of the soft palate or <u>uvula.</u>

NOTE: I have treated each consonant separately even in the case of those that correspond (as p and b), because usually not enough consideration is given to the fact that although similar, they are <u>not exactly alike.</u> It is the failure sometimes to observe this distinction that betrays the foreigner.

LAW OF ANTICIPATION
(LOI DE PRÉVOYANCE)

Before the articulation of a consonant, the lips must be, as nearly as possible, in the position required for the accompanying vowel. The term "accompanying vowel" indicates that vowel which either directly precedes or directly follows the consonant <u>in the same syllable.</u>

In French, it is the <u>vowel</u> which is all-powerful and which regulates the position of the organs for the articulation of the consonant, at every time it has the opportunity to do so.

<u>to</u>: The lips must be pushed very far forward for closed o even before t is pronounced. It is in this position that t should be pronounced.

<u>tɛ</u>: The corners of the mouth must be drawn far apart for open e, ɛ, even before t is pronounced. It is only in this position that t should be pronounced.

<u>ot</u>: The lips must remain pushed very far forward until t is pronounced. It is only in this position that t should be pronounced.

<u>ɛt</u>: The corners of the mouth must remain drawn far apart until t is pronounced. It is only

in this position that t should be pronounced.
I repeat that this law of anticipation operates with
all consonants.

RELEASE (Fr. DETENTE)

The release is the phase in the articulation of a consonant which is the opposite of the preparation--the
speech-organs suddenly leave the position which they have
assumed and their muscles become relaxed. This it is that
produces the clear-cut articulation of the last consonant
or consonants of a stress-group. Consequently, if a speaker has not kept his muscles extremely tense during the
pause, sufficiently complete and rapid relaxation is impossible, with the result that to a French person the last
consonant or consonants are audible only very slightly if
at all. This frequently causes him to misunderstand the
speaker, or (when an adjective or variable noun is in-
volved) to think that the masculine gender has been used
when the feminine is required.

From the very beginning therefore, the student should
make especial effort to articulate final consonants with
the greatest distinctness. It may even be useful to him to
pretend that a mute e, ə, exists after the final consonant.
In this way he will probably be more successful in attain-
ing sufficient articulation of the consonant or consonants.

Compare the following endings:

Il est Francais.
La prononciation française.

Dans le tas.
La grande table.

Le petit le fil.
La petite fille.

Dans le port.
J'ouvre la porte.

Un poisson frit.
Une pomme frite.

Le ruban vert.
La robe verte.

Le bon lait.
Le beau soleil.

Le beau genêt.
J'ouvre la fenêtre.

En tout cas.
Je vais à la cave.

Un sermon.
Une semonce.
C'est un monstre.

Il va à la mairie.
Il va en Amérique.

Dans la rue.
Il est Russe.
C'est un rustre.

P, *p*

TONGUE Inactive.

LIPS
- LIPS: pressed against each other just inside the visible part.
- CORNERS OF MOUTH: more or less far apart or close together, depending on accompanying vowel.
- MUSCLES: tense.

MECHANISM

P is a strong consonant. Larynx does not vibrate. At very beginning, lips are pressed tightly together; the pressure gradually diminishes until separation of lips. Volume of air very small.

AVOID

1. Bringing exterior part of lips together.
2. Separating lips too slowly.
3. Relaxing muscles from beginning.
4. Releasing too much air (whence sound of English h after p).
5. Making p insufficiently audible at end of word.

B, *p̸ b*

TONGUE Inactive.

LIPS
- LIPS: pressed against each other just inside visible part.
- CORNERS OF MOUTH: more or less far apart or close together, depending on accompanying vowel.
- MUSCLES: relaxed.

MECHANISM

B. is a gentle consonant.

At very beginning, as larynx is caused to vibrate, lips are pressed tightly together; the pressure gradually diminishes until separation of lips. Volume of air very small.

AVOID

1. Bringing exterior part of lips together.
2. Separating lips too slowly.
3. Releasing too much air (whence sound of English h after b).
4. Stopping vibrations of larynx partly or incompletely at end of word or when b is followed by l or r at end of word (whence sound of p).

FOR PRACTICE. Before mirror.
Do not pronounce while moving tongue, lips, or jaw. Pronounce only when in position.

I. TO REDUCE BREATH AND TO SUPPRESS POSSIBLE SOUND OF H:
Pronounce: *pa*, *pa*, *pa*, before a sheet of thin paper. During the pronunciation of correct French p, the paper barely moves, whereas with an English p, it shows a pronounced movement.

II. TO TRAIN LIPS: 1. *pa, po, pa, po, pa, po*
                     2. *ap, op, ap, op, ap, op*

READING LESSON

"Paix"| dit-il. "Père,| viens avec moi." "Pan,| pan,| pan!| Ouvrez-moi." Papa|n'y va pas. Paris|est une belle ville. Paul vient. Parlons-lui. Partons. Donne-lui une tape. C'est un type. Il fait la lippe. Je veux|qu'il le rompe. Il allume la lampe. Il l'attrape. Il s'en occupe. Hep!

Il avait trente ans; sa taille était assez élevée pour que Paul auprès de lui, parut transformé en pygmée; son expression était intelligente, hautaine, et telle que personne, à première et même à seconde vue, ne lui eût octroyé l'auréole de la sainteté. (Labiche)

FOR PRACTICE. Before mirror.
Do not pronounce while moving tongue, lips, or jaw. Pronounce only when in position.

I. TO REDUCE BREATH, TO SUPPRESS SOUND OF H, AND TO FORCE VIBRATIONS OF LARYNX: 1. *ba, be, bi, bo, bu*
Have larynx vibrate as soon as lips close.
                     2. *ab, εb, ib, ob, ub*
Do not stop vibrations between vowel and consonant.

II. TO TRAIN LIPS: 1. *ba, bo, ba, bo, ba, bo*
                     2. *ab, ob, ab, ob, ab, ob*

READING LESSON

Bien faire. Blanche|est venue me voir. Bonjour,| boulanger,| donne-moi du pain. Blond| comme un chérubin. Bouche d'or. Ce mot a deux syllabes. Un gros tube. Elle méprise la plèbe. La femme de l'Arabe. Le bel habit. L'abbé Constantin. Le jambon.Elle embellit. Il abolit. Il aborde. Buvez| le bon vin de la bonbonne.

grande
bouteille

Elle se rappelait bien l'histoire de la construction de cet étage; c'était à la suite d'une trouvaille de bateau abandonné faite en Manche par le père Gaos et son cousin le pilote; la nuit du bal, Yann lui avait raconté cela....Par un escalier de bois blanc tout neuf, on la fit monter dans la chambre d'en haut qui était la gloire du logis.
(Loti)

T, *t*

TONGUE
- TIP: behind and against upper incisors, touching them very firmly.
- SIDE-EDGES: against upper teeth and ridge.
- MUSCLES: tense.

LIPS
- Inactive for t itself, but in position of accompanying vowel.

MECHANISM

T is a strong consonant. Larynx does not vibrate. At very beginning, tip of tongue is strongly pressed against upper incisors; the pressure gradually diminishes until separation of tongue from teeth; tip then drops very rapidly, giving a clear-cut sound. Volume of air very small.

AVOID

1. Placing tip of tongue too far back in mouth.
2. Pressing tip of tongue insufficiently against teeth.
3. Relaxing muscles at very beginning.
4. Separating tip of tongue too slowly from teeth.
5. Releasing too much air (whence sound of English h after t).
6. Making t insufficiently audible at end of word.

D, *d*

TONGUE
- TIP: behind and against upper incisors.
- SIDE-EDGES: against upper teeth and ridge.
- MUSCLES: tense.

LIPS
- Inactive for d itself, but in position of accompanying vowel.

MECHANISM

D is a gentle consonant. At very beginning, as larynx is caused to vibrate, tip of tongue is strongly pressed against upper incisors; the pressure gradually diminishes until separation of tongue from teeth. Tip then drops very rapidly, giving a clear-cut sound. Volume of air very small.

AVOID

1. Placing tip of tongue too far back in mouth.
2. Pressing tip of tongue insufficiently against teeth.
3. Relaxing muscles at very beginning.
4. Separating tip of tongue too slowly from teeth.
5. Releasing too much air (whence sound of English h after d).
6. Stopping vibrations of larynx partly or completely at end of word (whence sound of t).

FOR PRACTICE. Before mirror.
Do not pronounce while moving tongue, lips, or jaw. Pro-
nounce only when in position.
I. TO REDUCE BREATH, TO SUPPRESS SOUND OF H, AND TO TRAIN
TIP OF TONGUE:
Pronounce: *ta*, *ta*, *ta*, before a sheet of thin paper. Dur-
ing the pronunciation of correct French t, the paper bare-
ly moves, whereas with an English t, it shows a pronounced
movement.
II. TO TRAIN JAW TO REMAIN MOTIONLESS AND TONGUE TO MOVE
RAPIDLY: *ta*, *ta*, *tà*
Do not move jaw.
III. TO TRAIN LIPS: 1. *ta*, *to*, *ta*, *to*, *ta*, *to*
                       2. *at*, *ot*, *at*, *ot*, *at*, *ot*
                    READING LESSON

Tiens! Tel fils, tel père.	Blanquette eut envie de re-
Tôt ou tard. Tandis qu'il	venir; mais en se rappelant
vient. Tapez fort. Il a hâte.	le pieu, la corde, la haie
Il parle à l'hôte. Vous êtes	du clos. elle pensa que
honnête. Le beau site. Sur la	maintenant elle ne pouvait
hatte La patte de la chatte.	plus se faire à cette vie
Il tape dans le tas.	et qu'il valait mieux res-
	ter. (Daudet).

FOR PRACTICE. Before mirror.
Do not pronounce while moving tongue, lips, or jaw. Pro-
nounce only when in position.
I. TO REDUCE BREATH, TO SUPPRESS SOUND OF H, AND TO FORCE
VIBRATIONS OF LARYNX: 1. *da*, *de*, *di*, *do*, *du*
Cause larynx to vibrate at very beginning of consonant.
                         2. *ad*, *εd*, *id*, *od*, *ud*
Do not stop vibrations between vowel and consonant.
II. TO TRAIN JAW TO REMAIN MOTIONLESS AND TONGUE TO MOVE
RAPIDLY: *da*, *da*, *da*
Do not move jaw.
III. TO TRAIN LIPS: 1. *dε*, *do*, *dε*, *do*, *dε*, *do*
                       2. *εd*, *od*, *εd*, *od*, *εd*, *od*
                    READING LESSON

Dis-le. Dix enfants. Donne-le.	"Monsieur le préfet, je
Dame fourmi. Dicte-lui la	crois devoir prévenir l'au-
fable. (Donnant, donnant.)	torité que deux insensés
D'ailleurs, dire n'est pas	ont l'intention de croiser
faire. Il est timide. Il est	le fer demain, à midi moins
malade. J'aime la salade. Je	un quart"...il suffit quel-
fais une promenade. L'onde est	quefois d'un quart d'heure!
profonde. Il doit. Il dit. Tu	..."A midi moins un quart...
diras à la grande amie. La	.Le rendezvous est à la
distance est grande.	porte du garde..."(Labiche)

K, k

TONGUE
{
TIP: behind and against lower incisors.
BACK: raised against hard palate.
POINT OF ARTICULATION: not always same: depending upon accompanying vowel:
  a. If accompanying vowel is posterior, point of articulation is against soft palate.
  b. If accompanying vowel is anterior, point of articulation is against back part of hard palate.
MUSCLES: tense.
}

LIPS { Inactive for k itself, but in position of accompanying vowel.

MECHANISM

K is a strong consonant. Larynx does not vibrate.
At very beginning, tip of tongue is placed behind and against lower incisors, and back of tongue is firmly pressed against hard palate; the pressure gradually diminishes until separation of tongue from palate. Then, back of tongue drops very rapidly, giving a clear-cut sound. Volume of air very small.

AVOID

1. Placing point of articulation too far back in mouth.
2. Pressing back of tongue insufficiently against hard palate.
3. Relaxing muscles from very beginning.
4. Separating back of tongue too slowly from hard palate.
5. Releasing too much air (whence sound of English h after k).
6. Making k insufficiently audible at end of word.

FOR PRACTICE. Before mirror.

Do not pronounce while moving tongue, lips, or jaw. Pronounce only when in position.

I. TO REDUCE BREATH, TO SUPPRESS SOUND OF H, AND TO TRAIN BACK OF TONGUE:

Pronounce: *ke, ke, ke,* before a sheet of thin paper. During the pronunciation of correct French k, the paper barely moves, whereas with an English k, it shows a pronounced movement.

II. TO TRAIN JAW TO REMAIN MOTIONLESS AND BACK OF TONGUE TO MOVE RAPIDLY: *ke, ke, ke*

Do not move jaw. After complete contact between back of tongue and hard palate, drop tongue as rapidly as possible.

III. TO TRAIN LIPS:
1. *ke, ko, ke, ko, ke, ko*
2. *ɛk, ok, ɛk, ok, ɛk, ok*

READING LESSON

Quiconque peut le casser. Coupable, |il l'est.
Quarante hommes. Qui vient? Que dit-il? Elle
est dans le hamac. J'ai un sac. Sur le lac.
J'apprends la physique. Il critique. L'oiseau|
ouvre le bec. Le trafic. Au Danemark. Le képi- *chapeau* ⌐
du soldat. Je vais à l'Académie. Un kilo de
concombres. Le choléra. Un chrétien. L'expression est exquise. Quelques caricaturistes|nous
prêteront leur concours. Que crie donc Christian,| là,| à côté? A Carcassonne|l'eau est calcaire. A New-York,| le trafic est considérable.
Isaac. J'ai un sac. Du tac au tac. Je vais à
Québec. Le long bec. Il est sec. Le pic. Le
diagnostic. Le Maroc. Jeanne d'Arc. Un viaduc.

De tous les jolis dictons, proverbes ou adages,
dont nos paysans passementent leurs discours,
je n'en sais pas un plus pittoresque ni plus
singulier que celui-ci. A quinze lieues autour
de mon moulin, quand on parle d'un homme rancunier, vindicatif, on dit: "Cet homme-là! méfiez-vous!...il est comme la mule du pape qui
garde sept ans son coup de pied!" (Daudet)

> La rumeur approche
> L'écho la redit;
> C'est comme la cloche
> D'un couvent maudit.
> (Victor-Hugo)

G, *g*

TONGUE
{
TIP: behind and against lower incisors.
BACK: raised against hard palate.
POINT OF ARTICULATION: not always same, depending
on accompanying vowel:
  a. If accompanying vowel is posterior, point of
    articulation is against soft palate.
  b. If accompanying vowel is anterior, point of
    articulation is against back part of hard
    palate.
MUSCLES: tense.
}

LIPS { Inactive for g itself, but in position of accompanying vowel.

MECHANISM

G is a gentle consonant.
At very beginning, as larynx is caused to vibrate, tip of
tongue is placed behind and against lower incisors, and
back of tongue is firmly pressed against hard palate; the
pressure gradually diminishes until separation of tongue
from palate. Then, back of tongue drops very rapidly, giving a clear-cut sound. Volume of air very small.

AVOID

1. Placing points of articulation too far back in mouth.
2. Pressing back of tongue insufficiently against hard
   palate.
3. Relaxing muscles from very beginning.
4. Separating back of tongue too slowly from hard palate.
5. Releasing too much air (whence sound of English h after
   g).
6. Stopping vibrations of larynx, partly or at end of word
   or when it is followed by l or r at end of word (whence
   sound of k).

FOR PRACTICE. Before mirror.

Do not pronounce while moving tongue, lips, or jaw. Pronounce only when in position.

I. TO REDUCE BREATH, TO SUPPRESS SOUND OF H, AND TO FORCE VIBRATIONS OF LARYNX: 1. *ga, ge, gi, go, gu*
Cause larynx to vibrate as soon as back of tongue comes in contact with hard palate. Test by placing fingers on larynx. 2. *ag, ɛg, ig, og, ug*
Do not stop vibrations between vowel and consonant; at first, one may even add a mute e, ǝ, to consonant to force vibrations of larynx.

II. TO TRAIN JAW TO REMAIN STILL AND BACK OF TONGUE TO MOVE RAPIDLY: *ga, ga, ga*
Do not move jaw. After complete contact between back of tongue and hard palate, drop tongue as rapidly as possible.
1. *ga, go, ga, go, ga, go*
2. *ag, og, ag, og, ag, og*

READING LESSON

Garde-la. Guide-le. Guy|est un petit garçon. Guiguite| est une petite fille. Gardons-nous| d'être goguenards. Garçon,| un café. Il donne la bague. Il est bègue. Il lègue. L'eau| a dépassé les digues. C'est un dogue. Il est rogue. Second. L'agrégé|a réussi à son agrégation. La guerre|a gagné la plus grande partie de la Gascogne. Gustave|se gargarise la gorge. Il est inexorable. En zigzag. Je vais à Dantzig. Je veux un grog. J'ai une bague. Mon collègue. Il se fatigue. Il parle plusieurs langues. Elle est longue. Un bouledogue. En Camargue.Les langues modernes. Je vais à Copenhague. Il est à Prague. C'est très vague. Il danse la gigue. Il est bilingue. Des meringues. Sur le catalogue.

Sa gaieté communicative, son esprit conciliant, le génie de l'organisation et des inventions drôlatiques qu'il possédait au plus haut degré en faisaient un compagnon charmant, égayaient notre vie et développaient mon amour.

(de la Brète)

Ce bruit vague
Qui s'endort
C'est la vague
Sur le bord;
(Victor-Hugo)

F, *f*

TONGUE   Inactive.

LIPS
{
LOWER LIP: internal part comes in contact with upper incisors, thus completely covering lower incisors.

UPPER LIP: does not touch lower lip.

CORNERS OF MOUTH: in position for accompanying vowel.

MUSCLES: tense.
}

MECHANISM

F is a strong consonant. Larynx does not vibrate.
Internal part of lower lip comes in contact with upper incisors, completely covering lower teeth and leaving enough space for air to pass out continuously; then, separation of lip and teeth is very rapid, articulation extremely precise. Volume of air small.

AVOID

1. Pressing upper incisors against external part of lower lip.
2. Relaxing muscles.
3. Releasing too much air.
4. When lip and teeth separate, dropping lower jaw too much
5. Making f insufficiently audible at end of word.

V, *v*

TONGUE   Inactive.

LIPS
{
LOWER LIP: internal part comes in contact with upper incisors, thus completely covering lower incisors.

UPPER LIP: does not touch lower lip.

CORNERS OF MOUTH: in position for accompanying vowel.

MUSCLES: tense.
}

MECHANISM

V is a gentle consonant.
As larynx is caused to vibrate, internal part of lower lip comes in contact with upper incisors, completely covering lower teeth and leaving enough space for air to pass out continuously; then separation of lip and teeth is very rapid, articulation extremely precise. Volume of air small.

AVOID

1. Pressing upper incisors against external part of lower lip.
2. Releasing too much air.
3. When lip and teeth separate, dropping lower jaw too much.
4. Stopping vibrations of larynx partly or completely, at end of word (whence sound of f).

FOR PRACTICE. Before mirror.
Do not pronounce while moving tongue, lips, or jaw. Pronounce only when in position.

I. TO REDUCE BREATH AND TO ACQUIRE CORRECT POSITION OF LOWER LIP AND UPPER TEETH: Pronounce: fa, fa, fa, before a sheet of thin paper. During the pronunciation of correct French f, the paper barely moves, whereas with an English f, it shows a pronounced movement.

II. TO TRAIN LIPS: 1. fa, fo, fa, fo, fa, fo
                     2. af, of, af, of, af, of

READING LESSON

Fais-le venir. Faites-la entrer. Faisons du bon travail. Faire une chose difficile. L'épitaphe. J'ai un phonographe. Le cinématographe. Un bon chef. L'affluence. C'est affreux. L'influence est bonne. Il a fait une affaire. Le fin fond de la France. Le fanfaron fanfaronne.
booster is bragging

Naïvement, Yann racontait sa vie de pêcheur, ses fatigues, ses salaires, les difficultés d'autrefois chez ses parents, quand il avait fallu élever les quatorze petits Gaos dont il était le frère aîné...
...Ainsi, cette année, notre père m'a fait faire ces habits neufs que je porte.
(Loti)

FOR PRACTICE. Before mirror.
Do not pronounce while moving tongue, lips, or jaw. Pronounce only when in position.

I. TO ACQUIRE CORRECT POSITION OF LOWER LIP AND UPPER TEETH AND TO FORCE VIBRATIONS OF LARYNX:
                     1. va, ve, vi, vo, vu
Cause larynx to vibrate at very beginning of consonant.
                     2. $a{:}v$, $\varepsilon{:}v$, $i{:}v$, $o{:}v$, $u{:}v$
Do not stop vibrations between vowel and consonant.

II. TO TRAIN LOWER JAW TO MOVE GENTLY: va, ve, vi, vo, vu
Drop jaw very little and very gently.

III. TO TRAIN LIPS: 1. va, vo, va, vo, va, vo
                     2. $a{:}v$, $o{:}v$, $a{:}v$ $o{:}v$, $a{:}v$, $o{:}v$

READING LESSON

Vas-y. Vont-elles à la gare? Vers elle. Vive l'Amérique. Viendra-t-il? Vaincre ou mourir. Je vais à la cave. Elle est brève. La veuve pleure. Elle est neuve. Qu'il vive. Un vilain voleur. Il casse la vitre. La vivacité d'Yvonne. Véra voyage avec ses voisins à travers les vallées.

On dansait à la vielle, au violon, les mêmes couples presque toujours ensemble. Quand lui venait la reprendre, après avoir par convenance dansé avec quelque autre, ils échangeaient un sourire d'amis qui se retrouvent et continuaient leur conversation d'avant...
(Loti)

S, s

TONGUE	TIP: behind ridge of lower incisors, touching it. FRONT PART: raised behind lower and upper incisors, leaving very narrow space between them and teeth. SIDE-EDGES: touching upper incisors, canines, premolars and molars as well as their ridge. MUSCLES: very tense.
LIPS	Inactive for s itself, but in position of accompanying vowel.
LOWER JAW	Slightly pushed forward so that lower teeth are as far forward as upper.

MECHANISM

S is a strong consonant. Larynx does not vibrate.
As tip of tongue is placed behind ridge of lower incisors so that it touches it, front part of tongue is raised behind lower and upper incisors, leaving very narrow passage between it and teeth; at same time, side-edges of tongue are raised and placed against incisors, canines, premolars and molars, and against their ridge as well, while lower jaw is pushed slightly forward. Articulation very precise. Muscles tense.

AVOID

1. Lowering tip of tongue insufficiently.
2. Leaving too large space between front part of tongue and upper incisors.
3. Leaving canal, from molars to molars, too narrow.
4. Relaxing muscles.
5. Pronouncing on too low a note.
6. Making s insufficiently audible at end of word.
7. Uncovering upper incisors insufficiently.
8. Pronouncing s when sign of plural:

les livres	leliʋrs	for	leli:ʋr
les tables	letabls	"	letabl
les filles	lefijs	"	lefij
les murs	lemyrs	"	lemy:r
les fauteuils	lefotœjs	"	lefotœj

FOR PRACTICE. Before mirror.

Do not pronounce while moving tongue, lips, or jaw. Pronounce only when in position.

<u>I. TO TRAIN TIP AND FRONT PART OF TONGUE:</u>

sa, se, si, so, su

Keep tip of tongue behind ridge of lower incisors so that it touches them. Raise front part behind lower and upper incisors, leaving very small space between tongue and teeth. Muscles must be very tense.

<u>II. TO TRAIN LIPS:</u> 1. *sa, so, sa, so, sa, so*
2. *as, os, as, os, as, os*

READING LESSON

Ça et là. Servez-vous. Si grand. Ciel et terre.
Sautez. Celle-là. Scandez ces vers. Je vais en
classe. Je suis lasse. Je vais en Suisse. J'aime
la sauce. Il faut qu'il finisse. Nous espérons.
C'est assez. Une grosse émotion. Il est pré-
tentieux. Je vais à Bruxelles. Sa soeur| s'as-
seoit sur le siège. Six chasseurs| sachant chas-
ser sans chien. Pour qui sont ces serpents| qui
sifflent sur nos têtes? Combien,| ces saucissons-
ci? Ces saucissons-ci,| six sous les six. Je de-
meure rue d'Assas. La rue Cujas|et.la rue Stanis-
las. Je vais à Arras. C'est un délice. Le train
express. Une_lettre expresse. Un edelweiss. Un
omnibus. L'oremus Vénus. Elle est basse. Qu'il
le fasse. Une déesse. La Suisse. Une brosse.
Elle est fausse.

Quand ils ont aperçu Monsieur le sous-préfet avec
sa belle culotte et sa serviette en chagrin gau-
fré, les oiseaux ont eu peur et se sont arrêtés
de chanter, les sources n'ont plus osé faire de
bruit, et les violettes se sont cachées dans le
gazon...Tout ce petit monde-là n'a jamais vu de
sous-préfet, et se demande à voix basse quel est
ce beau seigneur qui se promène en culotte
d'argent. (Daudet)

Il fuit, s'élance,
Puis en cadence
Sur un pied danse
Au bout d'un flot. (Victor-Hugo)

Z, *z*

TONGUE
{
TIP: behind ridge of lower incisors, touching it.
FRONT PART: raised behind lower and upper incisors,
leaving very narrow space between them and teeth.
SIDE-EDGES: touching upper canines, pre-molars and
molars as well as their ridge.
MUSCLES: very tense.
}

LIPS
{ Inactive for z itself, but in position of accompanying vowel. }

LOWER JAW
{ Pushed slightly forward so that lower teeth are as far forward as the upper. }

MECHANISM

Z is a gentle consonant.
As larynx is caused to vibrate, tip of tongue is placed
behind ridge of lower incisors so that it touches it, and
front part of tongue is raised behind lower and upper incisors, leaving very narrow passage between it and teeth;
at same time, side-edges of tongue are raised and placed
against upper canines, pre-molars, and molars, and against
their ridge as well. while lower jaw is pushed slightly
forward. Articulation, very precise. Muscles, tense.

AVOID

1. Lowering tip of tongue insufficiently.
2. Leaving too large space between front part of tongue
   and upper incisors.
3. Leaving canal, from molars to molars, too narrow.
4. Relaxing muscles.
5. Pronouncing on too low note.
6. Uncovering upper incisors insufficiently.
7. Stopping vibrations of larynx partly or completely at
   end of word (whence sound of s).

FOR PRACTICE.   Before mirror.

Do not pronounce while moving tongue, lips, or jaw. Pronounce only when in position.

I. TO TRAIN JAW, LIPS, AND FRONT PART OF TONGUE, AND TO FORCE VIBRATIONS OF LARYNX:

$$za, ze, zi, zo, zu$$

Push jaw forward so that it is as far forward as upper teeth. Keep tip of tongue behind ridge of lower incisors. Raise front part of tongue behind lower and upper incisors, leaving very small space between tongue and teeth; muscles very tense. Cause larynx to vibrate as soon as front part of tongue is raised. To test vibrations, place fingers on larynx.

II. TO TRAIN LIPS: 1. za, zo, za, zo, za, zo
2. $a:z, o:z, a:z, o:z, a:z, o:z$

READING LESSON

Zéro| est un chiffre. "Zouaves,| zouaves,| tenez ferme!" Zigzaguer| n'est pas marcher droit. Zézayer| est parler comme les petits enfants. J'aime les roses. Elle pause. Quelque chose. Une bonne cause. Les fleurs| sont dans le vase. Je l'ai mise. Elle use sa robe. Le cousin de Suzanne. Les enfants et les hommes. J'examine l'horizon. Zoé est inexorable. Le deuxième étage. Les hommes et les enfants| s'amusent. Le zézaiement de Suzanne| est chose désagréable. Suzanne| sème la zizanie| parmi les autres enfants. Le gaz. Berlioz. Trapèze. Ils sont treize. Il y en a quinze. Il est en bronze. J'en ai quatorze. La phrase. Le diocèse. Elle est Irlandaise.

Monsieur le sous-préfet, grisé de parfums, ivre de musique essaye vainement de résister au nouveau charme qui l'envahit. Il s'accoude sur l'herbe, balbutie encore deux ou trois fois:- messieurs et chers administrés...Messieurs et et chers admini...Messieurs et chers...(Daudet)

> Tandis qu'il se repose,
> Sa paupière rose,
> Pour la terre close,
> S'ouvre pour le ciel.
> (Victor-Hugo)

CH, ∫

TONGUE ⎰ TIP: wide, raised toward front palate far forward.
⎰ SIDE-EDGES: touching ridge of pre-molars and
⎱ molars.
⎱ MUSCLES: tense (pressure of tongue very strong).

LIPS ⎰ Play important part in articulation of ch, ∫:
⎱ pushed far forward, forming a small megaphone.

RESONANCE
There are three different places where sound is amplified:
1. Between tip of tongue and back of mouth.
2. Between tip of tongue and upper incisors.
3. Between lips and teeth.

MECHANISM
Ch, ∫, is a strong consonant. Larynx does not vibrate.
At the same time that tip of tongue is raised toward front
part of hard palate, side-edges come in contact with ridge
of pre-molars and molars, while lips are pushed very far
forward and form small megaphone; the different parts of
this composite position must be taken simultaneously and
before sound is uttered. Volume of air small. Muscles,
tense.

AVOID

1. Pressing side-edges of tongue insufficiently against
pre-molars and molars.
2. Lowering tip of tongue instead of raising it.
3. Bringing tip of tongue too far back.
4. Keeping lips inactive.
5. Pronouncing ch, ∫, on too low a note.
6. Making ch, ∫, insufficiently audible or even silent at
end of word.

FOR PRACTICE. Before mirror.

Do not pronounce while moving tongue, lips, or jaw. Pronounce only when in position.

<u>I. TO TRAIN TONGUE AND LIPS:</u>
$$\int a, \ \int a, \ \int a$$
Keep tip of tongue raised toward front part of hard palate. Side-edges of tongue must be brought into very firm contact with part of hard palate just above pre-molars and molars. Throw lips forward as much as possible.

<u>II. TO TRAIN LIPS:</u> 1. $\int a, \ \int o, \ \int a, \ \int o, \ \int a, \ \int o$
2. $a\int, \ o\int, \ a\int, \ o\int, \ a\int, \ o\int$

READING LESSON

Cher enfant. Chose vue. Chiffons. "Chauds,| chauds,| les marrons chauds". Chef de bande. Il triche. La jolie chatte. Elle est sèche. Cherchons. Le Général Hoche. Elle prend la hache. Elle apporte des bûches. Elle cherche. Il chérit son chat. Une hachette| est une petite hache. Elle cherche la chéchia. Le cheval de Charlotte. La vie est chère. Chacune a son cheval. La chevauchée des chevaliers. Six chasseurs| sachant chasser sans chien. Le chien| et le cheval de Chonchette. Dans la poche. Elle se cache. Elle est fraîche. En Autriche. C'est dimanche. Il marche. Il ouvre la bouche. Le maréchal Foch.

Tu penses, Gringoire, si notre ch<u>è</u>vre était heureuse. Plus de corde, plus de pieu...rien qui l'empê<u>ch</u>ât de gambader, de brouter à sa guise... C'est là qu'il y en avait de l'herbe! jusque pardessus les cornes, mon <u>ch</u>er!...et quelle herbe! Savoureuse, fine, dentelée, faite de mille plantes...C'était bien autre <u>ch</u>ose que le gazon du clos!...La <u>ch</u>èvre blan<u>ch</u>e, à moitié soûle, se vautrait là-dedans, les jambes en l'air et roulait le long des talus, pêle-mêle avec les feuilles tombées et les <u>ch</u>âtaignes.

(Daudet)

La rumeur appro<u>ch</u>e;
L'écho la redit.
C'est comme la clo<u>ch</u>e
D'un couvent maudit;

(Victor-Hugo)

J, ʒ

TONGUE
⎧ TIP: wide, raised toward front palate far forward.
⎪ SIDE-EDGES: touching ridge of pre-molars and
⎨ molars.
⎩ MUSCLES: tense (pressure of tongue very strong).

LIPS
⎧ Play important part in articulation of J, ʒ; push-
⎪ ed far forward, forming small megaphone.
⎨ CORNERS OF MOUTH: more or less far apart or close
⎩ together, depending on accompanying vowel.

RESONANCE

There are three different places where sound is amplified:
1. Between tip of tongue and back of mouth.
2. Between tip of tongue and upper incisors.
3. Between lips and teeth.

MECHANISM

J, ʒ, is a gentle consonant.
As larynx is caused to vibrate, tip of tongue is raised toward front part of hard palate, and side-edges come in contact with ridge of pre-molars and molars; at same time,
lips are pushed very far forward and form small megaphone.
The different parts of this composite position must be
taken simultaneously and before sound is uttered. Volume
of air, small. Muscles, tense.

AVOID

1. Pressing side-edges of tongue insufficiently against
   pre-molars and molars.
2. Lowering tip of tongue instead of raising it.
3. Bringing tip of tongue too far back.
4. Keeping lips inactive.
5. Pronouncing J, ʒ, on too low a note.
6. Stopping vibrations of larynx partly or completely at
   end of word (whence sound of ch, ʒ).

FOR PRACTICE. Before mirror.

Do not pronounce while moving tongue, lips, or jaw. Pronounce only when in position.

I. TO TRAIN TONGUE AND LIPS, AND TO FORCE VIBRATIONS OF LARYNX: 1. $\mathit{3^a, 3e, 3i, 3o, 3u}$
Keep tip of tongue raised toward front part of hard palate. Side-edges of tongue must be brought into very firm contact with part of hard palate just above pre-molars and molars. Throw lips forward. Cause larynx to vibrate as soon as side-edges come in contact with hard palate, and as soon as lips are thrown forward. Test vibrations of larynx by placing fingers on it.
2. $\mathit{a{:}3, \varepsilon{:}3, i{:}3, o{:}3, u{:}3}$
Do not stop vibrations between vowel and consonant; at first, one may even add a mute e, ə, to consonant to force vibrations of larynx.

II. TO TRAIN LIPS: 1. $\mathit{3^a, 3o, 3^a, 3o, 3^a, 3o}$
2. $\mathit{a{:}3, o{:}3, a{:}3, o{:}3, a{:}3, o{:}3}$

READING LESSON

J'ai, j'eus. J'avais. Joue. Jeanne| joue avec le joujou. Jacques est là-bas. Juge-la. Jouer est bien,| jurer est mal. Dans la loge du général. Le chien a la rage. Sur la plage. Le livre est jaune. Il fait le siège. Il est agile. Sur ses genoux. Elle agit bien. Elle s'agite. Elle est majeure. Elle nage. Je ne joue jamais| avec Jeanne. L'agile et joli petit Georges| joue à genoux sur la plage. La loge du concierge| est jolie. Georgette| est jeune et jolie. Dans la neige. En ai-je? Irai-je la voir? A son âge. Elle est Belge. Il a dit un mensonge. Il voit un singe. L'esclavage.

-Eh bien! écoute, Jan, si tu la veux tout de même, nous te la donnerons...Le père, rouge de honte, baissait la tête...Jan fit signe que non et il sortit....A partir de ce jour, il changea sa façon de vivre, affectant d'être toujours gai, pour rassurer ses parents.

(Daudet)

Levez, les gens, la barre en fer,
Ouvrez, les gens, je suis la Neige,
Mon manteau blanc se désagrège
Sur les routes du vieil hiver.

(Verhaeren)

M, m

TONGUE   Inactive.

LIPS   { LIPS: slightly pressed against each other just
inside visible part.
CORNERS OF MOUTH: more or less far apart or close
together, according to accompanying vowel.
MUSCLES: not very tense.

MECHANISM

M is a gentle consonant.

As larynx is caused to vibrate, lips are slightly pressed
against each other just inside visible part; at same time,
soft palate is lowered so that part of air passes out
through nose. Volume of air very small. Muscles not very
tense.

AVOID

1. Pressing lips together too firmly or too weakly.
2. Bringing external part of lips together.
3. Making m insufficiently audible at end of word.
4. Confusing m, mark of nasalization of a vowel, with m,
   consonant.

N, n

TONGUE   { TIP: against upper incisors.
SIDE-EDGES: touching pre-molars and molars and
their ridge.
MUSCLES: fairly tense.

LIPS   { Inactive for n, itself, but in position of accompanying vowel.

MECHANISM

N is a gentle consonant.

As larynx is caused to vibrate, tip of tongue is placed
behind and against upper incisors, and side-edges of
tongue come in contact with upper pre-molars, molars and
their ridge, while soft palate is lowered, so that part of
air passes out through nose. Volume of air, very small.
Muscles not very tense.

AVOID

1. Pressing tip of tongue against upper incisors too firmly or too weakly.
2. Bringing tongue insufficiently forward.
3. Relaxing muscles.
4. Making n insufficiently audible at end of word.
5. Confusing n, mark of nasalization of a vowel, with n,
   consonant.

FOR PRACTICE. Before mirror.
Do not pronounce while moving tongue, lips, or jaw. Pronounce only when in position.

I. TO TRAIN LIPS AND TO FORCE VIBRATIONS OF LARYNX:

1. *ma, me, mi, mo, mu*

Cause larynx to vibrate as soon as lips are closed.

2. *am, ɛm, im, om, um*

Do not stop vibrations between vowel and consonant.

II. TO TRAIN BACK OF TONGUE TO REMAIN MOTIONLESS:

a::m, a::m, a::m

Make a decided effort to refrain from raising back of tongue during whole vowel and consonant.

III. TO TRAIN LIPS:
1. *ma, mo, ma, mo, ma, mo*
2. *am, om, am, om, am, ·om*

READING LESSON

Ma robe. Mes enfants. Mot à mot. Maman. Moi, je viens. Mon enfant. Mari et femme. Mourir sans souffrir. Son âme. Il aime Marie. La grosse pomme. La jeune femme. C'est tout comme. Il s'amuse. Un mammifère. La minute.

Enorme, immobile, assis sur son train de derrière, il était là regardant la petite chèvre blanche et la dégustant par avance. Comme il savait bien qu'il la mangerait, le loup ne se pressait pas...(Daudet)

FOR PRACTICE. Before mirror.
Do not pronounce while moving tongue, lips, or jaw. Pronounce only when in position.

I. TO TRAIN TIP OF TONGUE AND TO FORCE VIBRATIONS OF LARYNX:

na, na, na

Cause larynx to vibrate at very beginning of consonant.

II. TO TRAIN BACK OF TONGUE TO REMAIN MOTIONLESS:

a::n, a::n, a::n

Make a decided effort to refrain from raising back of tongue at any time during emission of vowel and consonant.

III. TO TRAIN LIPS:
1. *na, no, na, no, na, no*
2. *an, on, an, on, an, on*

READING LESSON

Non, non. Ni moi ni toi. Notre livre. Naître et mourir. Nier la vérité. J'ai un âne. La haine. La pleine lune. La jeune personne est bonne. Elle a bonne mine. Il ne s'ennuie pas. La nuit noire. Le nouveau venu n'est pas né en novembre.

Quelle influence, l'ennui, chez nous? Mais énorme!... mais considérable! Le Français, vois-tu, a pour l'ennui une horreur poussée jusqu'à la vénération. Pour lui, l'ennui est un dieu terrible qui a pour culte la tenue.

(Pailleron)

GN, ɲ

TONGUE	TIP: behind and against lower incisors. TOP SURFACE: almost completely raised against hard palate. MUSCLES: fairly tense.

LIPS	Inactive for gn, ɲ, itself, but in position of accompanying vowel.

MECHANISM

Gn, ɲ, is a gentle consonant.
As larynx is caused to vibrate, tip of tongue is placed behind and against lower incisors, and top surface of tongue is raised in a single movement against hard palate, while soft palate is lowered so that part of air passes out through nose. The different parts of this composite position must be taken simultaneously; otherwise consonant is decomposed and loses its essential characteristic of being a simple consonant. Volume of air, small. Muscles, fairly tense.

AVOID

1. Raising tip of tongue toward hard palate.
2. Making too lax contact between top surface of tongue and hard palate and doing it too slowly.
3. Establishing contact at two different times or at two different places.
4. Causing larynx to vibrate too late.
5. Making gn, ɲ, insufficiently audible at end of word.
6. Confusing g+n, *gn* and gn, ɲ:

magnifique	*magnifik*	for	*maɲifik*
signification	*siɲifikasjɔ̃*	"	*siɲifikasjɔ̃*
ignorance	*ignorɑ̃:s*	"	*iɲorɑ̃:s*

FOR PRACTICE. Before mirror.

Do not pronounce while moving tongue, lips, or jaw. Pronounce only when in position.

<u>I. TO TRAIN TIP AND BACK OF TONGUE AND TO FORCE VIBRATIONS OF LARYNX:</u>

$$ɲa, ɲa, ɲa$$

Keep tip of tongue behind lower incisors. Raise remainder of tongue in a single movement against hard palate. Cause larynx to vibrate as soon as tongue and palate are in contact.

<u>II. TO TRAIN BACK OF TONGUE TO REMAIN MOTIONLESS TILL END OF PRECEDING VOWEL:</u>

$$a::ɲ, a::ɲ, a::ɲ$$

Make a decided effort to refrain from raising back of tongue before end of vowel. After finishing vowel, and not before, pronounce ɲ. When you have repeated this drill some time, try to pronounce syllable more rapidly. Same with: iɲ and oɲ.

<u>III. TO TRAIN LIPS:</u>

1. ɲa, ɲo, ɲa, ɲo, ɲa, ɲo
2. aɲ, oɲ, aɲ, oɲ, aɲ, oɲ

READING LESSON

Gnangnan. Gnognote. Je vais à la montagne. Tu es à la campagne. J'ai une compagne. Les belles vignes. Le roi| règne en Pologne. En Gascogne. Elle ment sans vergogne. Le bon compagnon. Le campagnard. Il est soigné| et soigneux. Charlemagne| eut un règne magnifique. Les montagnards| vivent dans les montagnes| et les campagnards| à la campagne. Le hargneux compagnon. La signification. Son compagnon| va à la campagne. Il va en Allemagne. La Champagne et la Bretagne| sont des provinces de France. Une ligne. Un peigne. La vigne. Il signe. Un ivrogne. Le cygne.

Quand la chèvre blanche arriva dans la montagne, ce fut un ravissement général...Les châtaigniers se baissaient jusqu'à terre, pour la caresser du bout de leurs branches...Toute la montagne lui fit fête...
...Jan couchait avec Cadet, tout près de la Magnanerie; la pauvre vieille se fit dresser un lit à côté de leur chambre...Les magnans pouvaient avoir besoin d'elle, dans la nuit.

(Daudet)

L, *l*

TONGUE
: TIP: wide, forming wall, behind and against upper incisors.
FRONT: lower than tip, not touching hard palate.
SIDE-EDGES: touching last molars and their ridge.
MUSCLES: tense.

LIPS
: Inactive for l itself, but in position of accompanying vowel.

MECHANISM

L is a gentle consonant.
As larynx is caused to vibrate, tip of tongue, widened, and forming a wall, presses behind and against four upper incisors, contact being established more firmly between tongue and two outer incisors. At same time, front part of tongue rises, but remains lower than tip and thus does not touch hard palate; front part of tongue seems to throw tip of tongue to a level higher than where it lies itself (this position is very important). At same time, too, side-edges are raised and come in contact with molars and their ridge; air passes out on both sides between front part of tongue and canines. All these movements are simul-taneous, and in order to avoid any extra or parasite sound, these positions are taken very rapidly, especially when l is placed after vowel at end of word. Resonance is in most forward part of mouth; l is pronounced on a sharp note.

AVOID

1. Bringing tip of tongue insufficiently forward.
2. Making contact insufficiently firm between tip of tongue and incisors.
3. Making contact of side-edges of tongue and hard palate too extensive.
4. Raising front part of tongue insufficiently.
5. Pronouncing l on too low a note.
6. Lowering larynx.
7. When l is at end of word or placed before another con-sonant, taking position for l too slowly, thus adding parasite sounds to preceding vowel and making a diph-thong.

FOR PRACTICE. Before mirror.

Do not pronounce while moving tongue, lips, or jaw. Pronounce only when in position.

I. TO TRAIN TIP OF TONGUE, AND TO FORCE VIBRATIONS OF LARYNX:

la, la, la

Bring tip of tongue into contact with upper incisors. Cause larynx to vibrate from very beginning.

II. TO TRAIN TONGUE TO A GREATER SPEED AFTER PRECEDING VOWEL IS PRONOUNCED AND TO FORCE RESONANCE FORWARD:

al, ɛl, il, ol, ul

1. Pronounce vowel very clearly, then throw tip of tongue rapidly against upper incisors, thus avoiding any extra or parasite sound.
2. Do not lower larynx or base of tongue so as to prevent a resonance in throat or in back of mouth. Pronounce l on a sharp note, bring resonance as far forward as possible.

III. TO TRAIN LIPS: 1. *la, lo, la, lo, la, lo*
2. *al, ɛl, al, ɛl, al, ɛl*

READING LESSON

Les enfants. Là, sur la chaise. L'eau est froide. L'un et l'autre. L'an prochain. L'année commence. J'ai un animal. Je joue à la balle. A la ville. J'ai du fil. La foule. Elle est folle. La Ligue des Nations. Elle a lu deux lignes| dans le journal. Le long conciliabule| de Lili et de Léon. La belle Isabelle| a lu le journal. Elle a lutté loyalement. Il mêle l'utile| à l'agréable. Je vais au bal. A Noël. Un cil. Il en a mille. Guillaume Tell. Dans un bol. Le calcul. C'est nul. Elle est pâle. Une balle. Tu appelles Estelle. Il est tranquille.

Puis elle lui parla tout bas, en montrant le malade. L'homme s'inclina sans répondre, sortit, siffla son chien et le voilà parti, le fusil sur l'épaule, sautant de roche en roche avec ses longues jambes. (Daudet)
Il les raille, il les hait, il les fuit comme peste, mais ils ont seuls son admiration secrète et sa confiance absolue.

Fort	Elle	Sort	Quelle
Belle,	Dort.	Frêle!	Mort!
			(de Rességuier)

FRONT LINGUAL ROLLED R, *r*
(French: R ROULÉ).

LOWER JAW ⎰Completely motionless; in position of accompany-
AND LIPS ⎱ing vowel.

TONGUE ⎰BACK: flat.
⎰TIP: raised toward front part of hard palate;
⎰must be very free and should not touch teeth or
⎰ridge.

MECHANISM

R is a gentle consonant.

As larynx begins to vibrate, tip of tongue rises toward
front part of hard palate, and as vibrating air is releas-
ed through mouth, tip of tongue gives rapid succession of
taps, usually not more than three. During r plus whole
accompanying vowel, lower jaw and lips remain absolutely
motionless.

AVOID

1. Moving lower jaw or lips.
2. Making r partly or completely voiceless, that is to
   say, without vibrations of larynx.
3. Bringing tip of tongue insufficiently forward.
4. Exaggerating taps in number or in intensity.
5. Making r insufficiently audible at end of word.

UVULAR R, *r*
(French: R UVULAIRE).

LOWER JAW ⎰Completely motionless; in position of accompany-
AND LIPS ⎱ing vowel.

TONGUE ⎰TIP: behind lower incisors, completely motion-
⎰less.
⎰BACK: slightly raised toward hard palate.

SOFT PALATE ⎰Lowered; uvula vibrates or rather gives sever-
⎰al taps in succession.

MECHANISM

R is a gentle consonant.

As larynx begins to vibrate, back of tongue rises slightly, soft palate is lowered, and as vibrating air is re-
leased through mouth, uvula gives a rapid succession of
taps. During emission of r and whole accompanying vowel,
lower jaw, lips, and tip of tongue remain absolutely motionless.

AVOID

1. Moving lower jaw, lips, or tip of tongue.
2. Raising tip of tongue toward hard palate.
3. Making r partly or completely voiceless (thus resembling German ch).
4. Exaggerating taps.
5. Making r insufficiently audible or even silent at end
   of word.

FOR PRACTICE. Before mirror.
Do not pronounce while moving lips or jaw. Pronounce only
when in position.
I. TO TRAIN BACK OF TONGUE, LIPS, AND JAW TO REMAIN MO-
TIONLESS WHILE TIP OF TONGUE IS RAISED BEHIND UPPER IN-
CISORS AND VIBRATES: *ra, ra, ra*
Have mouth open. Keep lower jaw motionless. Keep lips mo-
tionless. Keep back of tongue motionless. Then cause lar-
ynx to vibrate, and at same time raise tip of tongue be-
hind upper incisors and cause it also to vibrate--but very
gently and only once or twice.
II. TO TRAIN LARYNX TO VIBRATE: *a:r, ɛ:r, i:r, o:r, u:r*
Do not stop vibrations between vowel and r.
III. TO TRAIN LIPS: 1. *ra, ro, ra, ro, ra, ro*
                      2. *a:r, ɛ:r, i:r, o:r, u:r*

READING LESSON

Rire et pleurer. Rarement. Répéter sa leçon.
Retourner à sa place. Rapide comme l'oiseau.
Retirer sa plainte. Rayons X. Redire la poé-
sie. Etre à l'heure. J'ai peur. Son père. Ma
mère prend du beurre. Il est tard. Il est
mort. L'erreur. Ils font une ronde. Le ronron
du chat. Elle porte la lettre. Deux artistes.
Il est paternel. Il travaille. C'est drôle.
Le sourire aux lèvres,| Bernard réapparaît. La
robe de brocart|de Renée.
   (The student will find on p.81 selections
   for reading from Daudet and Victor-Hugo).

FOR PRACTICE. Before mirror.
Do not pronounce while moving tongue, lips, or jaw. Pronounce only when in position.
I. TO TRAIN TONGUE, LIPS, AND JAW TO REMAIN MOTIONLESS
WHILE UVULA VIBRATES, AND TO FORCE VIBRATIONS OF LARYNX:
                   1. *ra, ra, ra*
Have mouth wide open. Keep lower jaw motionless. Keep lips
motionless. Keep tip of tongue behind lower incisors. Then
cause larynx to vibrate just before uvula begins to vi-
brate; release of this vibrating air causes uvula to vi-
brate and produces uvular r.
               2. *a:r, ɛ:r, i:r, o:r, u:r*
Do not stop vibrations between vowel and r.
II. TO TRAIN LIPS: 1. *ra, re, ri, ro, ru*
                     2. *a:r, ɛ:r, i:r, o:r, u:r*

PARISIAN R   *r*
(French: R PARISIEN or GRASSEYÉ).

LOWER JAW {Completely motionless. In position of accompany-
AND LIPS {ing vowel.

TONGUE   {TIP: behind lower incisors and remaining com-
       {pletely motionless.

MECHANISM

R is a gentle consonant.

As larynx is caused to vibrate, back of tongue rises toward back of soft palate without touching it; the release
of vibrating air through narrow passage formed by back of
tongue and soft palate, produces the gentle Parisian r.
During emission of r and accompanying vowel, lower jaw,
lips, and tip of tongue remain absolutely motionless. A
person may at one and the same time pronounce both Parisian and uvular r.

AVOID

1. Moving lower jaw, lips, or tip of tongue.
2. Raising tip of tongue toward hard palate.
3. Making r partly or completely voiceless, that is to say,
   without vibrations of larynx, especially before consonant and at end of word.
4. Making r insufficiently audible or even silent at end
   of word.

SUPPLEMENTARY READING

Déjà s'éteint ma lampe,
Et l'ombre de la rampe,
Qui le long du mur rampe
Monte jusqu'au plafond.

D'étranges syllabes
Nous viennent encore;
Ainsi des Arabes
Quand sonne le cor,...

C'est la plainte
Presque éteinte
D'une sainte
Pour un mort.

Leur essaim gronde
Ainsi, profonde,
Murmure une onde
Qu'on ne voit pas.
(Victor-Hugo)

Une grenouille vit un boeuf
Qui lui sembla de belle taille.
Elle, qui n'était pas grosse en tout comme un oeuf,
Envieuse, s'étend, et s'enfle, et se travaille
Pour égaler l'animal en grosseur...
(La Fontaine)

FOR PRACTICE. Before mirror.

Do not pronounce while moving lips or jaw. Pronounce only when in position.

I. TO TRAIN TIP OF TONGUE, JAW, AND LIPS TO REMAIN MOTION-LESS WHILE BACK OF TONGUE RISES TOWARD HARD PALATE; TO TRAIN LARYNX TO VIBRATE: *ra, ra, ra*

Have mouth wide open. Keep lower jaw motionless. Keep lips motionless. Keep tip of tongue behind lower incisors. Then raise back of tongue toward back part of soft palate without touching it. Then drop tongue for next vowel. The release of vibrating air through narrowed passage formed between back of tongue and soft palate produces the gentle Parisian r.

II. TO TRAIN LIPS: 1. *ra, ro, ra, ro, ra, ro*
                       2. *a:r, o:r, a:r, o:r, a:r, o:r*

READING LESSON

(The student will find a reading lesson for r on p.79).

-Mais, malheureuse tu ne sais pas qu'il
y a le loup dans la montagne...Que fe-   Murs, ville
ras-tu quand il viendra?...   Et port,
-Je lui donnerai des coups de cornes,   Asile
Monsieur Seguin.   De mort
-Le loup se moque bien de tes cornes. Il   Mer grise
m'a mangé des biques autrement encornées   Où brise
que toi... Tu sais bien, la pauvre vieil-   La brise
le Renaude qui était ici l'an dernier?   Tout dort.

SUPPLEMENTARY READING

Un chant sur la grève   Elle brame
Par instants s'élève,   Comme une âme
Et l'enfant qui rêve,   Qu'une flamme
Fait des rêves d'or.   Toujours suit.
          (Victor-Hugo)   (Victor-Hugo)

C'est bien la pire peine
De ne savoir pourquoi
Sans amour et sans haine,
Mon coeur a tant de peine.
          (Verlaine)

Dans le verger et dans la vigne,
Il s'en va, furtif perruquier,
Avec une houppe de cygne.
Poudrer à frimas l'amandier.
          (Gautier)

82

P, p

L'époux. L'âpôtre. Il va l'é-
pouser. L'époux|fait du ta-
page. Papa[part pour Paris.
Les petites poupées|de la
pauvre petite Paulette|sont
perdues. Pensez-vous|qu'il
passe par la Pologne? Père,|
passe-moi le pain,| je te prie.
Il l'attrape. Une guêpe. Elle
anticipe. La tulipe. Il fume
la pipe. Il allume la lampe.
Il va en Europe. Le chien jap-
pe. Il s'en occupe. La soupe.
C'est un cap. "Hop!|la voilà
partie". Houp! Le pape. Ils
attrapent. Il dissipe. Ils
campent. Il trompe. Ils les
frappent. Elles enveloppent.

B, b

Buvez le bon vin de la bon-
bonne. Les beaux bébés blonds|
babillent. La bonne|berce les
bébés. Le bambin balbutie.
L'arabe. L'éphèbe. Le scribe.
Il imbibe. Il est ingambe. De
belles jambes. Le feu flambe.
La colombe. La bombe. Une
trombe. La rhubarbe est bonne.
Bêtement|est un adverbe. Le
beau Danube bleu.

T, t

Il termine le tableau. Quand
elle entra. C'est une enfant.
Ton thé| t'a-t-il ôté ta toux?
L'attentat| a attristé toute
la cité. L'entêté| n'entend
rien aux statistiques. Tiens-
toi tranquille. Tout vient à
point| à qui sait attendre. Le
riz tâté| tenta le rat;| le rat
tenté| tâta le riz tentant. Il

a hâte. Du tact. C'est di-
rect. Le verdict. C'est net.
Ils en ont huit. Une dot.
Ils sont sept. Une sonate.
Un acte. Ils achètent. Elle
est parfaite. La révolte.
Un alpiniste. Une patte.
Une trompette. La lutte.

D, d

Didon dîna,| dit-on,| du dos
d'un dodu Dindon. Daniel |
dédaigne la dot d'Adèle.
Dora|a dédommagé le descen-
dant du duc. Bagdad. Alfred.
Le Cid. David. Au sud. De
la marmelade. En Suède. Il
est candide. Tu te décides.
Une bande. Ils répondent.
Une ode. Ils tardent. Elle
est lourde. La tarte est
chaude.

F, f

Le froufrou| des fanfreluches
de Florence. "Un frais par-
fum| sortait des touffes
d'asphodèles". Il fait des
fautes. Il a fumé. Les cheveux frisés. En relief. Il
est naïf. Commémoratif.
C'est positif. Ils sont vifs.
Ouf! Une carafe. La girafe.
Elle se coiffe. De l'étoffe.
Tartufe. Il se chauffe. Tu
te chauffes. Ils étouffent.
Un golfe. Joseph. Adolphe.
Tu triomphes. Une nymphe.

V, v

Servez vivement la verveine.
L'avocat| avoue avoir volé.
Vivette va venir. Yvonne
l'a vue. Avez-vous vu| la

vitrine? Elle est vive. Elle est Slave. Il est brave. Je vais à Genève. Elle est naïve. Une initiative. Une valve. Il se conserve. Elle est mauve. Il l'approuve.Ève. Un élève. Geneviève. Il l'énerve. Le fleuve. Il cultive.

M, m

La mémoire. La marine marchande. Menez-moi au monument des morts. "Mais,| me mèneras-tu|au mémorable monument? "Le mur murant Paris." A Amsterdam. Il va à Jerusalem. Un beau géranium. C'est un maximum. Un post-scriptum. De la crème. Ils s'aiment. La victime. Il se calme. Une gamme. Un télégramme. Un dilemme. Il charme. Un psaume.

N, n

N'a-t-elle pas ennuyé| la bonne Nanette? "Non,| il n'est rien|que Nanine n'honore." N'as-tu ni haine|ni envie? Ni Janine ni Jeannette|ne sont venues. Un specimen. Il dit amen. Il joue du Beethoven. Les Djinns. Un âne. La cabane Il imagine. Il ne parle pas à Antoine. Une héroïne. C'est l'automne. La Marne.

(The following passage contains examples of all the consonants).

"C'était un long sentier tout pavé de braise rouge. Je chancelais comme si j'avais bu; à chaque pas je trébuchais; j'étais tout en eau, chaque poil de mon corps avait sa goutte de sueur, et je haletais de soif...Mais, ma foi, grâce aux sandales que le bon saint Pierre m'avait prêtées, je ne me brûlai pas les pieds.

"Quand j'eus fait assez de faux pas clopin-clopant, je vis à ma main gauche une porte...non, un portail, un énorme portail, tout bâillant, comme la porte d'un grand four. Oh! mes enfants, quel spectacle! Là, on ne demande pas mon nom; là, point de registre. Par fournées et à pleine porte, on entre là, mes frères, comme le dimanche vous entrez au cabaret.

"Je suais à grosses gouttes, et pourtant j'étais transi, j'avais le frisson. Mes cheveux se dressaient. Je sentais le brûlé, la chair rôtie, quelque chose comme l'odeur qui se répand dans notre Cucugnan quand Éloy, le maréchal, brûle pour la ferrer la botte d'un vieil âne. Je perdais haleine dans cet air puant et embrasé; j'entendais une clameur horrible, des gémissements, des hurlements et des jurements."

C'est sur ma petite colline verte qu'il est venu rêver aujourd'hui...Il est là, debout contre un pin, son tambour entre ses jambes et s'en donnant à coeur joie...Des vols de perdreaux effarouchés partent à ses pieds sans qu'il

s'en aperçoive. La férigoule embaume autour de lui, il ne
la sent pas.

Il ne voit pas non plus les fines toiles d'araignées
qui tremblent au soleil entre les branches, ni les aiguil-
les de pin qui sautillent sur son tambour. Tout entier à
son rêve et à sa musique, il regarde amoureusement voler
ses baguettes et sa grosse face niaise s'épanouit de plaisir à chaque roulement.

(Every consonant with the exception of gn, ɲ
is contained in the following poem).

Chanson

On est venu dire
(Mon enfant, j'ai peur)
On est venu dire
Qu'il allait partir...

Ma lampe allumée,
(Mon enfant, j'ai peur)
Ma lampe allumée,
Me suis approchée...

A la première porte
(Mon enfant, j'ai peur)
A la première porte
La flamme a tremblé...

A la seconde porte
(Mon enfant, j'ai peur)
A la seconde porte
La flamme a parlé...

A la troisième porte
(Mon enfant, j'ai peur)
A la troisième porte
La lumière est morte.
(Maeterlinck)

Chapter IX.
SYLLABIFICATION

A consideration of syllabification is important because
on it depends not only the question of the nasal vowel and
in part that of the mute e, but also because the <u>clear-cut</u>
effect so characteristic of French speech is the result of
a system of syllable division differing in many respects
from the English.

The phonetic or spoken syllable is the articulation of
one or several sounds in a single effort of the voice. Every syllable must contain one and <u>only one</u> vowel sound and
may contain one or more consonant sounds.

I. The phonetic syllable begins when possible with a
consonant:

> ca-pa-ci-té, dé-li-ca-tesse, etc.
>
> EXCEPTIONS:
> > a. When the word begins with a vowel sound:
> > then the first syllable begins with this
> > vowel:
> > > en-fant, é-lé-phant, a-do-
> > > rer, etc.
> >
> > b. When two vowel sounds are not separated
> > by any consonant:
> > > a-né-an-tir, cru-el, Ca-ïn,
> > > fa-ïence, etc.
> >
> > NOTE: The e which is inserted after g, before
> > a, o, u, in order to produce a soft
> > sound, does not count:
> > > nous man-geons, ils ju-
> > > geaient, etc.

The above phonetic division corresponds to the written
syllable division.

II. In words having a written double consonant, syllables are divided before the double consonant, which in
fact is pronounced as only one consonant:

> a-ller, a-nnée, te-rrain, etc.
>
> > NOTE: A written double consonant followed by a
> > mute e is considered as one consonant
> > belonging to the preceding syllable and
> > the mute e is disregarded:
> > > belle, telle-ment, etc.

The above phonetic division does not correspond to the
written division. In the latter, the division occurs between the two letters of the double consonant:

> al-ler, an-née, bel-le,

III. In words having a group of two inseparable consonants, the division comes before the group of consonants.

The groups of inseparable consonants are: b̲l, b̲r, c̲l, c̲r, d̲r, f̲l, f̲r, g̲l, g̲r, pl, pr, tr, v̲r:

> a-gré-men-te̲, con-flu-ent, etc.

The above phonetic division corresponds to the written division.

IV. When b̲, c̲, d̲, g̲, k̲, l̲, p̲, r̲, or s̲ precede:

    a. another single consonant except l or r

    b. any two consonants

        they belong to the first syllable, while the following consonant or group of consonants belongs to the second syllable:

> ab-di-quer, Ab-ner, ac-ti-vi-té, ad-mi-rable, cel-tique, mis-tral, per-du, res-plen-dir, somp-tueux, spec-tral, ver-tu, etc.

The above phonetic division corresponds to the written division.

V. When a word contains a written mute e which disappears in the pronunciation, the consonant that precedes the written mute e belongs to one syllable and the consonant or consonants that follow written mute e, to another syllable:

> env(e)-lo-pper, ãv-lo-pe ; él(e)-ver, el-ve ; am(e)-ner, am-ne; dév(e)-lopper, dev-lope , etc.

The above phonetic division does not correspond to the written division. In the latter, the division may occur before either of these consonants, but the mute e which does not exist in pronunciation must be written with the consonant that precedes it:

> en-ve-lopper, é-le-ver, a-me-ner, dé-ve-lopper, etc.

VI. When a written x̲ is placed between two vowels, it represents either k̲s̲ or g̲z̲. The first consonant belongs to one syllable and the second consonant to the following:

> examen, ɛg-za-mɛ̃; paradoxal, pa-ra-dok-sal ; etc.

The above phonetic division does not correspond to the written division. In the latter, the division occurs before x:

> e-xa-men, pa-ra-do-xal, etc.

VII. When x̲ precedes one or more consonants, it represents the two sounds k̲s̲. In that case, the consonants represented by x belong to the first syllable and the consonant or consonants which follow to the second syllable:

> ex-tra-or-di-naire, ex-plo-rer, etc.

The above phonetic division corresponds to the written division.

VIII. When the group b̲s̲ precedes a group of two inseparable consonants, it belongs to the first syllable, and the group of inseparable consonants, to the second:

abs-trac-tion, obs-tacle, etc.

The above phonetic division corresponds to the written division.

IX. All the consonants which follow the stressed vowel belong to the stressed syllable:

bel, arbre, I-sa-belle, pé-destre, terre, monstre, dé-montre, etc.

NOTE: Of course all the principles which I have described above apply not only to the grammatical but also to the phonetic word:

Tu ne-sais-pas.	*tyn-se-pa*
Job-a-sou-ffert.	*ʒo-ba-su-feːr*
La-gro-sse en-fant.	*la-gro-sã-fã*
Tu-vois le-ta-bleau.	*ty-vwal-ta-blo*
Un-mons-tre a-ffreux.	*œ̃-mɔ̃s-tra-frø*
Elle-sy-son-ta-llées.	*ɛl-ʒi-sɔ̃-ta-le*
Ma-me-illeu-re a-mie.	*ma-mɛ-jœ-ra-mi*
La-vi-lle é-ter-nelle.	*la-vi-le-tɛr-nel*
L'en-fant-a-é-té-ma-lade.	*lã-fã-a-e-te-ma-lad*
L'ad-mi-ra-ble (h) é-ro-ïne.	*lad-mi-ra-ble-ro-in*
La-f(e)-nê-tre es-tou-ver-te.	*laf-nɛ-tre-tu-vɛrt*
De-sa-mis mon-ta-por-té-de-grande-si-mages.	*de-ʒa-mi-mɔ̃-ta-por-ted-grãd-ʒi-maːʒ*

Chapter X.
INTONATION

For a correct French intonation one must group those units which are known grammatically as words but which are closely related in idea, and treat them phonetically as only one word (Fr. mot phonétique). These phonetic words are of two kinds:

1. Stress-group
2. Breath-group

1. STRESS-GROUP. In this case, since the individual words lose their independence, the last syllable, not of the grammatical word but of the phonetic word is stressed, and for this reason such a group is called a stress-group, (groupe rythmique). These stress-groups may consist of many words, of few words, or even of only one word:

'Viens.

Regarde 'bien.

C'est très impor'tant

Elle est devant les en'fants.

The first thing for a student to do is to determine the different stress-groups of a sentence. This is not diffi-cult, as the student has already discovered from Chapter IV, and the subsequent reading lessons.

2. BREATH-GROUP. A breath-group is a group that may be pronounced in only one breath. There is always a notice-able pause between such groups; this pause may be long or short according to the more or less close relation exist-ing between breath-groups. Although usually consisting of several stress-groups, a breath-group may contain only one. A single upright line, | , is used in this book to separate stress-groups; double upright lines, ‖ , to separate breath-groups.

The majority of sentences may be treated in more than one way:

I.
  a. Mon 'père‖qui est géné'ral‖a passé la re'vue‖'hier.‖

First breath-group, one idea:	{ Mon 'père
Second breath-group, one idea:	{ qui est géné'ral
Third breath-group, one idea:	{ a passé la re'vue
Fourth breath-group, one idea:	{ 'hier.

  b. Mon père|qui est général‖a passé la revue|hier.‖

| First breath-group, two ideas: | { Mon 'père qui est géné'ral |
| Second breath-group, two ideas: | { a passé la re'vue 'hier. |

In a., the speaker, being particularly desirous of bringing out every idea of his sentence, makes each stress-group correspond to a breath group.

In b., the more natural and normal division, there are only two breath-groups for four stress-groups.

II.
  a. A l'âge de vingt-deux, 'ans|en allant de Nevers à Mou'lins,‖il avait eu le bonheur de sau'ver|au péril de sa 'vie,‖un homme et un cheval|qui se noyaient| dans la 'Loire.‖

First breath-group, two ideas, age of the subject and location of the action:	$\Big\{$ à l'âge de vingt-deux 'ans, en allant de Nevers à Mou'lins,

Second breath-group, two ideas, the action and the circumstances under which the subject accomplishes the action:	$\Big\{$ il avait eu le bonheur de sau'ver, au péril de sa 'vie,

Third breath-group, three ideas, the person and the animal for which the subject accomplishes his action, the state in which they were, the place where the accident occurred:	$\Big\{$ un homme et un che'val qui se no'yaient dans la 'Loire.

b. If the speaker wishes to give, however, still more emphasis to the circumstances under which the subject accomplishes the action, he may arrange his groups as follows:
A l'âge de vingt-deux 'ans, ‖ en allant de Nevers à Mou'lins, ‖ il avait eu le bonheur de sau'ver ‖ au péril de sa 'vie, ‖ un homme et un che'val ┃ qui se no-yaient ┃ dans la 'Loire. ‖

Third breath-group, one idea:	$\Big\{$ il avait eu le bonheur de sau'ver

Fourth breath-group, one idea:	$\Big\{$ au péril de sa 'vie,

c. And if the speaker wishes to give more emphasis to the idea of the accident, he may group his words differently, make each group shorter, as follows:
A l'âge de vingt-deux 'ans, ‖ en allant de Nevers à Mou'lins, ‖ il avait eu le bonheur de sau'ver ‖ au péril de sa 'vie, ‖ un homme et un che'val ‖ qui se no-yaient ‖ dans la 'Loire. ‖

Fifth breath-group, one idea:	$\Big\{$ un homme et un che'val

Sixth breath-group, one idea: $\left\{ \underline{\text{qui se no'yaient}} \right.$

Seventh breath-group, one idea: $\left\{ \underline{\text{dans la 'Loire}} \right.$

The division as given in a., would be the normal one.

It is evident from the above examples that, in French as in English, the same sentence may be read or spoken differently according to the ideas which seem, at the moment, important to the reader or speaker. One may read or speak a sentence a first time, giving more importance to certain facts; the next time he may be more impressed by other facts and bring them out more conspicuously.

In order to give a stress-group or a breath-group its full value, the two following points must be taken into consideration:

    a. The normal stress
    b. The stress for emphasis

  a. NORMAL STRESS. (Fr. accent tonique). The normal French stress is marked by:

      1. Intensity (force) and duration
      2. Musical pitch

    1. INTENSITY. The intensity of a sound varies with the degree of force with which it is produced. For example, if one plays on the piano a given note, he may play it gently by touching the key lightly; or, on the contrary, he may play it heavily by touching the same key with force. The sound is the same in both cases; it is neither higher nor lower, but in the second case it is stronger...bigger, so to speak. Its intensity is greater.

    2. MUSICAL PITCH. The musical pitch of the voice varies with the number of vibrations of the vocal chords in a given time. The greater the number of vibrations, the higher the pitch; the smaller the number of vibrations, the lower the pitch.

In English, nearly every word in a group receives a stress on one of its syllables, and many words receive two. The syllable on which the stress falls is invariable--the word is stressed in the same way under whatever circumstances it occurs.

In French, however, only the last syllable of the stress-group receives the stress; usually all the other syllables, although clearly pronounced, are unstressed. So it is that the same grammatical word, used in two different stress-groups, may be stressed in one instance and not in the other, according to the place it occupies:

    Ta soeur est pe'tite.
    Ta petite 'soeur.
    J'ai une 'robe
    J'ai une robe 'rouge.
    J'ai une robe rouge et 'blanche.

When the stressed syllable is not the last of the sentence, a rise in the pitch of the voice is combined with the special intensity. At the end of the last stress-group of the sentence, a lowering of the pitch of the voice is usually combined with the special intensity given the syllable.

    b. STRESS FOR EMPHASIS. In any stress-group, to the normal stress, characterized by greater intensity and change in musical pitch, may be added another, the stress for emphasis, so called because it marks a word the speaker wishes to emphasize. We have seen that the normal stress falls on the last syllable (especially on the vowel of the last syllable) of the word. The stress for emphasis usually falls on the first consonant of the word to be emphasized, lengthening it, and at the same time, often raising it to a higher pitch. In this case, it is called a consonant stress.

    Imbécile.
    La*jolie robe.
    *Quelle surprise!
    La*douceur de vivre.

However, when the emphasized word begins with a vowel and more generally when it stands alone, the stress for emphasis may fall on the first vowel of the word. In this case, the stress is marked by a rise in pitch of the voice, a greater intensity, and also by a lengthening of the vowel.

    *E:pouvantable!
    *A:troce!
    *I:nique!

NOTE: It must be added that in French there are fewer accents for emphasis than in English. Whereas the latter may, without changing the construction of a sentence, emphasize the importance of almost any word by special stress, the former frequently prefers to produce the same effect, not so often by special stress as by constructing the sentence in such a way as to bring the word under consideration into a place where, by coinciding with the last syllable of a stress-group, it receives the normal stress.

    For instance, in the sentence, "I want to-speak to you", in English any one of five of the six

words may be emphasized in speaking without changing the
written form. The French would vary the construction.

There are three types of sentences:
1. The declarative
2. The interrogative
3. The exclamatory

In the treatment of this subject, I have relied chiefly
on the admirable little book of Maurice Grammont, La Prononciation française, Paris, 1926, and on the inspiring
teaching of M. Pierre Fouché from which I have greatly
benefited this last year in Paris.

DECLARATIVE SENTENCES

A declarative sentence is composed of two parts:
1. A rising part.
2. A falling part.

1. <u>THE RISING PART</u>. The rising part, which usually
arouses curiosity and makes the mind expectant of something to follow, may consist of one or more stress-groups
(groupes rythmiques).

However that may be:
- a. The note at the beginning is in general lower than
  in English.
- b. The highest note is that on which the speaker pronounces the last syllable of the rising part.
- c. In the interior of a stress-group, the rise of the
  voice seldom follows a perfectly straight line,
  but proceeds by means of modulations which may be
  represented in either one of the following ways:
  <u>En allant de Nevers à Moulins</u>

1.

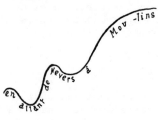

2.

1 is more often heard than 2. The latter is
rather difficult to imitate, but for one who has
thoroughly mastered the former, the study of 2 is
well worth while, since its use enables one to
avoid monotony in reading and speaking. It may be
heard over and over again in phonograph records
made by Madame Bara de Tovar, (Installation, from
Daudet's Lettres de mon moulin, Institut de Phonétique, Paris). For example, in the clause:

    La nuit de mon arrivée

the musical pitch of the voice is higher on nuit,
an unstressed syllable, than on -vée, the stressed
syllable, but nuit receives no added intensity or
length, whereas -vée receives intensity. Of the
three elements discussed--change in musical pitch,
increased intensity and length--nuit is marked by
only one:

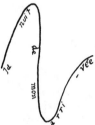

    When the rising part is composed of several
stress-groups, the ascent is usually progressive
and regular in the sense that the last syllable of
each successive stress-group is generally spoken
on a note somewhat higher than that of the preceding stress-group until the highest is reached. I
repeat that this is the last syllable of the entire
rising part, and I cannot insist too often that
the modulations within the stress-group are numerous, varied and delicate.

    One might represent as follows the rising part
of the sentence already studied;

94

    d. The musical note at the beginning of a stress-
       group is always much lower than that of the stress-
       ed syllable which immediately precedes. I can
       never overemphasize this fact or too often call
       the student's attention to it. Notice in the fol-
       lowing illustration the drop of the voice between
       -lées and co-, between bleu and et, between -lant
       and l'une, between l'autre and pour:
       Comme le fond des vallées| commençait à devenir
       bleu ‖et que les bêtes se serraient en bêlant|l'une
       contre l'autre| pour rentrer au parc,‖ j'entendis
       qu'on m'appelait| dans la descente.‖

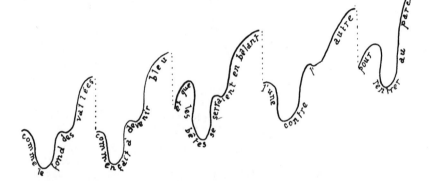

    2. THE FALLING PART. The falling part, which corre-
sponds to the satisfaction of curiosity, the knowledge for
which the mind was waiting during the rising part of the
sentence, follows the general laws for the rising part, as
far as the modulation and the drop of the voice between a
stressed-syllable and the following syllable are concerned.
The last group only of the falling part falls very low at
the end, lower, usually, than any other part of the sentence.

    The descent is progressive and regular in the sense
that the last syllable of each stress-group is on a note
somewhat lower than that of the last syllable of the preceding stress-group until the lowest note is reached; and
this, I repeat, is extremely low:

    ...il avait eu le bonheur de sauver| au péril de sa vie‖
un homme et un cheval| qui se noyaient dans la Loire‖:

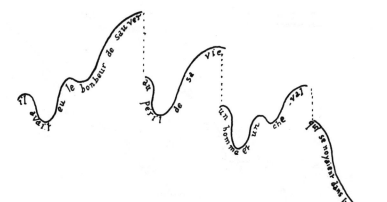

NOTE: Ordinarily, although there is no pause between simple stress-groups, there is a decided
pause between two breath-groups, and this is true
in either the rising or the falling part.

Comme le fond des vallées|commençait à devenir
bleu‖et que les bêtes se serraient en bêlant|l'une
contre l'autre|pour rentrer au parc,‖j'entendis
qu'on m'appelait|dans la descente.‖

Rising part:

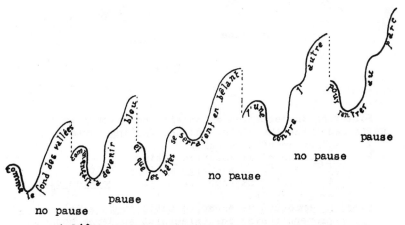

A l'âge de vingt-deux ans,|en allant de Nevers à
Moulins,‖il avait eu le bonheur de sauver|au peril
de sa vie,‖un homme et un cheval|qui se noyaient
dans la Loire.‖

Rising part:

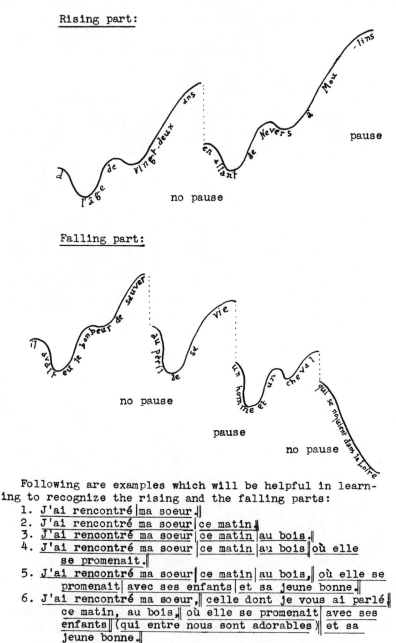

Falling part:

Following are examples which will be helpful in learning to recognize the rising and the falling parts:

1. J'ai rencontré | ma soeur. ‖
2. J'ai rencontré ma soeur | ce matin. ‖
3. J'ai rencontré ma soeur | ce matin | au bois. ‖
4. J'ai rencontré ma soeur | ce matin | au bois ‖ où elle se promenait. ‖
5. J'ai rencontré ma soeur | ce matin | au bois, ‖ où elle se promenait | avec ses enfants | et sa jeune bonne. ‖
6. J'ai rencontré ma soeur, ‖ celle dont je vous ai parlé ‖ ce matin, au bois, ‖ où elle se promenait | avec ses enfants ‖ (qui entre nous sont adorables) ‖ et sa jeune bonne. ‖

1. J'ai rencontré|ma soeur.‖

Rising part:

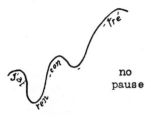

no
pause

(The elevation of the speaker's voice makes the hearer expect something more, something definite. He asks himself "Who? What?").

Falling part:

(The dropping of the voice indicates that there is nothing to add).

2. J'ai rencontré ma soeur| ce matin.‖

Rising part:

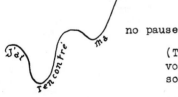

no pause

(The elevation of the speaker's voice makes the hearer expect something more: "Where? etc.).

Falling part:

(Curiosity is satisfied. By the dropping of the voice the speaker has indicated that he has given all his information. This drop shows that there is nothing to add).

3. J'ai rencontré ma soeur│ce matin│au bois.‖

Rising part:

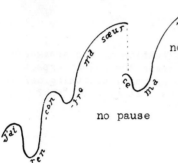

no pause

no pause

(The group of words adding
the idea of time belongs now
to the rising part. The elevation of the speaker's voice
keeps the hearer in suspense
and makes him expect additional information in answer
to the question: "Where?').

Falling part:

(The hearer is satisfied.
He knows now where the
meeting took place; and the
speaker, by lowering his
voice, indicates that he
has nothing to add).

4. J'ai rencontré ma soeur│ce matin│au bois‖où elle se
   promenait.‖

Rising part:

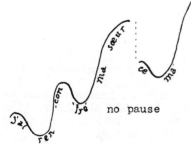

pause

no pause

no pause

(Three groups of words--
stress-groups--are now joined in the rising part. The
elevation of voice on bois
keeps the mind in suspense:
"What was she doing?").

Falling part:

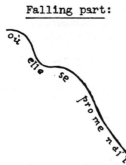

(By dropping his voice,
the speaker shows that
he has no further in-
formation to give).

5. J'ai rencontré ma soeur|ce matin|au bois‖où elle se
promenait|avec ses enfants|et sa jeune bonne.‖

Rising part:

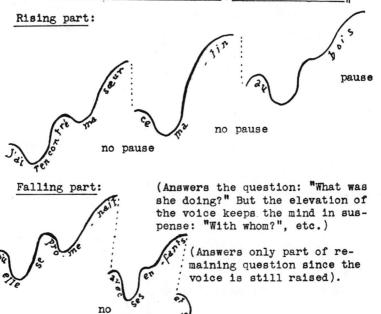

pause

no pause

no pause

Falling part:

(Answers the question: "What was
she doing?" But the elevation of
the voice keeps the mind in suspense: "With whom?", etc.)

(Answers only part of re-
maining question since the
voice is still raised).

no
pause

no
pause

(The speaker shows
that he has replied
completely to the last
unasked question:"With
whom?" by dropping his
voice. Curiosity is
entirely satisfied).

pause

6. When a sentence contains a parenthetical clause, whether or not enclosed by parentheses, this clause is spoken on a lower note with, however, a marked rising inflection at the end:

> J'ai rencontré ma soeur,‖celle dont je vous ai parlé‖ ce matin, au bois,‖ où elle se promenait|avec ses enfants,‖(qui entre nous sont adorables)‖ et sa jeune bonne. ‖

<u>Rising part:</u>

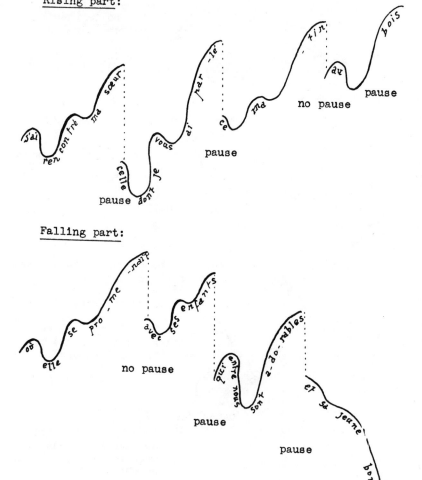

<u>Falling part:</u>

7. A phrase or clause introducing a direct quotation often ends on a very low note, corresponding generally to the end of the falling part.

Elle me dit:‖ "J'ai rencontré ma soeur,| ce matin."‖

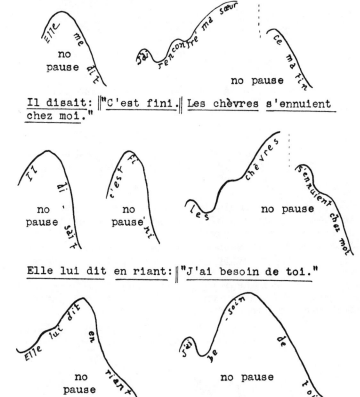

Il disait: ‖"C'est fini.‖ Les chèvres s'ennuient chez moi."

Elle lui dit en riant: ‖"J'ai besoin de toi."

In sentences in which the speaker stops abruptly or purposely interrupts himself--intensity, duration and musical pitch of the last syllable are those of a stressed syllable:

Je te dis que...‖

Tu viendras, sinon... ‖

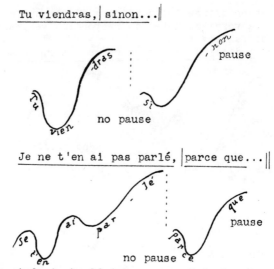

Je ne t'en ai pas parlé, parce que... ‖

The student should take care not to be misled by the
dots, ..., that are often found after a completed sentence.
He should never rely solely on the dots, ..., but should
determine from the sense whether the sentence is completed:

    1. <u>Blanquette</u>|<u>redoubla de coups de cornes,</u>‖ <u>le loup</u>|
<u>de coups de dents</u>...‖

    2. <u>Une lueur pâle</u>|<u>parut dans l'horizon</u>...‖(Daudet)

Here, in both sentences the sense is completed, and
each has a <u>rising</u> and a <u>falling</u> part:

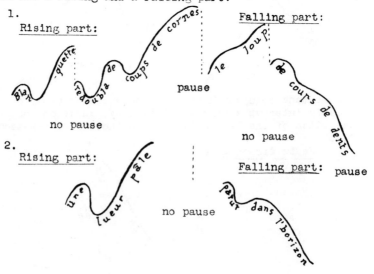

IMPORTANT NOTE: For the sake of variation, the student who has perfected himself in the use of more usual intonation may follow the model of other forms sometimes employed by French people. The ability to do this correctly requires not only intelligence and taste, but also skill. It should not be attempted by a beginner.

Some possibilities are:

a. To begin the stress-group on a very high note and finish on a very low one:

Quelquefois l'hiver,‖ quand les troupeaux┃ étaient descendus dans la plaine‖et que je rentrais le soir┃à la ferme pour souper...‖ (Daudet).

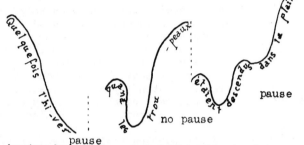

b. Or, having begun on a very high note, to drop the voice to a very low one near the middle of this stress-group and raise it at the end to a note as high as that of the beginning:

Ni les caresses de leur maître,‖ni la peur du loup, rien ne les retenait.‖

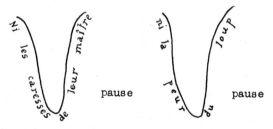

c. When two stress-groups are very closely related to each other, to place the last syllable of the first group on a very low note:

Le pauvre M. Seguin┃qui ne comprenait rien┃au caractère de ses bêtes‖était consterné.‖

(Daudet)

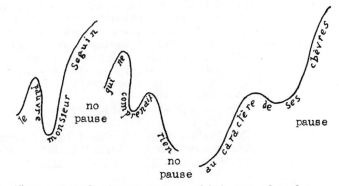

d. When several stress-groups which are <u>closely</u>
<u>related</u> in thought are placed in a sentence
among shorter ones which the reader intends to
speak with rich modulations, to pronounce these
closely related stress-groups on the same or
nearly the same note, without however diminish-
ing the intensity of every stressed syllable.
The contrast between monotony and variety of
intonation produces a striking and pleasing effect:

Enfin sur les trois heures,‖ le ciel étant lavé,
la montagne│luisante d'eau et de soleil,‖ j'en-
tendis│parmi l'égouttement des feuilles │et le
débordement│des ruisseaux gonflés,│ les son-
nailles de la mule,‖aussi gaies,‖aussi alertes‖
qu'un grand carillon de cloches│un jour de
Pâques.‖ (Daudet)

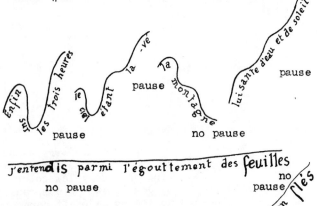

e. When a stress-group, particularly at the beginning of the sentence, really <u>stands out</u> to mark
the time or place of the event or scene which
follows, to place the last syllable of that
group on a higher note than the last syllable
of the subsequent groups but rarely higher than,
or even as high as, the last syllable of the
entire rising part:

<u>Quelquefois l'hiver,</u>‖ <u>quand les troupeaux</u> |
<u>étaient descendus dans la plaine</u> ‖<u>et que je</u>
<u>rentrais le soir</u> |<u>à la ferme pour souper...</u>‖
(Daudet)

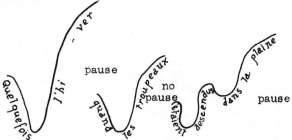

(Compare e. with a., p.103).

f. To transfer the high musical pitch, generally
associated with the last syllable, to the next-
to-the-last, while taking great care that the
greater intensity still falls upon the last
syllable:

<u>Pas un sac,</u>‖ <u>pas un grain de blé,</u>‖ <u>pas la</u>
<u>moindre farine</u>‖

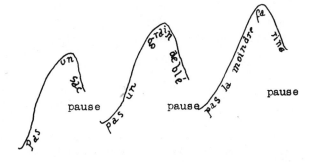

(To transfer <u>intensity</u> and <u>duration</u> as well
as the higher musical pitch from the last

to the next-to-the-last syllable is to use
an intonation characteristic of the speech
of the <u>uneducated Parisian</u>, and consti-
tutes an error against which the foreigner
should be constantly on his guard).

<u>Note 1</u>. It is evident that the student should not at-
tempt any one of the six variations of French intonation
described above, if he has not already learned to recog-
<u>nize and dissociate</u> the three elements of intonation--in-
tensity, duration, and musical pitch.

<u>Note 2</u>. My readers who have spent some time in France
have perhaps noticed that some French people in <u>rapid con-
versation</u> permit the voice to rise even at the end of a
declarative sentence. The student may use this intonation
in conversation on condition that he take care to follow
the diagram for the whole sentence as has been indicated
above, with the exception that at the end he may permit
his voice to rise to a very high note as in an exclamatory
sentence (see page 116). But he should be careful when using this intonation <u>not to drag</u> the next-to-the-last syllable, and he should <u>raise</u> his voice to a very high note.
This intonation should be used only in reading passages
which are composed of conversation.

<u>Note 3</u>. When the principles described above have been
thoroughly mastered, let the student add, in his reading
and speaking, color, life, life, and still more life.

MISTAKES TO AVOID.

Americans should avoid:

1. Beginning the sentence on a note which is insufficiently low:

<u>Elle est venue me voir</u>

instead of:

2. Transferring American stress to the French sentence,
especially in the case of a word similar in the two languages, by giving intensity, length and high pitch to the
wrong syllable:

<u>Elle est arrivée</u>

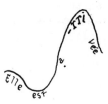 instead of:

3. "Wavering" in a monotonous manner between two musical notes far less widely separated than in French, and
insufficiently marking the modulations:

    <u>J'ai rencontré ma soeur</u>

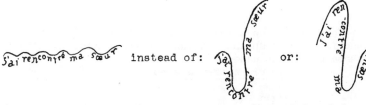

4. Raising the voice and at the same time giving intensity to the highest note of the rising group on the next-
to-the-last-syllable instead of on the last only:

    <u>J'ai rencontré ma soeur</u>

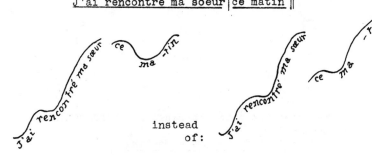

5. Beginning the initial syllable of a stress-group on
a note too near in pitch to the final syllable of the preceding stress-group:

    <u>J'ai rencontré ma soeur</u>|ce matin ‖

6. Reducing the intensity as well as the pitch on the last syllable or syllables of the falling group:

J'ai rencontré ma soeur|ce matin|

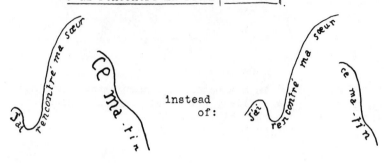

instead of:

7. Letting the voice fall insufficiently at the end of the falling group and singing the last vowel on two or three different notes:

J'ai rencontré ma soeur

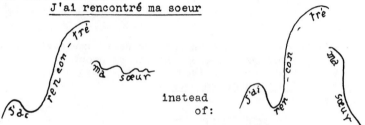

instead of:

8. When occasionally an unstressed syllable receives very high musical pitch, giving it also intensity and length:

La nuit de mon arrivée

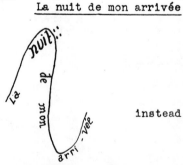

instead of:

9. Permitting the voice to rise in a straight line, without modulation:

En allant de Nevers à Moulins

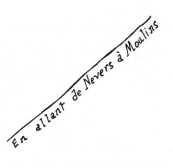

<u>NOTE</u>: If one makes the mistake indicated above he obtains a melody--if melody it may be called!-- which is opposed to the true music of the French sentence. The diagram above is one artificially created by some teachers of French intonation in order "to simplify" the subject. The result is double--the music of our language is incorrectly represented, and the student acquires, in his so-called French intonation, an unbearably monotonous delivery, of which later he finds it difficult to rid himself.

10. Always pronouncing the unstressed syllables on the same note and raising the voice only on the stressed syllable. Although it is true that some French people employ this intonation under certain circumstances, it is not sufficiently customary to justify its constant use (p.104).

A l'âge de vingt-deux ans,│ <u>en allant de Nevers à Moulins</u>║

instead of:

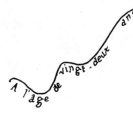 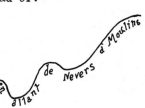

11. Pronouncing all the stressed syllables on the same note:

<u>Monsieur le sous-préfet,</u>‖ <u>grisé de parfums,</u>‖ <u>ivre de musique,</u>‖ <u>essaye vainement de résister</u> |<u>au nouveau charme qui l'envahit</u>‖

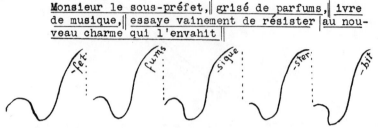

instead of:

12. Making too many breath-groups, that is to say, too many pauses:

<u>En allant de Nevers à Moulins,</u>‖ <u>il avait eu le bonheur</u>‖<u>de sauver au péril de sa vie</u>‖<u>un homme</u>‖et <u>un cheval</u>‖<u>qui se noyaient</u>‖<u>dans la Loire</u>‖

instead of

<u>En allant de Nevers à Moulins,</u>| <u>il avait eu le bonheur de sauver</u>| <u>au péril de sa vie</u>‖<u>un homme et un cheval</u>|<u>qui se noyaient dans la Loire</u>‖

NOTE: This is a mere sketch of the rhythm of the sentence. French intonation is far more varied, more subtle, more flexible than what I show here; but to treat it in an adequate manner would require much more space than the character of this book permits. An admirable work on this subject has recently been published. The author, Madame Bara de Tovar, discusses French intonation very clearly and in great detail (Principes généraux de la diction française, Institut de Phonétique, Paris).

INTERROGATIVE SENTENCES

The interrogative sentence corresponds, in general, to the rising part of the declarative sentence, for it arouses curiosity; but, although a complete sentence, it does not satisfy it, as is the case in the declarative sentence.

The highest syllable of the interrogative sentence is generally the same as in the corresponding rising part of the declarative sentence, but as a musical note it is much higher.

This highest note may be:

    a. At the end of the question, on the last syllable:

       1. <u>Est-elle ici?</u>   2. <u>Tu iras là-bas?</u>

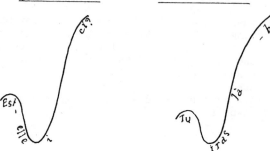

       3. <u>Est-ce que j'ai</u>   4. <u>Pourquoi venez-vous?</u>
          <u>pris mon livre?</u>

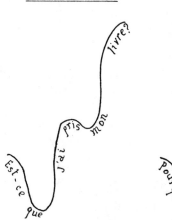
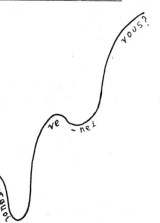

5. N'est-elle pas   6. Est-elle partie ce matin?
   venue nous voir?

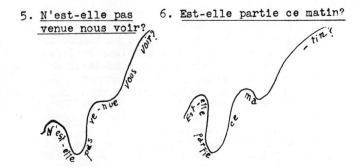

    b. In the middle of the interrogative sentence, according to the position of the most important word (that is to say, the word which would be the last of the rising part of the corresponding declarative sentence).

    Compare:

1. Vous lui avez parlé? de-   with: Vous devez parler
   manda-t-elle.   à Jean.

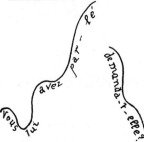

2. Vous les avez vues,   with: Vous avez vu ses
   vous, ses filles?   filles.

3. <u>Que va-t-il faire là</u>
<u>bas, cet enfant?</u>

with: <u>Il va là-bas, cet</u>
<u>enfant.</u>

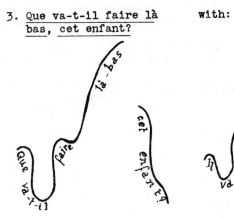

4. <u>Est-ce à lui que tu as</u>
<u>parlé?</u>

with: <u>C'est à lui que tu</u>
<u>as parlé.</u>

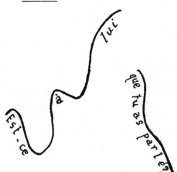

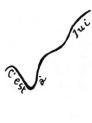

5. <u>A qui ont-elles écrit?</u>

with: <u>C'est à eux qu'el-</u>
<u>les ont écrit.</u>

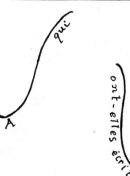

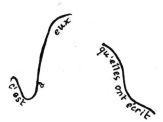

114

Note 1. The part of the interrogative sentence which immediately follows the highest note is pronounced on relatively low notes.

Note 2. The interrogative words such as: quoi, que, qui, comment, pourquoi, etc...are not necessarily the most important:

Pourquoi venez-vous ce soir, Marguerite?

Quoi de plus drôle, que ce jeu-là?

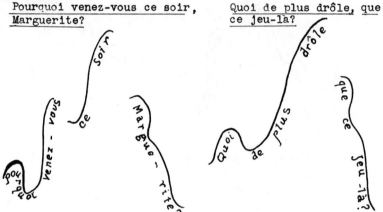

EXCLAMATORY SENTENCES

Contrary to what usually happens in an interrogative sentence, words of an exclamatory nature such as: que, quel, comment, etc...as well as the interjections, are pronounced on the highest note. This may be as many as five or six musical notes higher than the others.

1. Quel enfant!

2. Que de beaux paysages!

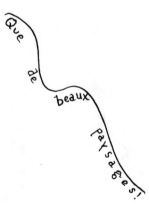

3. <u>Comment</u>!

4. <u>Combien j'ai douce souvenance</u>!

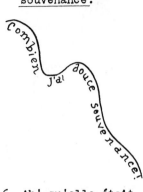

5. <u>Oh</u>! l'amour chéri!

6. <u>Ah</u>! qu'elle était belle!

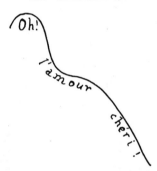

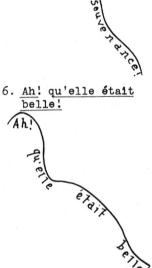

But more often than not, the exclamation is connected with the stress for emphasis (the most important word in the sentence):

    1. L'imbécile qui s'est <u>per·du</u>!

    2. <u>Merveilleux</u>!

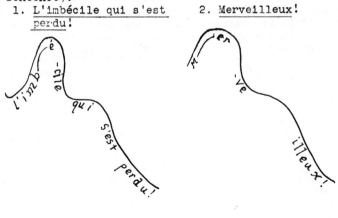

3. <u>Admirablement beau</u>!　　　4. <u>Bandit</u>!

5. <u>Maudit sois-tu</u>!　　　6. <u>Un amour de petite</u>
　　　　　　　　　　　　　<u>chèvre</u>!

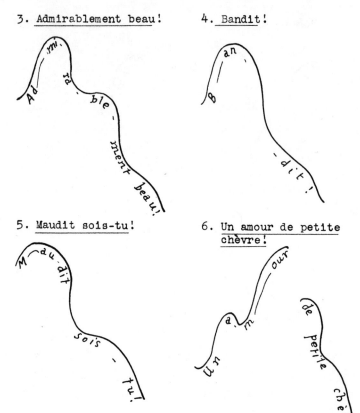

Unlike the examples already given, in those exclamatory sentences which express surprise, astonishment, or incredulity, it is the last syllable which usually receives greater intensity and a very high musical note.

1. <u>Comment</u>!　　　　　2. <u>Par exemple</u>!

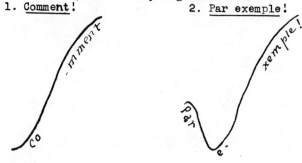

3. C'est fort!   4. Elle n'est pas **venue**!

5. C'est impossible!   6. Je ne le crois pas!

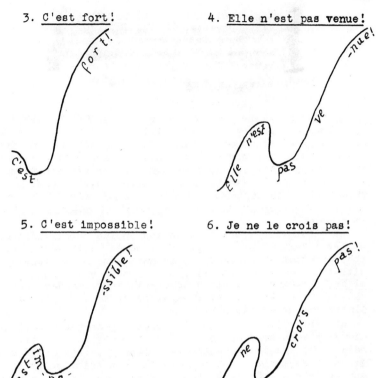

Chapter XI.
MUTE E, ə

SPELLINGS:
1. -<u>e</u>-, -<u>e</u>:
   la table, la **porte**, une chaise, telle-
   ment, etc.
2. -<u>es</u>: when mark of plural or of personal verb endings:
   les tables, les portes, tu parles, que
   tu sentes, etc.
3. -<u>ent</u>: when mark of third person plural:
   ils aiment, ils disent, ils paient,
   elles aimaient, etc.
4. -<u>ai</u>-: in the following words only:
   je faisais, tu faisais, il faisait,

nous faisions, vous faisiez, ils faisaient, nous faisons, faisant; faisan,
faiseur,-euse, bienfaisance, bien-
faisant,-e, malfaisant,-e, malfaisance,
satisfaisant,-e, faisandé, faisanderie.
 5. -on-: in the following word only:
 monsieur

GENERAL CONSIDERATIONS

Mute e by nature is a vague, obscure, neutral vowel.
Sometimes, depending on the position it occupies in a word
or in a group of words, it is completely silent, and the
consonants thus brought into contact through its silence
are pronounced as if there were no letter between them.
This is the only case when the name of mute e (that is,
silent e) is justifiable. In this, there is no phonetic
symbol to represent this letter, since it does not exist
as a sound.

At other times, still depending on the position it occupies in a word or in a group of words, although mute e
is not completely silent, it is not pronounced clearly
with all the characteristics of a French vowel: one
slides over the mute e, so to speak, very rapidly. In
this case, mute e is represented by an e of very small
dimension, upside down:ᵊ.

At other times, too, still depending on the position it
occupies in a word or in a group of words, mute e is a
real vowel and is pronounced as clearly as any other vowel.
It is then represented in phonetic transcription by an e
upside down of the same size as the other vowels: ə .

The question of the pronunciation of mute e depends upon the consonants which surround it.

Before studying the rules themselves, the following
questions must be considered:

 1. WHICH CONSONANTS ARE TO BE TAKEN INTO CONSIDERATION?
It is understood that only pronounced consonants are to
be considered; silent consonants are never counted, for
pronunciation deals with sounds and not with mere letters.
 Tu me dis de partir
 Il me sert de bureau
The s of dis and the t of sert are not to be counted
because they are silent.

 II. HOW SHOULD THE CONSONANTS BE COUNTED?
When determining whether a mute e is to be pronounced
or not, the consonant should be counted beginning with the
first after the preceding vowel, to and including the last
before the following vowel:
 a. Tu veux le finir
 First consonant after the preceding vowel: l(preceding vowel: eu).

Last consonant before the following vowel:_f_(following vowel: <u>1</u>).
In the above example there are <u>two</u> consonants to
deal with, and to determine whether mute e is to
be silent or not, one must understand the rules
concerning a mute e between two consonants.

2+1   b. Edit̸ me l'a dit
First consonant after the preceding vowel: <u>t</u>(preceding vowel: <u>1</u>).
Last consonant before the following vowel: <u>1</u>(following vowel: <u>a</u>).
In the above example there are <u>three</u> consonants to
deal with; and to determine whether mute e is to
be silent or not, one must understand the rules
concerning mute e with three consonants.

III. IS MUTE E IN THE SAME WORD ALWAYS SILENT OR ALWAYS
PRONOUNCED?
From the rules which will be explained later, it will
be evident that in many words the same mute e may be silent or pronounced, depending on the position of the word
and its surroundings.

MUTE E IS COMPLETELY SILENT: ✗

I. At the end of a breath-group:

Sur la chais̸	Jean l'ouvr̸
Tu mets la rob̸	Il parl̸
Il prend des not̸s	La pest̸
Tu chant̸s	La maison vert̸
Il dans̸	J'ai vu le chantr̸ _singer / chorister_
Elle est bell̸	C'est la nôtr̸
Tu l'appell̸s	Ce sont les vôtr̸s _silent_
Sur la terr̸	C'est un monstr̸ _when next_
Voici la tabl̸	Un bel arbr̸ _word begins with a vowel._

II. Between two consonant sounds, and only two. (That
is to say, when preceded by one consonant only):

Voici l̸ chien
La ch̸minée fume
Il es̸ d̸vant la f̸nêtre
On l̸ dit
On n̸ veut pas
Vous v̸nez m̸ voir   / + /
Nous sommes dans l̸ salon
Il a trois ans d̸ moins qu̸ moi
Enfin, j̸ suis là
———— Vous donn̸rez l̸ livre au p̸tit garçon
———— Il a enl̸vé les env̸loppes et l̸ papier
Il est bien él̸vé et vous l'aim̸rez
Bien qu̸ tu n̸ sois pas allé l̸ voir, Jean
n̸ t'en veut pas l̸ moins du monde.

120

EXCEPTIONS:

   a. At the beginning of a breath-group,
      mute e between two consonants usu-
      ally is pronounced:
         Compare:
            { Le tableau noir
            { J'ai vu lé tableau noir
            { Ne dis rien
            { Tu né dis rien
            { Tenez; le voilà
            { Vous ténez
            { Venez avec moi
            { Vous vénez avec moi
            { Toi, le père, tu dois lui parler
            { Tu es lé père tu dois lui parler
            { Depuis huit jours, il est là
            { Il y est dépuis huit jours
            { De loin, il l'a vu
            { Il l'a vu dé loin
            { Serez-vous prêt à temps
            { Vous sérez prêt à temps
            { De toi, ça m'étonne
            { Il rit dé toi
            { Remettez-vous
            { Il faut vous rémettre

   b. When the stress for emphasis falls
      on the syllable containing the mute
      e, mute e is pronounced, and it is
      pronounced as clearly and with as
      much intensity as any other vowel:
         Compare:
            { Debout les morts
            { Je suis débout
            { Il faudra recommencer
            { Tu récommences demain
            { L'auteur s'appelle Lenormand
            { C'est lé Normand
            { Je vous en prie, de la tenue
            { Elle n'a pas dé tenue
            { Restons-nous dedans ou dehors?
            { Il est dédans
            { Il jura devant Dieu et devant
              les hommes
            { Je suis dévant vous
            { Savez-vous la différence entre
              recommander et raccommander?
            { Je lui ai récommandé de venir

   c. In a few words of which the first
      syllable contains a mute e, this

mute e is always pronounced. Following is the list of the more usual words of this type:

besace – *begging bag;*
celui
devers
menu
menuet   *woodworkers sawyer, joiner*
menuisier and words of same
  family
pelouse
peser and words of same family
querelle
sedan
vedette

d. In the first and second persons
plural of the conditional, mute e
is always pronounced:

nous danserions
vous chanteriez
nous ferions
vous feriez, etc.

e. -elier. In the words ending in
-elier, mute e is always pronounced:

atelier
bâchelier ← *scholar; someone with baccau-*
laureat
chancelier
chandelier
coutelier
ficelier
hôtelier, etc.

f. Before the word rien:

Tu ne manges rien
Il ne demande rien

III. With three consonant sounds:

a. When the second and third belong to the same syllable and are inseparable. The groups of inseparable
consonant sounds are:

1. bl, br, cl, cr, dr, fl, fr, gl, gr, pl, pr,
tr, vr.
2. ks, sk, ps, sp, ts, st, sf, sm, sn.

Then, it may be said that mute e is silent with
three consonants when they are grouped 1+2, that is
to say, when the syllable-division is after the
first, leaving the inseparable consonants together:

Dans le clair-obscur
Un amas de glace
J'en ai de plus belles
Donnez-lui le bras

1+2
(cl)
cluster

Il fait lé snob
Saluez lé drapeau
Vous êtes dans lé vrai
Prends lé gros crayon
Vous mettez lé smoking?
Elle a des yeux dé sphynx
Rien dé spécial, aujourd'hui?
On dansait beaucoup chez lé tsar
Il travaillait lé xylophone (x=ks)
retrouver = to discover Vous n'avez pas retrouvé vos gants?
retrieve   Nous irons dé préférence en autobus
C'est lé scandale qui lui fait peur
Cette expression est dans lé psaume 37
Vous né frémissez pas à cette idée-là?
Les coureurs entrèrent dans lé stade
Prends lé flambeau
Préférez-vous lé blanc ou lé bleu?
Elle a lé gros chien
Elle étudie lé pluriel des adjectifs, etc.

b. When the first and second consonant sounds belong
to the last syllable of a word and the third is the
initial consonant of a following word. It is to be
noted that the consonants are grouped --in two different grammatical words--2+1.(In such cases the
second consonant becomes partly or completely voiceless, p.141):

2+1 Les Chevaliers de la Tablé Ronde
2+1 Elle a un immeublé neuf
2+1 L'inaccessiblé sommet
2+1 Il ronflé fort
2+1 C'est un célèbré savant
2+1 C'est un vrai diablé noir
2+1 C'est du sablé jaune
2+1 Il a un cartablé noir
2+1 C'est la porté verte
2+1 Il voit l'onclé Pierre
2+1 Le gesté du chanteur
2+1 La gardé du malade
2+1 Presqué pas
2+1 Inculpé-la
2+1 Crispé-les
2+1 Désaxé-la
2+1 L'éclipsé du soleil
2+1 Le torsé nu, etc.

Note 1. But one must take care to pronounce the
three consonants very distinctly; if at first this
is too difficult, the student should insert a
slight mute e after the second consonant sound.
Even some French people, in such expressions,

sometimes pronounce not only a slight but even a complete mute e, although this practice is infrequent.

Note 2. When such words as those given in the above examples precede one of the eight monosyllables in which there is a mute e (ce, de, je, le, me, ne, que, te), the mute e of the monosyllable is very clearly pronounced:

> La tablé de Jean
> L'immeublé que tu possèdes
> Son onclé ne voit rien, etc.

MUTE E IS PRONOUNCED:

I. With three consonants, if the first and second precede a mute e, even though in spelling there may be another mute e, between the first and second consonants. This is called the "Rule of the three consonants", because with the omission of both the mute e's, three consonants would come together. These consonants are grouped either 2+1--that is, in a single grammatical word--or 1+1+1--that is, in three consecutive grammatical words--but not in two consecutive grammatical words (page 122):

> 2+1 Il sort librement
> 2+1 Elle est dans l'appartement   *tristement*
> 2+1 Il est du Parlement   *1 + 1*
> 2+1 Il agit noblement
> 2+1 C'est terriblement triste
> 2+1 Il l'a fortement soutenu
> 2+1 Il l'avait préalablement regardé
> 2+1 Il fait partie du gouvernement
> 1+1+1 Elle jouait avec le chat
> 1+1+1 Il me l'a dit
> 1+1+1 Ellé te voit
> 1+1+1 Il me parle
> 1+1+1 Il ne peut pas attendre
> 1+1+1 Poussé le verrou
> 1+1+1 Il est arrivé sur le sommet
> 1+1+1 Il reparlera
> 1+1+1 La curé de silence
> 1+1+1 Des aiguillés de cette grosseur-ci
> 1+1+1 Madamé de Sévigné
> 1+1+1 Madamé de Maintenon
> 1+1+1 Professeur de littérature
> 1+1+1 Encoré de la soupe
> 1+1+1 Toujourś de la viande

II. Between two consonants, and only two, in the following cases only:

1. At the beginning of a breath-group.
2. When the stress for emphasis falls on the syllable containing the mute e.

3. In a few words of which the first syllable contains
   a mute e.
4. In the first and second persons plural of the conditional.
5. In the ending -elier.
   (Examples have been given in the exceptions to rule II on pages 119 and 120).

MONOSYLLABLES

I.
1. When, at the <u>beginning</u> of a stress-group, there
   are two monosyllables in succession, each containing a mute e, the <u>first</u> mute e usually is <u>retained</u>
   and the <u>other</u> <u>dropped</u>. However, in the combinations <u>ce que</u> and <u>je te</u>, the first mute is
   dropped and the second kept:

   Ne mø dis rien
   Que cø fut lui, je nø le croyais pas
   Que dø toi je m'éloigne et c'en est fait
   Que jø parte ou non
   Que lø soleil luise ou non, je partirai
   Que mø fait ton récit?
   Que tø dirai-je encore?
   Te lø dire et mourir
   Se lø répéter
   Ce mø semble parfait
   Ce nø peut pas être vrai
   Ce tø paraît gai, n'est-ce pas?
   Je nø veux pas
   Que nø lui en parles-tu?
   Ne tø mets pas en route
   De cø beau jour je me souviendrai
   Je mø suis fait mal
   Je lø ferai volontiers
   Me lø faut-il vraiment faire?
   Ne lø prends pas
           BUT
   Cø que tu as dit
   Cø que j'aime
   Jø te parle
   Jø te raconterai une histoire

2. When, <u>within</u> a stress-group, there are two monosyllables in succession, usually <u>either one</u> may be
   retained and the other dropped:

Et je le lui donnai	je lø	or	jø le
André ne se rase pas	ne sø	"	nø se
Qu'on se le dise	se lø	"	sø le
Et je me suis fait mal	je mø	"	jø me
Il veut me le faire faire	me lø	"	mø le
Tu ne le prends pas	ne lø	"	nø le

Vous ne me dites rien   ne m<u>e̸</u>   "   n<u>e̸</u> me
Léon te le dira   te l<u>e̸</u>   "   t<u>e̸</u> le
Jean ne te verra pas   ne t<u>e̸</u>   "   n<u>e̸</u> te

Note the three following exceptions:

  a. If one of the monosyllables is <u>que</u>
     or <u>de</u>, this monosyllable rather than
     the other retains the mute e:
        Que fais-tu de c<u>e̸</u> tableau
        Tu as besoin <u>de</u> l<u>e̸</u> dire
→   Il vient <u>de</u> m<u>e̸</u> parler
        Il oublie <u>de</u> s<u>e̸</u> taire
        Il essaie <u>de</u> s<u>e̸</u> voir
        Tu feras bien de n<u>e̸</u> pas la voir
        Tu as dit <u>que</u> c<u>e̸</u> livre était à toi
        Il n'a parlé <u>que</u> d<u>e̸</u> géographie
        Tu ne veux <u>que</u> l<u>e̸</u> sien
        Il ne veut que m<u>e̸</u> parler
        Marie ne fait que t<u>e̸</u> louer
        Il ne faut que s<u>e̸</u> coucher. etc.

  b. In the following combinations begin-
     ning with <u>ce</u>:   ce me, ce te, ce ne,
     ce le, and in the combination je ne,
     the <u>first</u> mute e is kept and the sec-
     ond dropped:
        Mais <u>ce</u> m<u>e̸</u> semble parfait
        Et <u>ce</u> t<u>e̸</u> paraît très gai
        Mais <u>ce</u> n<u>e̸</u> sera rien
        Et <u>ce</u> l<u>e̸</u> semblera ainsi
        Et <u>je</u> n<u>e̸</u> sais rien de plus

  c. And in the combinations: ce que, que
     je, the first mute e is dropped and the
     second kept:
        Tu sais c<u>e̸</u> <u>que</u> tu veux
        Il veut qu<u>e̸</u> <u>je</u> lui donne ma réponse
        Mais j<u>e̸</u> te parle

(handwritten left margin: "not on test", "skip")

II. When there is a group of more than two monosylla-
bles, usually it is the mute e of the <u>first</u> that is kept,
then the second dropped, the third kept, and so forth:
        Jean me l<u>e̸</u> demande
        Tu m<u>e</u> l<u>e̸</u> red<u>e̸</u>mandes
        Tu n<u>e</u> l<u>e̸</u> ref<u>e̸</u>ras pas
        Tu n<u>e</u> l<u>e̸</u> ref<u>e̸</u>ras qu<u>e̸</u> si tu t<u>e̸</u> souviens
        de c<u>e̸</u> <u>que</u> j<u>e̸</u> te dis
        Et <u>je</u> n<u>e̸</u> le r<u>e̸</u>verrai plus
Ne parl<u>e̸</u> pas de c<u>e̸</u> qu<u>e</u> l<u>e̸</u> devin t'a dit
        EXCEPTIONS:
        a. When the combination <u>ce que</u> occurs
           in a long group of monosyllables, the
           <u>e</u> of <u>que</u> is kept, the <u>e</u> of <u>ce</u> dropped,

and the other mute e's are suppressed
alternately on either side:
Je suis content de ce que le profes-
seur dit
Parce que tu la demandes
Parce que je me le redemande
Et ce que ce salon est sombre!
C'est ce que je te redis depuis long-
temps. etc.

b. When the combination je te occurs in
a long group of monosyllables, the e
of te is kept, the e of je dropped:
and the other mute e's are suppressed
alternately on either side:
Quand je te le dis
Si je te le redonne
Et je te le redemande
Mais je te le redemanderai

NOTE: Although other pronunciations of groups of monosyllables containing mute e are sometimes heard, the rules
explaining them are very complicated. A foreigner who follows those given above may be sure that his treatment of
the mute e will always be considered correct by a French
person.

SPECIAL OBSERVATIONS

I. The mute e of le, pronoun, when the last syllable of
a phonetic group placed after the affirmative imperative,
is always pronounced:

Prends-le   Attrapez-le
Dis-le   Rendez-le
Redis-le   Chantons-le, etc.

II. When one of the eight monosyllables containing mute
e, or one of the conjunctions ending in -que is stressed,
the mute e is pronounced very clearly--as a real vowel:

Et ce,
Parce que, étant donné---
Sur ce, elle partit.

III. Mute e is always pronounced, and very clearly pronounced when it is placed before an aspirated h or a word
which does not permit liaison (p.131) or linking (p.140):

le héros   Elle parle haut
le hameau   Qu'elle dise oui
le houx   Le oui de Juliette
le haut perron   Presque onze heures
se hausser   Puisque Hortense le dit.

IV. From the preceding rules it may very easily be understood that the pronunciation of a given mute e may de-
pend on its position in a word or group of words:

	{La petite fille	{C'est à moi qu'il parle
	{Une petite fille	{Il parle_haut
\+|	{Je suis debout	{Je n'ai pas de papier
	{Il chante debout	{Le professeur de littérature

Note 1: These rules apply to delivery of medium speed--
neither very slow, as in the oratorical style, nor very
fast, as is apt to be the case in familiar speech. As the
general tone of a single conversation changes, the foreigner will find variations. Let him not be surprised,
however, for French is a living language, and as such,
subject to change. At the present time a real evolution is
taking place, especially with regard to liaison and mute e.

Note 2: The student will do well not to ask his French
friends for rules with regard to the omission or retention
of the mute e, for unless a French person has studied the
phonetics of his own language, he will stoutly assert and
maintain that he pronounces mute e's which in reality he
omits. Of this fact phonograph records, which may be retarded at will, furnish irrefutable proof.

<h1 style="text-align:center">Chapter XII.</h1>
LIAISON

Liaison is that phenomenon by which a final consonant
silent in the isolated word, is sounded before a word beginning with a vowel or mute h. In pronunciation, this
consonant then loses its connection with the first word
and becomes the first consonant of the second word. Petit
enfant is pronounced as if it were peti tenfant. Liaison
is indicated as follows: petit_enfant.

GENERAL CONSIDERATIONS

Liaison takes place only between words closely connected in thought.

Some liaisons are obligatory; but in rapid speech, the
liaison has a tendency to disappear. Thus in many cases, a
liaison which in oratorical and formal speech is optional,
is avoided in conversation.

It is not that the succession of two or more vowel
sounds is disagreeable in French. Within a word or within
a stress-group, if two or more vowels are in contact,
there is always something which approximates a liaison
from vowel to vowel, and this is shown by the inflexion of
the voice as well as in the continuity of the vibrations
of the vocal chords. The sentence: "Papa a à aller à Paris"
is not shocking to a French ear, if the vibrations of the
vocal chords are not interrupted after each a; even a
short cessation of the vibrations however will at once re-
veal the foreigner.

Failure to make an obligatory liaison shocks the ear of

an educated Frenchman therefore, not because of the succession of two vowel sounds but because of usage, which
demands the combination of a consonant and a vowel in that
special case.

Liaison is unusual between two stress-groups and consequently between two breath-groups. Even within a stress-
group, liaison occurs only between words closely related
in thought. "Dans la prononciation courante d'aujourd'hui
les mots accessoires, articles, pronoms, adjetifs posses-
sifs et démonstratifs, prépositions, conjonctions, ad-
verbes, se lient toujours quand ils sont préposés et ne se
lient pas quand ils sont postposés." M. Grammont, La Prononciation française, page 130.

Within a stress-group, liaisons are either:

        1. obligatory
        2. prohibited
        3. optional

        OBLIGATORY LIAISONS

I. ARTICLES

  a. Between the definite articles les, and the follow-
     ing noun, adjective, pronoun:

       Les enfants
       Les adorables bébés
       Les uns et les autres

  b. Between the indefinite articles, un, des, and the
     following noun, adjective, or pronoun:

       Un autre   Des hirondelles
       Un oiseau   Des enfants
       Un heureux mélange   Des immenses espaces

II. ADJECTIVES

  a. Between the possessive adjectives (mon, ton, son,
     mes, tes, ses, nos, vos, leurs) and the following
     noun or adjective:

    Ses autres filles   Vos immortels poèmes
    Leurs images   Ses admirables livres

  b. Between the demonstrative adjective ces, and the
     following noun or adjective:

       Ces usages
       Ces autres livres

  c. Between a qualitative, indefinite, or numeral ad-
     jective and a following noun:

    Les grands animaux   Vingt enfants
    Les belles histoires   Tout homme
    Le grand⁺enfant   Second acte
    Le petit homme   Plusieurs histoires
    Cent hommes   Deux cents hommes

    NOTE: There are only three adjectives ending in -ier
    which may be placed before the noun: premier, der-
    nier, singulier. After them liaison always takes

place:

Son dernier atout   Premier avril

Un singulier ami   Au premier étage

III. PRONOUNS

a. Between the indefinite pronoun <u>tout</u> used as subject and the following <u>verb</u>:

       Tout est dit

       Tout a disparu

b. Between a <u>personal pronoun</u> used as subject and the following <u>verb</u>:

       Nous avons   Ils aiment

       Vous avez   Elles amusent l'enfant

c. Between the <u>personal pronoun</u> used as direct or indirect object and its <u>verb</u>:

       Il vous écrit   En a-t-elle?

       Elle vous aime   Il y en a

d. Between the relative pronoun <u>dont</u>, and the following <u>word</u>:

       Ce dont il parle

       Les tableaux dont elle est fière

IV. VERBS

a. In an <u>interrogative</u> sentence between the <u>verb</u> and a following <u>pronoun</u> used as subject:

       Voit-il?   Parleront-elles?

       Peut-on?   Ont-elles parlé?

       Peuvent-ils?   avaient-elles dansé?   *sont-ils entrés*

b. Between the auxiliary <u>avoir</u>, in the <u>third person</u> of the plural, and a following <u>past participle</u>:

       Ils ont eu

       Ils ont augmenté leurs prix

c. Between the <u>third person</u> singular or plural of the verb <u>être</u> (in every tense and mode) and the <u>following word</u>:

Il est en voyage   Elle était ici

Ils y sont encore   Ils seraient entre eux

Ce sont eux   Qu'il soit ici avant midi!

Ce furent eux   Qu'elle soit à Paris demain!

d. Between any verb used as an <u>auxiliary verb</u> and a following <u>infinitive</u>:

       Il faut aller le voir

       Je dois être à New-York demain

       Ils pourraient entendre

       Nous voudrions entendre cet artiste

V. PREPOSITIONS

Between a <u>preposition</u> and a following <u>word</u>:

       Avant eux   Dans une salle

       Sous une étagère   Après elle

       Devant elle   Pendant un mois

       Chez elle   Sans eux

EXCEPTION: No liaison is made after the
following prepositions:

selon‿	nonobstant‿
dès‿	vers‿
moyennant‿	hors‿

VI. CONJUNCTIONS

a. Between the conjunction <u>quand</u> and the following
   word:

   Quand‿elle entra   *kãtɛlãtra*
   Quand‿on perd la tête *kãtɔperlatɛt*

b. Between the conjunctions <u>soit...soit, tant...que,</u>
   and the following word:

   Elle ira le voir soit‿à Paris soit‿à
   Londres.
   Elle est heureuse tant‿ici qu'à la ville.

Optional:
Les chats‿et
les chiens

c. Between <u>plural nouns</u> or <u>plural adjectives</u>, used
   without articles or other determinatives, and the
   conjunction <u>et</u> or <u>ou</u>.

Ponts‿et chaussées	Beaux‿ou laids
Forts‿et faibles	Gras‿ou maigres
Grands‿ou petits	Contes‿et légendes

VII. ADVERBS

a. Between adverbs ending in <u>-ment</u> and the word they
   modify:

   Tendrement‿aimé
   Admirablement‿écrit

b. Between the adverbs <u>tout, très, fort</u>, and a following <u>adjective</u> or <u>past participle</u>:

Il est tout‿autre	Ils l'ont fort‿applaudi
Il est très‿heureux	Elle l'a fort‿apprécié

c. Between <u>two adverbs</u> in the same stress-group:

   Pas‿encore
   Mieux‿encore

d. Between <u>quant</u> and <u>à</u>:

Quant‿au jour	Quant‿à cette enfant
Quant‿à vous	Quant‿aux autres

e. Between <u>comment</u> and the verb <u>aller</u>, in the expression used to inquire about <u>health</u>:

   Comment‿allez-vous?
   Comment‿alliez-vous?

Comment est-il?

> But in all other cases, there is no liaison be-
> tween comment and the next word.

VIII. IDIOMATIC PHRASES AND EXPRESSIONS

With some words, in idiomatic phrases and in certain
other expressions, there are no rules; usage alone
prevails. The student should learn such expressions
by heart.

Accent‿aigu	Dos‿à dos	Pot-au-feu
Avant‿hier	D'un bout‿à l'autre	Pot‿au lait

Bout à bout *end to end* Franc-alleu   Pot-aux roses *secret*
But à but *even*   Franc-archer *yeoman* Respect humain
De but en blanc *point blank* Franc-étrier *free reign* Sang impur
De fond en comble *head to foot* Le fait est   Suer sang et eau
De haut en bas   Les Champs-Elysées Tout à coup
De mieux en mieux   Les Etats unis   Tout à fait *completely*
De moins en moins   Le Tiers-Etat   Tout à l'égout *sewage*
De pied en cap   Mot à mot   Tout à l'heure
De plus en plus   Pas à pas   Un croc-en-jambes *trip (so you fall)*
De temps en temps   Petit à petit   Un guet-apens *ambuscade*
Deux à deux   Pied à terre *extra apartment* Un pis-aller *last resort*
Deux ou trois   Pot à eau   Vis-à-vis

NOTE: These rules concerning obligatory liaisons are
based on the every day speech of the majority of cultured
Frenchmen, but one will occasionally discover some variations in usage among equally cultured French people. As I
have said, the phenomenon of liaison is in evolution, and
will be as long as French is a living language. However,
if a foreigner observes the rules given herewith he will be
certain neither to make incorrect liaisons, nor to omit
those that are indispensable.

PROHIBITED LIAISONS

I. PRONOUNS

   Between the personal pronouns elles and ils used as
   subject, when placed after the verb, and the following word:

          Ont-elles étudié?   Vont-elles y aller?
          Ont-ils appris?   Apprendront-ils une fable?

II. NOUNS

   a. Between a noun or word used by exception as a
      noun in the singular and a following qualitative *optional*
      adjective: *les filles, intel*

          Un chat étique   Un front adorable
          Un lit immense   Un nez épaté
          Un cas inouï *unheard of* Un garçonnet étrange
          EXCEPTIONS: In the following expressions,
              liaison takes place:
                  Accent aigu
                  Sang impur   *sãkẽpy:r*

   b. Before the word uhlan or ululer, and words derived
      from ululer: *to hoot*
          Des uhlans   Les affreux ululements
          Les uhlans   Les grands uhlans

   c. Before a word beginning with y + a vowel:
          Des yachts   Des yes
          Des yatagans   Des yoles
          EXCEPTIONS:
                      des yeuses *yew trees*
                      des yeux

S / V

d. Between a <u>noun</u>, a <u>pronoun</u> (with the exception of
nous, vous, ils, elles, on, tout) or any word used
as subject, and a <u>following verb</u>:

    Ces cahiers⌐ont une jolie couleur
    Ces personnes⌐iront vous voir
    Ce jouet⌐a besoin de réparation
    Le tout⌐est de savoir (<u>tout</u> here used as
      noun)
    Le fermier⌐est parti
    D'autres⌐ont dansé
    Trois⌐est son nombre favori
    Deux⌐est la moitié de quatre
    Aimer⌐est un joli verbe

e. With the <u>s of the plural</u>, within <u>compound words</u>:

    Des arcs-en-ciel   Des salles à manger
    Des pots-au-feu   Des chambres à coucher

f. Before <u>oui</u>:

    Mais⌐oui   Pour un⌐oui ou pour un non
    Elle t'a dit⌐oui   Les⌐oui qu'elle t'a dits

III. CONJUNCTIONS

a. Between the conjunction <u>et</u> and the following word:

Marguerite et⌐Yvonne   Des roses et⌐une violette
Une robe et⌐un manteau   Elle est grande et⌐élevée

IV. INTERJECTIONS

Before an <u>interjection</u>:

    Les⌐oh! et les⌐hi! de Jean
    Elle faisait des⌐ah! et des⌐oh! très
      amusants

V. ADVERBS

Between <u>comment</u> and the <u>next word</u>--except in the expression used to inquire about health:

    Comment| iras-tu à l'école?
    Comment| a-t-il fait?
    Comment| allons-nous au théâtre?
    Comment| êtes-vous?
        but
    Comment‿allez-vous?
    Comment‿allait-il?

VI. NUMERALS

Before the numerals <u>un</u>, <u>huit</u>, and <u>onze</u>:

    Quatre-vingt-huit   Les numéros⌐un et deux
    Tous les⌐huit   Louis⌐onze
    Tous les⌐onze   Ils sont⌐onze
    Les⌐onze enfants   Quatre-vingt-un
    NOTE: In the following numerals, liaison occurs:
      dix-‿huit   soixante-dix-‿huit
      vingt-‿huit   quatre-vingt-dix-‿huit

VII. ASPIRATE H

Before a word beginning with an aspirate h:

Un⁊ héros	Les⁊ huit de coeur
Un⁊ héron	Ces⁊ hauts murs
De grands⁊ héraut	Deux⁊ homards

VII. TO AVOID LACK OF HARMONY IN SOUND

Vous êtes‿ aisée	Six heures‿ et demie
Comment‿ êtes-vous?	Nous sommes allés‿ aux eaux

IX. IN CERTAIN EXPRESSIONS:

Au doigt‿ et à l'oeil	Nez‿ à nez
Chaud‿ et froid	Riz‿ au lait
	Pot‿ à tabac

All cultured people strictly observe the preceding
rules in oratorical, formal and every day speech.

OPTIONAL LIAISONS

I. ADJECTIVES

Between an adjective and a following preposition:

> Prêt‿ à parler
> Haut‿ en couleur

But in rapid speech, this liaison is usually avoided.

II. NOUNS

a. Between a plural noun and a following preposition:

> Des appartements‿ à louer
> Des petites filles‿ à élever
> Les héros‿ en question

But in rapid speech, this liaison is usually avoided.

b. When two plural nouns that are determinated are
united by the conjunctions et or ou, the liaison
is optional between the first noun and the following conjunction:

> Des filles‿ et des garçons
> Des fleurs‿ et des feuilles
> Des livres‿ et des cahiers

c. Between a plural noun and a following adjective:

> Des personnes‿ aimables
> Des bouquets‿ exquis
> Des chapeaux‿ adorables

> NOTE: When in either the singular or the
> plural the noun ends with a consonant
> sound or sounds especially in rapid speech,
> linking (p.140)may take place:

>> Des personnes aimables
>> Des livres ennuyeux

> But the liaison is correct also.

d. Before proper names:

> Chez‿ Yvonne
> Chez‿ Hédiard

But this liaison is more and more avoided.

134

III. PRONOUNS

Between personal pronoun _eux_ placed at beginning or in middle of a stress-group and the following word:

Eux‿aussi
Eux‿et moi

But in rapid speech, this liaison is usually avoided.

IV. VERBS

a. Between the auxiliary verbs _avoir_, _être_, and the following _past participle_ (exception: with the third person the liaison is obligatory):

Nous avons‿eu
Vous l'aviez‿abandonné   Je suis‿allé en ville
Tu eus‿aimé à le faire   Nous sommes‿allés les voir
Tu l'avais‿organisé   Nous serions‿enchantés

But in rapid speech, this liaison is usually avoided.

b. Between the _verb_ and a following _object_:

Nous avons‿un beau livre
Nous jouons‿une sonate

But in rapid speech, this liaison is avoided more and more often.

c. Between _infinitives_ ending in _-er_ and the following word:

Aimer‿à parler   Jouer‿aux cartes
Aimer‿et chanter   Jouer‿aux échecs
Monter‿à cheval   Se promener‿en auto

But in rapid speech, this liaison is avoided more and more often.

d. Between the _verbal ending -ent_ (mark of the third person plural) and the following word:

Elles aiment‿à parler
Ils dansent‿un tango

But in rapid speech, this liaison is usually avoided.

e. Between a _past participle_ and a following _preposition_:

Mis‿en demeure
Remis‿à neuf

f. Between a _present participle_ and a following _preposition_:

En allant‿à Paris
En venant‿au moulin
En répondant‿à Marguerite

V. CONJUNCTIONS

Between the conjunction _mais_ and the following word:

Mais‿il viendra
Mais‿aujourd'hui même
Mais‿encore plus

REMARK: Liaison never takes place between mais and oui.

VI. ADVERBS

  a. Between the adverbs beaucoup, trop, or jamais, and a following past participle, adjective, or the preposition à.

        Elle a beaucoup‿appris
        Elle a trop‿à dire
        Elle n'en a jamais‿eu

  But in rapid speech, this liaison is more and more avoided.

  b. Between an adverb placed at the beginning of a stress-group and the following word:

        Aussitôt‿arrivé
        Cependant‿on le lui répétait
        Partout‿où elle ira
        Elle ne pense à rien, tant‿elle est sotte
        Elle ne part plus, tellement‿elle se plaît
        ici

  But in rapid speech, this liaison is more and more avoided.

  c. When two adverbs are united by the conjunctions et or ou, the liaison is optional between the first adverb and the following conjunction.

        Rapidement‿et lestement
        Longuement‿ou rapidement

NOTE: Most of these liaisons are avoided in rapid speech but observed in oratorical and formal speech.

CHANGES OF SOUND IN LIAISON

I. C-K. In the following expressions:

        Franc-alleu
        Franc-archer
        Franc-étrier

II. CT=K. In the following expression only:

        Respect‿humain

III. D=T:

        Il prend‿une pomme
        Quand‿il viendra
        Son second‿enfant
        Grand‿homme

IV. G=K. In the following expressions:

        Suer sang‿et eau
        Sang‿impur

        NOTE: With all other words ending in -g, and with sang placed before words other than the two above, there should be no liaison:

          Un long| exorde
          Il perd du sang| en quantité

V. <u>-RC</u>, <u>-RD</u>, -RF, -RG, <u>-RS</u>, -RT=R.

Un clerc̸ ͜intelligent	Vers̸ ͟elle
Un abord̸ ͟aimable	Envers̸ ͟eux
Sourd̸ ͟et muet	Vert̸ ͟et jaune
Un cerf̸ ͟aux abois	Il part̸ ͟au matin
Un iceberg̸ ͟énorme	Toujours̸ ͟immense

EXCEPTIONS:

1. -RD, -RT $=$ RT.

In the interrogative verbal forms before a pronoun used as subject.

Perd-͟il?
Sert-͟elle?

Usually with the adverb fort.

Fort ͟ɦeureusement
Fort ͟adroit
Fort ͟ɦabile
Fort ͟intelligent

2. -RS=RZ:

With the following indefinite adjectives:

Plusieurs ͟enfants
Divers ͟autres

NOTE: Final <u>s</u>, mark of the plural, placed after an <u>r</u> pronounced in the isolated word, may form the liaison instead of the <u>r</u>. Either is correct, unless <u>s</u> is required to indicate plural (in case the context is not clear).

Des airs˥ ͟ingénus	(With or without liaison,
Des ports˥ ͟étendus	since the plural is indicated by <u>des</u>).

BUT

Airs ͟ingénus	(With liaison, since there
Ports ͟étendus	is no other way of indi-
Mers ͟immenses	cating plural).

VI. <u>S</u>=Z:

Vas-y	Gros ͟ɦomme
Perds-͟en	Dans ͟un mois
Donnes-͟en	Sans ͟elle
Bas ͟étage	

VII. <u>X</u>=Z:

Dix ͟ɦommes	Tu peux ͟aller la voir
Je veux y être	De mieux ͟en mieux

Chapter XIII.
LIAISON OF THE N OF THE NASAL VOWELS

GENERAL RULE: Liaison <u>never</u> takes place between a noun in the singular or a word used by exception as a noun and the following word. Therefore, between such a noun when ending with a nasal vowel and the initial vowel of the following word, liaison never occurs:

Adam est le premier homme	Le marchand est parti
Aucun est un pronom	Le mien est plus joli
C'est un parfum enivrant	Le second est parti
C'est un rien auquel il faut penser	On est un pronom
	Quelqu'un a dit
Chacun en voulait	Quelqu'un en voulait
Combien a coûté ce livre?	Sottement est un adverbe
En est une préposition	Un a pour pluriel des
En voulez-vous chacun un	Une conversation agréable
Il a faim et soif	Une leçon admirable
Il est à Caen ou à Rouen	Un est un article
Jean est venu	Un nom agréable
Jean et Jacques sont sortis	Un ruban orange
Le bien et le mal	Un son affreux

NOTE: Unless otherwise indicated, the nasal vowel retains its nasal quality.

I. AN, ã

1. EN, préposition. Liaison always takes place after en, préposition:

Nous sommes en Autriche
Il est en Europe
En avant, marche

2. EN, pronoun. Liaison takes place after en, pronoun, when it is placed before the verb:

S'en est-il allé?
Il en a pris trois
Tu en apportes deux

NOTE: When en pronoun, is placed after the verb, no liaison takes place:

Allez-vous-en ailleurs
Donnez-m'en un peu
Parlez-lui-en un peu

After all other words ending with the nasal vowel ã, whatever its spelling, no liaison takes place.

II. ON, ɔ̃

1. MON, TON, SON. Liaison takes place after any of these three words, and the vowel may either retain its nasal quality or be pronounced like an open o:

Mon école
Ton enfant

2. ON. When on is the subject of a declarative sentence, liaison takes place:

On aime la tranquillité
On espère une amélioration
On y va souvent

NOTE: In other cases, no liaison takes

        place after <u>on</u>, pronoun:

      a. When <u>on</u> follows the verb and is placed before either the past participle or another word:

A-t-on eu des nouvelles?
Est-on arrivé à le voir?
A-t-on envoyé la lettre?

      b. When <u>on</u> is used to take the place of a noun:

On est un mot vague
On est un pronom indéfini
On a plusieurs significations

3. <u>BON</u>. When <u>bon</u> is placed before the noun, liaison takes place. In this case, the vowel loses its nasal quality and is pronounced like an open o (as if it were the feminine form: bonne):

Un bon ami   Un bon enfant
Un bon exercice   Bonheur

NOTE: In expressions where <u>bon</u> precedes the preposition <u>à</u> no liaison takes place and the vowel retains its nasal quality:

Bon à tirer
Bon à prendre

After all other words ending with the nasal vowel ɔ̃, (whatever its spelling) no liaison takes place.

III. IN, ɛ̃

1. <u>RIEN</u>, indefinite pronoun. Liaison takes place after rien, indefinite pronoun:

Vous n'avez rien à faire?
Il n'a rien obtenu
Rien à penser

2. <u>BIEN</u>, adverb. Liaison takes place after bien, adverb.

Nous sommes bien à plaindre
Vous êtes bien en retard
Est-il bien arrivé?

NOTE: After bien used as an adjective no liaison takes place:

Ils sont bien ensemble

3. <u>BIEN ENTENDU</u>. In this expression, liaison takes place:

Bien entendu

4. <u>ANCIEN</u>, <u>CERTAIN</u>, <u>HAUTAIN</u>, <u>HUMAIN</u>, <u>LOINTAIN</u>, <u>MOYEN</u>, <u>PLEIN</u>, <u>PROCHAIN</u>, <u>SOUDAIN</u>, <u>SOUVERAIN</u>, <u>VAIN</u>, <u>VILAIN</u>. When these adjectives are placed before a noun, liaison takes place, but the vowel loses its nasal quality and is pronounced like an open e, thus giving the sound of the feminine form:

C'est un ancien amiral   En plein air
Une dame d'un certain âge   Au prochain arrêt

Un hautain accueil   Un soudain éclat
L'humain espoir   Un souverain empire
Dans un lointain avenir   Le vain espoir
Au moyen âge   Quel vilain oiseau

5. **DIVIN**. When this adjective is placed before a noun, liaison takes place and the vowel loses its nasal quality and is pronounced i, thus giving the sound of the feminine form:

Divin enfant

After all other words ending with the nasal vowel $\tilde{\epsilon}$, (whatever its spelling) no liaison takes place.

IV. UN, $\tilde{\infty}$

1. **AUCUN**, adjective. Liaison takes place after **aucun**, adjective:

Aucun homme ne l'a jamais vu
Pourquoi n'a-t-il aucun ami?
NOTE: No liaison takes place after **aucun**, pronoun:
Je n'en ai vu aucun ici

2. **UN, article**. Liaison takes place after **un**, article:

Un heureux caractère
Un enfant très sage
NOTE: No liaison takes place after **un**, pronoun:
En veut-il un aussi?
J'en ai un orange

3. **UN, numeral**. Liaison takes place with **un**, numeral, if **un** multiplies the following noun:

Vingt et un arbres
Trente et un hommes
Quarante et un élèves
Cet homme a cinquante et un ans
Note 1. In dates before a noun beginning with a vowel, liaison is optional:
vingt-et-un avril
Note 2. In other cases, there is no liaison:
un Hollandais
un et un font deux

4. **D'UN COMMUN ACCORD**. In this expression, liaison takes place:

D'un commun accord

5. **OPTIONAL LIAISONS**. In all expressions beginning with **un** or **l'un**, except those already noted, liaison is optional:

Un à un
L'un ou l'autre
L'un avec l'autre

L'un et l'autre
L'un auprès de l'autre
After all other words ending with the nasal vowel œ̃
(whatever its spelling), no liaison takes place.

Chapter XIV.
LINKING

In some words the final consonant or group of consonants is always pronounced whatever the position of the
word. When it appears before a word beginning with a vowel
or mute h, such a final consonant or final group of consonants is not only pronounced but also linked with the
initial vowel of the following word. This phenomenon,
called <u>linking</u>, is similar to liaison in that it has the
effect of producing that smoothness of sound so characteristic of spoken French.

It is by his failure to observe this phenomenon that
the foreigner is easily detected. He inserts a slight mute
e which often exists in the spelling but never in the
spoken word.

Linking is usually required <u>within a breath-group:</u>

Cette idée-là	Naître et mourir
Chère enfant	Noble enfant
Cher enfant	Paraître et disparaître
Entre eux	Pour avoir
Heureuse et confiante	Quatre hommes
Le beau lys en fleur	Sain et solide
La belle amie	Se mettre au lit
La fleur en bouton	Tout à toi
La grande enfant	Un arbre en fleur
La petite Isabelle	Un brave homme
Légère ironie	Victor-Hugo
Modeste auberge	Votre ami

Note 1. In the following expressions in
which liaison does not occur, linking
takes place:

de part et d'autre
de part en part
bord à bord
mort ou vif
à tort et à travers
corps a corps

Note 2. In the following expressions either linking or liaison may take place:

nord-est
nord-ouest

But <u>linking</u> is used more and more.

EXCEPTIONS: The only exceptions are the following:
1. NUMERALS
   Before the numerals <u>un</u>, <u>huit</u>, and <u>onze</u>:
   Le nombre⌉ un
   Le nombre⌉onze
   Le nombre⌉huit
2. OUI, UHLAN, ULULEMENT
   Before <u>oui</u>, <u>uhlan</u>, or <u>ululement</u>:
   La particule⌉oui
   Ce seul⌉oui
   D'admirables⌉uhlans
   L'effroyable⌉ululement
3. Y+VOWEL
   Before a word beginning with <u>y+ vowel</u>:
   Une belle⌉yole
   Un superbe⌉yacht
      EXCEPTIONS:
         des‿yeuses *yew trees*
         des‿yeux

4. ASPIRATED H
   Before a word beginning with <u>aspirated h</u>:
   L'horrible⌉honte
   Le fidèle⌉héros
   La belle⌉housse
   Quelle⌉haute⌉haie
5. INTERJECTIONS
   Before an interjection:
   De terribles⌉ah! s'échappaient
      de sa poitrine
   D'admirables⌉oh!

IMPORTANT NOTE: A consonant or a group of consonants used in linking, belong not to the vowel that precedes but to the vowel that follows, thus forming a normal French syllable: <u>consonant plus vowel</u>. Linking is usually required between stress-groups. It is even heard, at times between breath-groups.

Chapter XV.
ASSIMILATION
(CONSONANT HARMONY)

Assimilation is the phenomenon involving the modification of a voiced consonant by a voiceless consonant, or vice versa.

This modification occurs whenever the two consonants are in <u>complete contact</u>, that is to say, when they are not separated by a sounded vowel. A mute e, in case it is not pronounced, does not prevent the complete contact of two consonants.

This modification may take place between consonants that are in the same word or between consonants that are in different words.

Assimilation does not occur between stress-groups.

There are two kinds of assimilation:

1. Regressive, which is the more usual.
2. Progressive, which does not often occur.

I. REGRESSIVE ASSIMILATION

1. When a voiced consonant occurs before a voiceless consonant the voiced consonant, through the influence of the voiceless becomes <u>partly</u> voiceless itself:

absolument, abcès, médecin, je tiens, grande table

2. When a voiceless consonant occurs before a voiced consonant, the voiceless consonant, through the influence of the voiced consonant, becomes <u>partly</u> voiced itself:

cette jeune fille, petite violette, une pêche verte

la puissante dame, un vif bavardage

In rapid pronunciation, the assimilation occurs naturally. In slow pronunciation it very seldom occurs.

Assimilation does not completely transform the nature of the assimilated consonant. One cannot say, for instance, that the <u>t</u> of <u>puissante dame</u> becomes a real <u>d</u>: the beginning of the consonant remains voiceless, that is to say, without vibrations, and part only of the consonant becomes voiced through the influence of the following voiced consonant. It is a <u>voiced t</u> and not a veritable d.

PROGRESSIVE ASSIMILATION

When voiceless <u>s</u> is placed before voiced <u>m</u>, m through the influence of <u>s</u> becomes voiceless too:

enthousiasme, journalisme, romantisme,
scepticisme, cataplasme, sarcasme, spasme,
judaïsme, catholicisme, paroxysme, organisme,
égoïsme, schisme

> Note 1. In English the inverse is true.
> Note 2. Some French people make the inverse assimilation here, that is to say, they permit voiced <u>m</u> to influence voiceless <u>s</u> so that it sounds nearly like <u>z</u>. But this pronunciation should be carefully avoided by the foreigner.

Chapter XVI.
VOWEL HARMONY
(Fr: HARMONIE VOCALIQUE)

Contamination

Vowel harmony is the result of the influence of one vowel, (usually stressed) on the closing or opening of the preceding vowel.

Vowel harmony occurs in the following cases:

I. A <u>closed e closes an open e</u> which precedes:
  a. When the two vowels are separated by only one consonant:
  ailé, *ele*, aider, *ede*, démêler, *demele* , vous aimez, *vuzeme*, fêté, *fete*
  b. When the two vowels are separated by a double consonant (only one sound):
  guettez, *gete*, mettez, *mete*
  c. When the two vowels are separated by two insepara-ble consonants of which the second is <u>l</u> or <u>r</u>: Such groups are <u>bl</u>, <u>br</u>, <u>cl</u>, <u>cr</u>, <u>dr</u>, <u>fl</u>, <u>fr</u>, <u>gl</u>, <u>gr</u>, <u>pl</u>, <u>pr</u>, <u>tr</u>, <u>vr</u>:
  guettrez, *getre*, mettrez, *metre*
  > NOTE: In all other cases, a <u>closed e</u> <u>does</u> <u>not close</u> a preceding open e:
  >> chercher, *ʃerʃe*, détester, *deteste* perler, *perle*, pester, *peste*

II. An <u>i</u> or <u>u</u> <u>closes an open e</u> which precedes:
  a. When the two vowels are separated by only one consonant:
  aigu, *egy*, aiguë, *egy*, engrêlure, *ãgrely:r*, plaisir, *plezi:r*
  b. When the two vowels are separated by a double consonant (only one sound):
  épaissir, *epesi:r*, blessure, *blesy:r*
  c. When the two vowels are separated by two insepara-ble consonants: (<u>bl</u>, <u>br</u>, <u>cl</u>, <u>cr</u>, <u>dr</u>, <u>fl</u>, <u>fr</u>, <u>gl</u>, <u>gr</u>, <u>pl</u>, <u>pr</u>, <u>tr</u>, <u>vr</u>).
  maigrir, *megri:r*
  > NOTE: In all other cases i or u does not close a preceding open e:
  >> architecture, *arʃitekty:r*, lecture, *lekty:r*, Mercure, *merky:r* perdit, *perdi*, perdu, *perdy*

III. A <u>closed eu closes an open eu</u> which precedes:
heureux, *ørø*, malheureusement, *malørøzmã*, peureux, *pørø*, valeureux, *valørø*

IV. An <u>open o</u> preceded by the sound <u>z</u> <u>opens</u> a preceding <u>closed o</u>:
myosotis, *mjozotis*, philosophe, *filozof*, théosophie, *teozofi*

V. <u>Rarely</u>, <u>open e</u> opens a <u>closed e</u> which precedes:
J'étais, ʒɛtɛ, il répétait, *ilrepɛtɛ*
> NOTE: The foreigner will notice that many
> French persons use indifferently the two
> different pronunciations:
>
> ʒetɛ and ʒɛtɛ

IMPORTANT REMARKS

I. Vowel harmony occurs only in the cases explained above. Contrary to what is often said, closed o <u>does not</u> <u>close</u> an open o which precedes:
copeau,*kɔpo* , dotaux,*dɔto* , loto,*lɔto* , pommeau, *pomo*
In words of the type of <u>roseau</u>, the first o is closed through the influence of z and not through the influence of vowel harmony.

II. Vowel harmony is a phenomenon essentially Parisian. The speech of many cultivated French persons who are not Parisian by birth or breeding has not yet been influenced by it. Consequently one often hears with an <u>open e</u> words such as:
plaisir, *plɛziːr̩* aimer, ɛmɛ, mettez, mɛtɛ
That is why in the selections from French authors quoted in the Reading Lessons, the sounds susceptible to modification through vocalic harmony have not been underlined. For example, the first vowel of the word <u>peignée</u>, occurring on page 31, may through the influence of vocalic harmony be pronounced as a closed e, *peɲe*, but many French people prefer to preserve the open e, without however exaggerating the sound: *pɛɲe*.

Chapter XVII.
THE DOUBLE CONSONANT

As has been shown in the discussion of Syllabification and elsewhere, double consonants are generally pronounced as one single consonant. Under certain circumstances, however, they are pronounced, not as two separate consonants, it is true, but <u>as one very much prolonged</u>. This is the case as follows:

I. In future and conditional of the verbs <u>courir</u>, <u>mourir</u>, <u>acquérir</u>, <u>conquérir</u>:
> Je courrais, nous mourrons, vous acquerriez, nous conquerrons

II. When the <u>two letters</u> of the double consonant are separated by a mute e:
> Nous n~~e~~ nommons pas, nett~~e~~té, mêm~~e~~ment, un aid~~e~~ désireux d'agir, la petit~~e~~ terrasse, une grand~~e~~ dame, vous l~~e~~ lirez, écout~~e~~-t-il?

III. When the stress for emphasis falls on the double
   consonant. (In this case even a single consonant
   is sounded like a double consonant):
      Immense
      C'est *ravissant
      Elle est *jolie au possible
      Et votre *fier dédain
      *Vivez, si m'en croyez
      Je te dis *non, *non et *non
IV. In all words beginning with ill-:
      Illustre, illogique, illettré
V. In rare, scientific, or literary words having a double
   consonant:
      distiller, intelligence
REMARK. More and more the pronunciation of the double
consonant as such is tending to disappear except in the
three first cases.

Chapter XVIII.
PRONUNCIATION OF H

The letter h is not a sound in French. It is merely an
orthographic sign, and therefore may be pronounced only in
combination with the consonants c and p whose pronunciation is thus modified.

Placed at the beginning or in the middle of a word, it
is said to be mute when its presence does not prevent
liaison or elision:
   l'Homme, un Homme, l'Héroine, bonHeur
   aux Hommes

It is said to be aspirate when its presence indicates
the impossibility of liaison or elision:
   des Héros, la Haine, en Haut, deHors

The presence of an aspirate h causes a mute e which
precedes to be pronounced with the value of a true vowel:
   une Honte, l'horrible Haine, la grande Hâte

There are about six hundred words in French that begin
with an aspirate h. The majority of these words are rare or
scientific and generally of Germanic origin. The most common are:
   SUBSTANTIVES
     la hache, la haie, le haillon, la haine,
     le hâle, le hall, la halle, la hallebarde,
     la halte, le hamac, le hameau, la hanche,
     le hanneton, la harangue, le hareng, le
     haricot, la harpe, le hasard, la hâte, La
     Havane, Le Hâvre, La Haye, le héraut, le
     hère, le héros, le héron, le hêtre, le hibou,

la hiérarchie, la Hollandaise, le Hol-
andais, La Hollande, La Hongrie, la horde,
la hutte

Note 1. Words derived from héros have mute
h:

l'Héroïne, l'Héroïsme

Note 2. In the expression:

par hasard

linking takes place.

ADJECTIVES

hagard,-e; nardi,-e; haut,-e; hideux,
-euse

VERBS

haïr, hanter, haranguer, harasser, heur-
ter (se), hurler

MISCELLANEOUS

en haut, hors, dehors, hormis

Chapter XIX.
PRONUNCIATION OF X

I. At the beginning of a word x is pronounced:
  a. k in the two following words:
       Xérès, $keres$ Ximénès, $kimenes$
  b. gz in the following words:
       Xantippe, $gz\tilde{a}tip$, Xénophon, $gzenɔfɔ̃$,
       Xerxès, $gzerses$
  c. z in the following word:
       Xavier, $zavje$
  d. s in the following word (often written with an s):
       Xaintonge, $s\tilde{e}tɔ̃:ʒ$
  e. ks in the following word:
       xylophone, $ksilɔfon$
II. In the middle of a word, x is pronounced:
  a. gz in words containing the prefixes; ex-, hex-,
     inex-, before a vowel or a mute h:
       exact, $egza$, examen, $egzam\tilde{e}$, exhumer, $egzyme$
                hexagone, $egzagon$, inexorable,
                $inegzorabl$
  b. z in the following words and words derived from
     them:
       deuxième, $døzjem$, dixième, $dizjem$,
       sixième, $sizjem$, dix-huit, $dizɥit$
     as well as in liaison:
       dix ouvrages, $dizuvra:ʒ$, heureux ami,
       $ørøzami$, malheureux hommes, $malørøzom$
  c. s in the following words:
       Auxerre, $oser$, Bruxelles, $brysel$,

dextrier, *destrije*, Saulxure, *sosy:r* ,
soixante, *swasã:t*, and words derived from it.
d. <u>ks</u> in all other words:
    expatrier, *ɛkspatrije*, inexplicable,
    inɛksplikabl , paradoxal, *paradoksal*
III. At the end of a word, <u>x</u> is pronounced <u>ks</u>:
  1. In the following words only, having the termina-
     tions:
     <u>-ax</u>:
        Ajax, pax, thorax
     <u>-aix</u>, <u>-eix</u>, <u>-ex</u>:
        Aix, Aix-la-Chapelle, Aix-les-Bains,
        codex, index, vertex, vortex
            In all other common words ending in
            -<u>aix</u>, <u>x</u> is not pronounced:
               paix̸, Roubaix̸
    <u>-ix</u>:
        Cadix, Félix, phénix, préfix,
        Vercingétorix
            In all other common words ending in
            -<u>ix</u>, <u>x</u> is not pronounced:
              perdrix̸, prix̸
            For the numerals <u>six</u> and <u>dix</u>, see
            Chapter XXI.
    <u>-inx</u>, <u>-ynx</u>:
        larynx, linx or lynx, pharynx
    <u>-ux</u>:
        fiat lux, Pollux
    <u>-yx</u>:
        onyx, Styx
  2. In all words having the terminations:
     <u>-xe</u>:
        boxe, complexe, fixe, luxe,
        paradoxe
     <u>-xes</u>:
        tu boxes, tu fixes, tu luxes

Chapter XX.
PRONUNCIATION OF DONC, PLUS, SENS, TANDIS QUE, TOUS.

DONC
I. When <u>donc</u> has the meaning of <u>consequently</u>, <u>there-
fore</u>, or when it stands alone, <u>c</u> is pronounced
(like <u>k</u>):
    Je pense, don<u>c</u> je suis
    Je vois son chapeau, don<u>c</u> il est là
    Tu iras don<u>c</u> à la poste
    Don<u>c</u>, ainsi que je vous le faisais prévoir

II. In exclamatory sentences, where <u>donc</u> loses the meaning of <u>consequently</u>, the articulation of <u>c</u>, though most people make it silent, is optional:

Allons donc! or Allons donc!
Dis donc or Dis donc
Dites donc or Dites donc
Comment donc or Comment donc
Ne pleure donc pas or Ne pleure donc pas
Finissez donc or Finissez donc

PLUS

I. The <u>s</u> of plus is pronounced:

  a. When <u>plus</u> is the sign of an addition:

    2+3+5
    C'est mille francs plus dix pour cent
    Vous êtes quatre plus vos cousins

  b. When <u>plus</u> meaning <u>more</u> follows the verb (to avoid confusion with the negation):

    Elle n'en veut pas plus
    J'en ai plus
    Il en faut plus
    Elle veut plus

  c. In the following expression:

    Plus-que-parfait

II. The pronunciation of <u>s</u>, in plus, is optional, when <u>plus</u> meaning <u>more</u>, is not placed after the verb and is not the mark of the comparison:

    Un peu plus et vous tombiez à l'eau, *ply* or *plys*
    Il y restera tout au plus deux ans, *ply* or *plys*

III. In all the other cases, <u>s</u>, in <u>plus</u>, is not pronounced:

  a. In the negation:

    Il n'est plus dans sa chambre
    Jamais plus je ne vous croirai
    Je n'en ai plus
    Il n'en faut plus

  b. When <u>plus</u> is used to form a comparison:

    Est-elle plus grande ou plus petite que moi?
    Il est plus tard que je ne pensais

  c. In the expression <u>plus de</u> and <u>plus que</u>:

    J'ai plus de livres que vous
    Pas plus d'une heure
    A votre place, plus d'un accepterait
    Pas plus que vous

  d. In the following expressions:

    Tant et plus   Sans plus
    Ni plus ni moins   D'autant plus
    Bien plus   Tout au plus

De plu~~s~~   Au plu~~s~~
> In the following expressions, there is a
> liaison, s sounding like z:
>> Qui plus est
>> De plus en plus
>> Plus ou moins

SENS

I. In the following expressions the final s of sens is
silent:
> sen~~s~~ dessus dessous
> sen~~s~~ devant derrière

II. In the following expressions, the pronunciation of
the final s of sens is optional:
> sens commun or sen~~s~~ commun
> bon sens   or bon sen~~s~~

III. In all other cases, final s of sens is pronounced
(always like s):
> j'ai cinq sens
> le sens de l'odorat
> dans un autre sens
> sens unique

TANDIS QUE

S should be silent in tandi~~s~~ que. Some cultured French
people, however, sound it.

TOUS

I. In tous, pronoun, s is pronounced (always like s):
> Tous sont venus
> Ils les ont tous invités
> Ils les veut tous.

II. In tous, adjective, s is silent.
> Tou~~s~~ les enfants
> J'ai vu tou~~s~~ ceux dont il parle

PUIS, PUISQUE

Although in puis the s is silent, in puisque it is
sounded.

Chapter XXI.
PRONUNCIATION OF THE NUMERALS

A

PRONUNCIATION OF THE TEN FIRST NUMBERS, ACCORDING
TO THEIR POSITION IN THE SENTENCE

I. Un
   a. Before a noun or adjective beginning with a vowel
   or mute h, when un limits the noun, liaison takes
   place without denasalization:
   > un arbre, un autre arbre, vingt et un
   > arbres, quatre-vingt-un arbres, un homme

b. In dates, before a noun beginning with a vowel, liaison is optional:
> vingt-et-un‿avril, trente et un‿août

c. In other cases, there is no liaison:
> un‿Hollandais, un‿et un font deux

II. Deux

a. Before a noun or adjective beginning with a vowel or mute h, when deux multiplies the noun, liaison takes place, the x being pronounced like z:
> deux‿enfants, deux‿autres enfants, deux‿hommes

b. In dates, before a noun beginning with a vowel, liaison is optional:
> le deux‿avril

c. In other cases, the x is not pronounced:
> deux tables, deux hêtres, le deux mai, j'en ai deux

> EXCEPTIONS: In expressions such as the following, liaison usually takes place:
> deux‿à deux, deux‿ou trois, deux‿ou quatre, deux‿et deux font quatre

III. Trois

a. Before a noun beginning with a vowel or mute h, when trois multiplies the noun, liaison takes place, the s being pronounced like z:
> trois‿élèves, trois‿aimables dames, trois‿horaires

b. In dates, before a noun beginning with a vowel, liaison is optional:
> le trois‿août, le vingt-trois‿octobre

c. In other cases, the s is not pronounced:
> trois, trois professeurs, trois homards, trois et trois font six, le trois mai, le trois avril, j'en ai trois, une heure trois, Henri trois

> EXCEPTIONS: In expressions such as the following, liaison usually takes place:
> trois‿à trois, trois‿ou quatre

IV. Quatre

a. Before words beginning with a consonant, the r, as well as the mute e, disappears, unless the pronunciation is extremely slow, as is sometimes the case when a teacher speaks to a class. The disappearance in rapid speech of these two sounds may be compared to a similar phenomenon in the English expression, "I'll do it." Although it is frequently written, "I will do it", there are few persons who do not, when speaking, use the contracted

form:
> quat~~re~~ tables, quat~~re~~ livres, le quat~~re~~ mai

b. In all other cases r is pronounced very distinctly, and when followed by a word beginning with a vowel or mute h it is linked very closely with the first vowel of this word, so that in pronunciation the r becomes a part of its syllable (the mute e being suppressed):
> quatr~~e~~ oncles, quatr~~e~~ horloges, le quatr~~e~~ août, quatr~~e~~ et quatr~~e~~ font huit, Henri quatr~~e~~, j'en ai quatr~~e~~

c. Before a noun or an adjective beginning with an aspirate h, the r and the mute e are both pronounced:
> quatre͡ homards, quatre͡ hautes fenêtres, quatre͡ hardis voyageurs

V. Cinq

a. Before a noun or adjective beginning with a consonant or aspirate h, when cinq multiplies the noun, the q is not pronounced:
> cin~~q~~ pupitres, cin~~q~~ petites filles, cin~~q~~ hussards

b. Although the pronunciation of q is optional when cinq occurs before the expression pour cent or in date before the name of a month beginning with a consonant, the present tendency is to sound q under such circumstances:
> cinq pour cent, le cinq mai, le vingt-cinq septembre

c. In other cases q is pronounced like k, and when preceding a word beginning with a vowel or mute h, q is linked to its first vowel:
> cinq, cinq ans, cinq anciens professeurs, cinq heures, une heure cinq, j'en ai cinq, Georges cinq

VI. Six

a. Before a noun or adjective beginning with a consonant or aspirate h, when six multiplies the noun, the x of six is not pronounced:
> si~~x~~ crayons, si~~x~~ hamacs

b. Before a noun or adjective beginning with a vowel or mute h, when six multiplies the noun, the liaison takes place, the s sounding like z:
> six articles, six héroïnes

c. Although the pronunciation of x is optional when six occurs before the expression pour cent or in a date before the name of a month beginning with a consonant, the present tendency is to sound x--like s--under such circumstances:

six pour cent, le six novembre

d. In other cases, that is to say at the end of a
stress-group or before any word which six does not
multiply, the s of six is pronounced like s:

j'en ai six, le six avril, nous sommes six,
nous sommes six en tout, une heure six,
Charles six

VII. Sept

NOTE: p in sept is never pronounced.

a. Before a noun or adjective beginning with a consonant or aspirate h, when sept multiplies the
noun, t may or may not be pronounced:

sept plumes, sept haies

b. Although the pronunciation of t is optional when
sept occurs before the expression pour cent or in
a date before the name of a month beginning with a
consonant, the present tendency is to sound t under such circumstances:

sept pour cent, le vingt-sept septembre,
le dix-sept novembre

c. In other cases, t is pronounced, and when the word
which follows begins with a vowel or mute h, t is
linked to its first vowel:

sept, sept hirondelles, sept oracles,
j'en ai sept, une heure sept, Alphonse
sept

VIII. Huit

a. Before a noun or adjective beginning with a consonant or aspirate h, when huit multiplies the
noun, t is not pronounced:

huit jeunes filles, huit haricots

b. Although the pronunciation of t is optional when
huit occurs before the expression pour cent or in
a date before the name of a month beginning with a
consonant, the present tendency is to sound t under such circumstances:

huit pour cent, le huit mai, le vingt-
huit juin

c. In all other cases, t is pronounced, and when the
word which follows begins with a vowel or mute h,
t is linked to its first vowel:

huit, huit incidents, huit hérésies,
j'en ai huit, une heure huit, Léon
huit

IX. Neuf

a. Before a noun or adjective beginning with a consonant, when neuf multiplies the noun, f may or
may not be pronounced:

neuf chiens, neuf tables, neuf livres, etc.

b. Although the pronunciation of <u>f</u> is optional when <u>neuf</u> occurs before the expression <u>pour cent</u> or in a date before the name of a month beginning with a consonant, the present tendency is to sound <u>f</u> under such circumstances:

> neu<u>f</u> pour cent, le neu<u>f</u> mai, le dix-neu<u>f</u> juin

c. In other cases, <u>f</u> is pronounced and when the word which follows begins with a vowel or mute h, <u>f</u> is linked to its first vowel:

> neu<u>f</u>, neu<u>f</u> accidents, neu<u>f</u> ḥistoires, neu<u>f</u> ḥiboux, etc.

d. In two cases only, liaison of f takes place, <u>f</u> sounding like <u>v</u>:

> neuf ans, neuf ḥeures, *nœvã, nœvœ:r*

X. <u>Dix</u>

The same rules as for <u>six</u>.

B

11, *ɔ̃:z*	39, *trãtnœf*
12, *du:z*	
13, *trɛ:z*	40, *karã:t*
14, *katorz*	41, *karãteœ̃*
15, *kɛ̃:z*	42, *karãtdø*
16, *se:z*	43, *karãttrwa*
17, *disɛt*	44, *karãtkatr*
18, *dizɥit*	45, *karãtsɛ̃:k*
19, *diznœf*	46, *karãtsis*
	47, *karãtsɛt*
20, *vɛ̃*	48, *karãtɥit*
21, *vɛ̃teœ̃*	49, *karãtnœf*
22, *vɛ̃tdø*	
23, *vɛ̃ttrwa*	50, *sɛ̃kã:t*
24, *vɛ̃tkatr*	51, *sɛ̃kãteœ̃*
25, *vɛ̃tsɛ̃:k*	52, *sɛ̃kãtdø*
26, *vɛ̃tsis*	53, *sɛ̃kãttrwa*
27, *vɛ̃tsɛt*	54, *sɛ̃kãtkatr*
28, *vɛ̃tɥit*	55, *sɛ̃kãtsɛ̃:k*
29, *vɛ̃tnœf*	56, *sɛ̃kãtsis*
	57, *sɛ̃kãtsɛt*
30, *trã:t*	58, *sɛ̃kãtɥit*
31, *trãteœ̃*	59, *sɛ̃kãtnœf*
32, *trãtdø*	
33, *trãttrwa*	60, *swasã:t*
34, *trãtkatr*	61, *swasãteœ̃*
35, *trãtsɛ̃:k*	62, *swasãtdø*
36, *trãtsis*	63, *swasãttrwa*
37, *trãtsɛt*	64, *swasãtkatr*
38, *trãtɥit*	65, *swasãtsɛ̃:k*

66, swasãtsis

67, swasãtset

68, swasãtчit

69, swasãtnœf

70, swasãtdis

71, swasãteõ:z

72, swasãtdu:z

73, swasãttrɛ:z

74, swasãtkatorz

75, swasãtkɛ̃:z

76, swasãtsɛ:z

77, swasãtdisɛt

78, swasãtdizчit

79, swasãtdiznœf

80, katr(ə)vɛ̃

81, katr(ə)vɛ̃æ

82, katr(ə)vɛ̃dø

83, katr(ə)vɛ̃trwa

84, katr(ə)vɛ̃katr

85, katr(ə)vɛ̃sɛ̃:k

86, katr(ə)vɛ̃sis

87, katr(ə)vɛ̃sɛt

88, katr(ə)vɛ̃чit

89, katr(ə)vɛ̃nœf

90, katr(ə)vɛ̃dis

91, katr(ə)vɛ̃õ:z

92, katr(ə)vɛ̃du:z

93, katr(ə)vɛ̃trɛ:z

94, katr(ə)vɛ̃katorz

95, katr(ə)vɛ̃kɛ̃:z

96, katr(ə)vɛ̃sɛ:z

97, katr(ə)vɛ̃disɛt

98, katr(ə)vɛ̃dizчit

99, katr(ə)vɛ̃diznœf

100, sã

101, sãæ

102, sãdø

103, sãtrwa

110, sãdis

111, sãõ:z

112, sãdu:z

120, sãvɛ̃

121, sãvɛ̃teæ

122, sãvɛ̃tdø

200, døsã

201, døsãæ

202, døsãdø

300, trwasã

301, trwasãæ

302, trwasãdø

400, katr(ə)sã, katsã

401, katr(ə)sãæ, katsãæ

402, katr(ə)sãdø, katsãdø

500, sɛ̃sã

501, sɛ̃sãæ

502, sɛ̃sãdø

600, sisã

601, sisãæ

602, sisãdø

700, sɛtsã

701, sɛtsãæ

702, sɛtsãdø

800, чisã

801, чisãæ

802, чisãdø

900, nøsã, nœfsã

901, nøsãæ, nœfsãæ

902, nøsãdø, nœfsãdø

1000, mil

1001, milɭæ, milæ

1002, mildø

1,000,000, æmiljõ

1,000,000,000, æmilja:r

Cent never pronounced

IMPORTANT REMARKS.

1. In dix-huit, the x is pronounced like z even before huit, which ordinarily does not permit liaison;

in vingt-ḥuit, trentḛ-ḥuit, etc., the t of vingt, trente, etc., is thrown forward to become the first letter of the following syllable.

2. In quatre-vingt⌐un, cent⌐un, deux cent⌐un, etc., there is no liaison between t and the following vowel.

3. There is strong assimilation:
   a. In dix-neuf, which causes x to sound like z.
   b. In vingt-deux, trente-deux, etc., which causes t to become voiced (but not in 82).
   c. In vingt-neuf, trente-neuf, etc., which causes t to become voiced (but not in 89).

4. The t, though sounded in 21, 22, 23, 24, 25, 26, 27, 28, 29, is silent in 81, 82, 83, 84, 85, 86, 87, 88, 89.

5. In soixante, x, although between two vowels, is pronounced, not like z but like s.

Chapter XXII.
PRONUNCIATION OF WRITTEN OU+VOWEL, U+VOWEL, AND I+VOWEL

Written ou, u, or i plus a vowel, is pronounced in a single syllable:

a. alouette, *alwɛt*; allouons, *alwɔ̃*; jouer, *ʒwe*; Rouen, *rwɑ̃*; silhouette, *silwɛt*; Louis, *lwi*.

b. duel, *dɥɛl*; nuage, *nɥa:ʒ*; puis, *pɥi*; Ruy, *rɥi*; celui, *səlɥi*; afféctueux, *afɛktɥø*.

c. bien, *bjɛ̃*; rien, *rjɛ̃*; siège, *sjɛ:ʒ*; pied, *pje*; voyage, *vwaja:ʒ*; assiette, *asjɛt*; vous alliez, *vuzalje*; nous apportions, *nuzaportjɔ̃*; Assomption, *asɔ̃psjɔ̃*; congestion, *kɔ̃ʒɛstjɔ̃*; version, *vɛrsjɔ̃*.

EXCEPTIONS:

1. Written ou, u, or i plus a vowel if preceded by two consonants forming a so-called inseparable group belonging to the same syllable, is pronounced in two syllables. Such groups (of which the second consonant is always l or r) are: bl, br, cl, cr, dr, fl, fr, gl, gr, pl, tr, vr.

   a. brou-ette, *bru-ɛt*; é-blou-is-se-ment, *e-blu-is-mɑ̃*; trou-er, *tru-e*.
   b. cru-el, *kry-ɛl*; mons-tru-eux, *mɔ̃s-try-ø*; obs-tru-er, *obs-try-e*.
   c. cen-dri-er, *sɑ̃-dri-je*; s'é-cri-a,

se-kri-ja ; ouv-ri-er, u-vri-je ;
en-cri-er, ã-kri-je; pri-ère,
pri-jɛ:r ; su-**ppl**i-er, sy-pli-je ;
tri-angle, tri-jã:gl .

In such cases i is pronounced
twice, i in the first syllable,
and yod, j , in the second.

2. In the first and second person plural
of the imperfect indicative and present
subjunctive, written ou, or u, plus a
vowel is pronounced in two syllables:

que vous nou-iez, kǝ-vu-nu-je;
que nous allou-ions, kǝ-nu-za-lu-jõ;
que vous pollu-iez, kǝ-vu-po-ly-je;
que vous tu-iez, kǝ-vu-ty-je

Note 1. When u, y , is followed by the vowel i, the combination is regularly pronounced in a single syllable:

autrui, o-trɥi; bruit, brɥi ; druide,
drɥid

Note 2. Those forms of the verbs lier and rire in which
the combination in either of the above ways (one or two
syllables):

nous rions, nurjõ or nuri-jõ
vous liez vulje or vuli-je

Note 3. Those forms of the verb nier in which the combination i plus a vowel occurs are pronounced in two syllables:

nier, ni-je ; nous nions, nuni-jõ

PART III

LEXICON

As has been said before, French is not a phonetic language. Not only may different combinations of letters be
pronounced in the same way (as é, -er, -ez, etc.), but the
same combinations of letters may be pronounced in different ways (as -tien, *tjɛ̃*, in chrétien, but *sjɛ̃* in Egyptien).
Naturally, inasmuch as it is usage alone which deter-
mines the pronunciation of such letters or groups of letters in different words, they often prove puzzling to a
foreigner.
In the following pages will be found lists of such
spellings and the indication of their pronunciation, together with exceptions in common use. Thus, when a student
in his reading outside this book comes across a word containing a group of letters for which he knows that different pronunciations exist under different circumstances, he
may easily find which is the correct pronunciation by reference to this condensed lexicon. Immediately below the
name of the sound under consideration I have placed the
spellings which represent it. Sometimes the same spelling
represents two different sounds--depending on the word in
which it is located, the position which it occupies in the
word, etc. This spelling therefore appears on two different pages, but with sufficient explanation so that the
student need never be at a loss. The order will be seen to
correspond to that in Part I, with the exception that I
treat first of all the four principal vowels which may be
either open or closed.
In general, I have treated the various sounds according
to their position in the word--the four vowels just mentioned, first, when in the last pronounced syllable, second, when in other syllables; the vowels ou, *u*, u, *y*, i,
and the nasal vowels, first, when the last sound, second
when not the last sound of a word; yod, first, when at the
end, second, when in the middle, third, when at the beginning of a word; the consonants, first, when at the beginning or in the middle, second, when at the end of a word;
the semi-vowels ou, *w*, and u, *ɥ*, in one way only, by spelling. The student should always remember that since I am
dealing primarily with sounds, the expression "last syllable" means last pronounced syllable. When, in order to
show the timbre of a vowel, I include among the examples
the first, second, or third person singular of a regular
verb, it will of course be understood that this timbre remains unchanged throughout the conjugation of the verb.
Plural forms are indicated in the list of spellings immediately following the title--op(s)--but among the examples

will be found only the singular form.

1 have included very few scientific words, and have
used phonetic symbols only when I considered them absolutely necessary.

Parts I and III are designed to be used together. By
study of the former the student will be enabled to produce
the sound correctly; by reference to the latter he will be
able to recognize the various orthographic forms under
which the sound may appear.

Chapter XXIII.
POSTERIOR A, α

A-, -A-, Â-, -Â-, -AE-, -EA-, -(O)I-; -A(S), -ACS, -ARS,
-AS, -AT(S), -ÂT(S), -(O)İ(S), -(O)İD(S), -(O)İDS, -(O)İE,
-(O)İES, -(O)İE(S), -(O)İS, -(O)İT(S), -(O)İT, -(O)İX.

-A-

In the last syllable of a word, a is posterior:
I.When it is the last sound of a word and is written:
   1.-a.In the three following words only:
   fa (music), la (music), bêta.
   2.-acs.In the following word only:
   lacs (Eng. net; nets).
   3.-as.In the following words and their derivatives:
   amas, ananas, appas, bas, cas, cervelas, compas,
   coutelas, Dumas, échalas, fatras, fracas, glas,
   gras, Judas, las, lilas, Nicolas, pas, patatras,
   plâtras, ras, repas, tas, Thomas, tracas, trépas.
   4.-ars.In the following word only:
   gars.
   5.-at.In the following words only:
   chocolat, climat.
   6.-ât:
   bât, mât, etc.
          EXCEPTIONS (a).Verbal forms:
             qu'il allât, qu'il parlât, etc.
   7 -(o)i, -oî-, -(o)id, -(o)ids, -(o)ie, -(o)ies,
   -(o)is -(o)it, -(o)ît, -(o)ix.(In these combinations
o represents w, i and the following silent letters, if
any, represent posterior a, α; the combination oi represents wα).
   a.When preceded by r, except in the endings -roisse,
   -roite:
   roi, froid, je crois, trois, endroit, il croît,

croix, etc.
b.When <u>not preceded by r</u>, in the following words only:
foi, loi, poids, j'emploie, joie, que je noie,
oie, soie, voie, courtois, mois, pois, toit,
choix, noix, poix.
II.When it is not the last sound of the word and is written:
   1.<u>â-</u>, <u>-â-</u>:
   âge, albâtre, plâtre, etc.
                   ONLY EXCEPTIONS (a):
                   All verbal forms:
                      nous aimâmes, vous parlâtes,
                      vous dansâtes, etc.
   2.<u>a-</u>, <u>-a-</u>:
  a.In the following spellings:
   α.<u>-abre</u>, <u>-adre</u>, <u>-afle</u>, <u>-afre</u>, <u>-affre</u>, <u>-ase</u>, <u>-ases</u>,
   <u>-avre</u>, <u>-az</u>, <u>-aze</u>:
   candélabre, cadre, rafle, balafre, affre,
   base, Le Hâvre, gaz, topaze, etc.
   β.<u>-able</u>.In the three following common words only:
   diable, il l'accable, sable.
   γ.<u>-ace</u>.In the two following words only:
   elle lace, espace.
   δ.<u>-acle</u>.In the following words only:
   miracle, oracle, tabernacle.
   ε.<u>-aille</u>, <u>-ailles</u>.In nouns:
   bataille, fiançailles, Versailles, etc.
                   ONLY EXCEPTIONS (a):
                    médaille, de Noailles.
   ζ.<u>-ame</u>.In the following words only:
   il acclame, elle déclame, je proclame, il
   s'exclame, il réclame.
   η.<u>-ape</u>:
   il dérape.
   θ.<u>-asse</u>.In the following words only:
   basse, casse, classe, grasse, lasse, passe.
   ι.<u>-ate</u>.In the following word only:
   Ponce-Pilate.
  b.In the following words:
  Anne, crabe, damne, gagne, flamme, Isaac,
  Jacques.
  3.<u>-aë-</u>.In the two following proper names:
  Ruisdaël, Staël.
  4.<u>-(o)i-</u>, <u>-(o)î-</u>.(In this combination o represents ŭ
  i, posterior a, α; the combinations <u>oi</u>, <u>oî</u>, represent
  wα).
When <u>preceded by r</u>, except in the endings -roisse,
-roite:
 froide, roide, croître, etc.

-B-

In any syllable in a word except the last, a is posterior when it is written:
  I. â-, -â-:
  ânonner, bâton, pâlir, etc.
  II. -a-:
    1. In the following terminations:
      a. -ason, -azon:
      blason, gazon, Jason, etc.
                    ONLY EXCEPTION (a):
                         diapason.

      b. -assion, -ation:
      conversation, location, passion, etc.
    2. In the following common words and their derivatives:
      baron, bazar, brasier, carré, carreau, carosse,
      charron, graillon, haillon, Jacob, jadis, maçon,
      madré, marron, masure, poulailler, quasi, sar-
      reau, satan, scabreux.
    3. In general in the words derived from those which
    have a posterior a in the last syllable:
      batailleur from bataille; cadrer from cadre;
      damner from damne; endiablé from diable; espacer
      from espace; gagner from gagne; passage from pas-
      se; troisième from trois, etc.
IN OTHER CASES A IN ANY SYLLABLE OF A WORD EXCEPT THE
LAST IS ANTERIOR.
  REMARK. Posterior a varies progressively in degree from
a sound produced only slightly farther back in the mouth
than anterior a to one produced as far back as possible.
The degree depends upon the word, the circumstances, the
speaker.

                    Chapter XXIV.
                    ANTERIOR A, a

A-, -A-, -Â-, -E-, -(O)E-, -(O)Ê-, (O)I-, -(O)Î-, -(O)Y-;
-A, -A(S), -AC(S), -AP(S), -AS, -AT, -AT(S), -ÂT, -ATS,
-ÂT(S), -(O)Í, -(O)Í(S), -(O)ÍE, -(OÍE(S), -(O)ÍENT,
-(O)ÍES, -(O)ÍGT(S), -(O)ÍS, -(O)ÍT, -(O)ÍX.
_____

  In the last syllable of a word a is anterior:
  I. When it is the last sound of a word and is written:
    1. -a:
      ça, il a, opéra, va, etc.
                    ONLY EXCEPTIONS (ɑ):
                         fa (music), la (music), bêta.

    2. -ac, -ap:
      drap, estomac, tabac, etc.

3.<u>-as</u>.In the following common words:
 bras, cadenas, canevas, chasselas, débarras,
 embarras, galetas, maletas, taffetas.
And in all verb forms:
 tu as, tu chantas, tu feras, tu iras, etc.
4.<u>-at</u>:
 avocat, délicat, etc.

ONLY EXCEPTIONS (a):
chocolat, climat.

5.<u>-ât</u>:In verb forms only:
 qu'il parlât, qu'il chantât.
6. <u>ats</u>:
 je bats.
7.<u>-(o)i</u>, <u>-(o)ie</u>, <u>-(o)ient</u>, <u>-(o)ies</u>, <u>-(o)igt</u>, <u>-(o)is</u>,
<u>-(o)it</u>, <u>-(o)ix</u>.(In this combination o represents w, i
and the following silent letters, if any, represent anterior a, a; the preceding combinations represent <i>wa</i>).
<u>Not preceded by r</u>, in the majority of words:
 moi, quoi, qu'il voie, qu'ils soient, que tu
 voies, doigt, je dois, voix, etc.

ONLY EXCEPTIONS (a):
foi, loi, poids, j'emploie,
joie, que je noie, oie, soie,
voie, courtois, mois, pois,
toit, choix, noix, poix.

II.When it is not the last sound of the word and is written:
 1.<u>-a-</u>:
 a.In the following spellings:
  α.<u>-able</u>:
  adorable, aimable, épouvantable, etc.

ONLY EXCEPTIONS (a):
diable, il l'accable, sable.

  β.<u>-ace</u>:
  il l'agace, place, surface, etc.

ONLY EXCEPTIONS (a):
espace, elle lace.

  γ.<u>-acle</u>:
  obstacle, spectacle, etc.

ONLY EXCEPTIONS (a):
miracle, oracle, tabernacle.

  δ.<u>ail</u>, <u>-ail</u>:
  ail, détail, travail, etc.
  ε.<u>-aille</u>, <u>-ailles</u>.In the two following nouns only:
  médaille, de Noailles.
And in verb forms:
 tu travailles, il taille, etc.
  ʒ.<u>-am</u>, <u>-ame</u>:
  Abraham, dame, drame, etc.

ONLY EXCEPTIONS (*a*):
déclame, elle acclame, il s'exclame, elle le proclame, il réclame.

η.-asse:
chasse, je tracasse, masse, que j'embarrasse,
que tu aimasses, terrasse, etc.

ONLY EXCEPTIONS (*a*):
basse, casse, classe, grasse,
lasse, passe.

b.Before a double consonant:
balle, bizarre, datte, gramme, nappe, etc.

ONLY EXCEPTIONS (*a*):
Anne, enflamme, flamme.
NOTE: Double s (ss) has already
been explained.

c.Before the consonant sounds: b, d, f, g, ʒ, k, l,
n, p, r, t, v, ʃ,ɲ :
arabe, salade, girafe, bague, page, bac, balle,
Diane, j'attrape, art, fat, brave, vache, bagne,
etc.

ONLY EXCEPTION (*a*):
Ponce-Pilate.

d.Before the other groups of consonants which have
not yet been mentioned either for posterior a or anterior a, namely: c+consonant, g+consonant, l+con-
sonant, p+consonant, r+consonant, s+consonant, t+con-
sonant, x=(ks):
acte, Ajax, algue, arme, astre, calme, marbre,
Marne, quatre, remarque, enthousiasme, syntaxe,
valse, etc.

2.-â-.In verb forms only:
nous aimâmes, vous dansâtes, etc.

3.-e-, -ê-.In the following words:
femme, moelle, poêle.

4.(o)i-, -(o)i-, -(o)î-.(In these combinations o represents *w*, i and the following silent letters, if any,
represent anterior a, *a*; the combinations oi, oî, represent *wa*).

a.Preceded by r in the following terminations only:
-oisse, -oite:
froisse, paroisse; droite, étroite; etc.

b.Not preceded by r, in the majority of words:
oiseau, angoisse, boîte, étoile, villageoise,
etc.

Note 1.In solennel and its derivatives, in the derivatives of femme, moelle, poêle, as well as in adverbs in
-emment, e is pronounced like anterior a, *a*:
solennité, femmelette, poêllée, moelleux, évidemment,

intelligemment, etc.

Note 2.In the proper name Jeanne, a may be either posterior or anterior.

Note 3.In any syllable in a word except the last, a is
usually anterior, except in the cases already mentioned
(p.160).

Chapter XXV.
CLOSED O, *o*

AU-, -AU-, HO-, O-, Ô-, -O-, -Ô-; -AO, -AU, -AU(X), -AUD(S)
-AULD, -AULT, AULX, -AUT, -AUT(S), -AUX, -EAU(X), -O(S),
-Ô, -OC(S), -OD, -OP, -OP(S), -OS, -OST, -OT(S), -ÔT(S).

-A-

In the last syllable of a word, o is closed:

I.When it is the last sound of the word and is written:

1.-ao, -au, -aud, **auld**, -ault, **aulx**, -aut, -aux, -eau,
-o, -ô, -oo, -ost, -ôt:
curaçao, Pau, chaud, La Rochefoucauld, Hérault,
aulx, il faut, faux, beau, domino, Pô, Waterloo,
Prévost, rôt, etc.

2.-oc.In the following words only:
accroc, broc, croc, escroc, raccroc.

3.-od.In proper names only:
Gounod, Monod, Pernod, etc.

4.-op.In the following words only:
galop, sirop, trop.

> NOTE: Some French people make
> the o of trop open, but this
> practice is not to be recommend-
> ed.

5.-os.In the following common words:
à propos, campos, chaos, clos, dispos, dos,
éclos, enclos, gros, héros, os (plural), nos,
propos, repos, vos.

> Note 1.In the following words, s
> is pronounced:
> albatros, albinos, Burgos,
> Calvados, Carlos, intra-muros,
> mérinos, tétanos.
> Note 2.In the following word, o
> is open and s pronounced:
> os (singular), *os*.
> Note 3.In the following word, s
> is pronounced and o is either
> closed or open:
> rhinocéros, *rinoseros* , or

rinoseros.

6.-ot;
escargot, Margot, etc.
> NOTE: In the following words, t
> is pronounced and o is open:
> dot, *Lot.*

II.When it is not the last sound of a word and is written:

1.-aô-.In the following word:
Saône.

2.au-, -au-:
autre, Paule, pauvre, saute, etc.
> EXCEPTIONS (ɔ):
> a.Before r:
> Centaure, Laure, maure, etc.
> b.In the following words:
> Faust, Paul (compare with
> Paule).

3.-o-.In the following terminations:

a.-ome.In the following common words:
arome, atome, axiome, Chrysostome, idiome, tome.
> Note 1.In the following words, o
> is.open:
> agronome, astronome, économe,
> métronome, Sodome.
> Note 2.In the following words, o
> may be open or closed:
> autonome, gnome, hippodrome,
> majordome, vélodrome.

b.-one.In the following common words:
cyclone, zone.
> Note 1.In the following words, o
> may be open or closed:
> amazone, aphone, atone, au-
> tochtone, décagone, hexagone,
> octogone, ozone, polygone.
> Note 2.All the other words in
> -one, have an open o.

c.-ose:
arrose, chose, rose, etc.

d.-osse.In the following words only:
adosse, désosse, endosse, fosse, grosse.

4.-ô-:
drôle, j'ôte, le nôtre, le vôtre, etc.

5.-os-.In the following word:
Vosges.

-B-

In any syllable in a word except the last, o is closed,
when it is written:

I.au-, -au-:
autrement, Pauline, pauvreté, etc.
EXCEPTIONS ($\mathfrak{o}$):
a.Before r:
j'aurai, Laurence, restaurant,
etc.
b.In the following words:
cauchemar, encaustique, mauvais.
c.In augmenter and its derivatives:
augmentatif, augmentation, etc.
d.In all the words beginning with
auto:
autobus, automobile, autorité,
BUT
auto with closed o,oto,
as well as compound words in
which auto, as a prefix, is
joined to the remainder of the
word by a hyphen:
auto-suggestion.

II.o-, -o-:
1.Before the sound z:
j'oserai, position, rosette, etc.
EXCEPTIONS ($\mathfrak{o}$):
cosaque, losange, myosotis,
philosophe and its derivatives;
théosophe and its derivatives;
sosie.
2.In words derived from dos, gros, fosse, os:
adosser, désossement, dossier, endosser, fossé,
grossir, grossier, ossement, etc.
EXCEPTION ($\mathfrak{o}$):
fossette.
NOTE: In the following words, o
may be open or closed:
fossoyement, fossoyer, fosso-
yeur.
3.In the termination -otion:
devotion, notion, etc.
4.In the following words·
momie, odeur. odieux, vomir, etc.

III.ô-, -ô-, hô-:
j'ôterai, drôlerie, enrôlé, hôtesse, etc.
NOTE: In the following words, ô
may be open or closed, but open
o is preferred:
côté, côtelette, hôpital, hôtel,
rôti, rôtir.

IN OTHER CASES <u>O</u>, IN ANY SYLLABLE OF A WORD EXCEPT THE LAST, IS OPEN.

Chapter XXVI.
OPEN O, ɔ

AU-, -AU-, O-, -O-, -ô-, U(M).

In the last syllable of a word, <u>o</u> is open when it is written:

1.-au-:
  a.Before the sound <u>r</u>:
  Centaure, Laure, maure, Minotaure, etc.
  b.In the following words only:
  Faust, Paul (but Paule with closed <u>o</u>).

> NOTE: In all other words, -au- in the last syllable is closed.

2.-o-:
  a.In the following terminations:
  α.-ome. In the following common words:
  agronome, astronome, économe, métronome, Rome, Sodome.

> Note 1.In the following words, <u>o</u> is closed:
> arome, atome, axiome, Chrysostome.
> Note 2.In the following words, <u>o</u> may be open or closed:
> autonome, gnome, hippodrome, majordome, vélodrome.

  β.-one. In the following common words:
  anémone, Babylone, Barcelone, carbone, madone, matrone, monotone, Simone, téléphone, etc.

> EXCEPTIONS (*o*):
> cyclone, zone.
> NOTE: In the following words, <u>o</u> may be open or closed:
> amazone, aphone, atone, autochtone, décagone, hexagone, octogone, ozone, polygone.

  γ.-osse:
  bosse, brosse, gosse, etc.

> EXCEPTIONS (*o*):
> In the following words and their derivatives:
> adosse, désosse, endosse, fosse, grosse.

  b.And in all other cases where <u>o</u> is followed by one

or several pronounced consonants:
adopte, divorce, dogme, médiocre, quatorze,
porte, école, globe, féroce, o<u>s</u> (singular),
moque, code, pope, dot, etc.
3.-u(m).In this combination, <u>m</u> is sounded:
albu<u>m</u>, maximu<u>m</u>, pensu<u>m</u>, rhu<u>m</u>, etc.

> EXCEPTION (*Œ*):
> The only exception is the fol-
> lowing word, in which <u>um</u> is pro-
> nounced like the nasal <u>un</u>, *Œ* :
> parfum, *parfŒ*.

IMPORTANT NOTE.O is never open when it is the last
sound of a word.
GENERAL REMARKS.
1.<u>O</u> is silent in the following words:
fa<s>o</s>n, La<s>o</s>n, La<s>o</s>nnois, pa<s>o</s>n, pa<s>o</s>nne, ta<s>o</s>n.
2.Two successive o's are pronounced in two syllables
and both are open (*oɔ*):
co-opérative, zo-ologie, etc.

> EXCEPTION (*ɔ*):
> alcool and its derivatives are
> pronounced with only one <u>o</u>, and
> that is open: *alkɔl*

3.ao is usually pronounced in two syllables (*aɔ*):
a-oriste, a-orte, extra-ordinaire.

> EXCEPTIONS (*ɔ*):
> In the following words -ao- and
> -aô- are pronounced in one syl-
> lable and sound like closed <u>o</u>:
> curaçao, Saône.

Chapter XXVII.
CLOSED E, *e*

AI-, -AI-, -AIE-, E-, -É-, -ÉE-; -AI, -AI(S), -AIS, -AIT,
-É(S), -ÉE(S), -EF(S), -ER, -ER(S), -(ERS), -EZ, ET conjunction.

-A-
In the last syllable of a word, <u>e</u> is closed when it is
written:
1.-ai.
a.In verb forms:
j'ai, j'aimerai, je chantai, je donnerai, etc.
b.In the following words:
gai, quai.
2.-ais, -ait.In the following words only (verb forms):
je sais, tu sais, il sait, je vais.

> NOTE: Some French people pro-
> nounce these verb forms with an
> open e̲.

3.-é, -ée:
  bonté, clé, donné, donnée, poupée, etc.
4.-e̲ without written accent, in all Italian or Latin
words:
  fac simile, tolle, etc.
5.-ed.In the following word and its derivatives only:
  pied.
6.-ef.In the following word:
  clef.
7.eh, -eh.
  eh! nargileh, (or nargilé).
8.-er, -ers:
  aimer, boucher, léger, mener, porter, etc.
and the adverb:
  volontiers.

> EXCEPTIONS (ε):
> In the following common words, e̲
> is open and r̲ pronounced:
> amer̲, cancer̲, cher, enfer̲,
> éther̲, fer̲, fier̲ (adjective) but
> fier (verb) with closed e and
> silent r; hier̲, hiver̲, mer̲, re-
> volver̲, ter̲, ver̲.

9.-es.In the six monosyllables:
  ces, des, les, mes, ses, tes.

> NOTE: In poetry, the e̲ of these
> six monosyllables is open.

10.et.In the conjunction:
  et.
11.-ez:
  assez, dansez, nez, parlez, vous aimez, vous
  chantez, voyez, etc.

-B-

In any syllable in a word except the last, e is closed
when written:
 I.-ae:
 Maeterlink.
 II.-aie-.In derivatives of gai:
  gaiement, gaieté, etc.
III.é-, -é-, -ée-:
  édifice, Américain. bénéfice, général, phonétique,
  féerie, etc.
IV.-e-, without written accent when it is the last sound
of a syllable in words of Latin, Italian, or English origin:
  brasero, Montenegro, revolver, vice-versa, etc.

V.-oe:
Oedipe, oesophage, etc.

Note 1. In case of vowel harmony, any of the spellings
of open e may become closed:
aigu, *egy*; aisé, *eze*; bêtise, *beti:z*; plaisir,
plezi:r; etc.

Note 2. In the following prefixes e may be open or
closed:
desc-, dess-, eccl-, eff-, ex-:
descendre, dessiner, ecclésiastique, effacer, examen,
exhumer, etc.

IN OTHER CASES E, IN ANY SYLLABLE OF A WORD EXCEPT THE
LAST, IS OPEN.

Chapter XXVIII.
OPEN E, ɛ

AI-, -AI-, -AIE-, -E-, -È-, -Ê-, -Ë-, -EI-, -EY-; -AI,
-AID(S), -AIE, -AIE(S), -AIENT, -AIES, -AIS, -AIT, -AÎT,
-AY, -AIX, -E-, -È-, -Ê-, -EI-, -EY-, -ECT(S), -EGS, -ES,
-EST, -ET(S), -ÊTS, -EY, HAIE, HAIS, HAIT.

In the last syllable of a word, e is open:
I. When it is the last sound of a word and is written:
1. -ai, -aid, -aie, -aient, -aies, -ais, -ait, -aît, -ay
-egs, -es, est, -et, -ets, -êt, -ey, haie, hais, hait.
geai, laid, baie, qu'ils aient, que tu aies,
j'aimerais, il prendrait, il paraît, Charlotte
Corday, legs, tu es. il est, jouet, je mets,
genêt, Vevey, haie, hais, il hait, etc.

> EXCEPTIONS (e):
> a. -ai. In verb forms:
> je danserai, je parlai, etc.
> and in the following words:
> gai, quai.
> b. -ais, -ait. In the following
> words:
> je sais, tu sais, il sait, je
> vais.
> NOTE: Some French people pro-
> nounce these verb forms with an
> open e.

2. -aix:
faix, paix, Roubaix, etc.

> NOTE: In the following words x
> is pronounced ks:
> Aix, Aix-la-Chapelle, Aix-les
> Bains.

3.**-ect**.In the following words only:
anspe¢ȼ, aspe¢ȼ, circonspe¢ȼ, suspe¢ȼ, respe¢ȼ.

> Note 1.In derivatives of the preceding words, <u>ct</u> is pronounced:
> respe<u>ct</u>ueux, suspe<u>ct</u>er, etc.
> Note 2.In the following words and their derivatives, <u>ct</u> is pronounced:
> abje<u>ct</u>, corre<u>ct</u>, dire<u>ct</u>, infe<u>ct</u>.

4.**-ès**:
expr**ès**, pr**ès**, succ**ès**, tr**ès**, etc.

> NOTE: In the following common words, <u>s</u> is pronounced:
> Agnè<u>s</u>, aloè<u>s</u>, cacatoè<u>s</u>, Cérè<u>s</u>, Damoclè<u>s</u>, è<u>s</u>, Méphistophélè<u>s</u>, palmarè<u>s</u>, pataquè<u>s</u>, Périclè<u>s</u>, Xérè<u>s</u>.

II.When it is not the last sound of a word and is written:
1.**-ai-**, **-aie-**, **-è-**, **-ê-**, **-ë-**, **-ei-**, **-ey-**:
laide, paiement, zèle, bête, Ismaël, reine, Seyne, etc.
2.**e** without written accent, when it is followed by one or more pronounced consonants in the same syllable:
Albert, amer, avec, chef, commerce, Elizabeth, mettre, reste, romanesque, terre, etc.

Chapter XXIX.
CLOSED EU, ø

-EU, -EU-, -EÛ-, HEU-, -HEU-; -EU(X), -EUE(S), -OEUD(S), -OEUF(S), -EUT.

-A-

In the last syllable of the word, <u>eu</u> is closed:
I.When it is the last sound and is written:
-eu, -eue, -oeu, -oeud, -oeufs, -eus, -eut, -eux:
adieu, queue, voeu, noeud, boeufs, je me meus, il peut, je veux. etc.
II.When it is not the last sound of a word and is written:
-eu, -eu-, -eû-, heu-:
1.Before the sound <u>z</u>:
creuse, heureuse, Meuse, etc.
2.In the following terminations:
a.**-eude**, **-eudes**, **-euges**, **-eûne**, **-eute**, **-eutre**:
leude, Eudes, Maubeuge, jeûne (fasting) but jeune (young) with open <u>eu</u>; emeute, neutre, etc.
b.**-eugle**.In the two following words:

il beugle, il meugle.
  c.-eule.In the two following words:
  meule, veule.
 3.In unusual or scientific words:
  Zeus, Pentateuque, etc.
-B-
In any syllable of a word except the last, eu is closed:
 I.In all words derived from those in which eu is closed
in the last syllable:
  bleuir from bleu; deuxième from deux; meuglait
  from meugle; neutralité from neutre; veulerie from
  veule, etc.
 II.In the following words also:
  Eugène, Eugénie, Eulalie, jeudi, meunier, Meurice
  (Hôtel).
III.In unusual or scientific words:
  Deutéronome, eucalyptus, euphonie, leucocyte,
  thérapeuthie.
 IV.As a result of vowel harmony:
  heureux, peureux, etc.
IN OTHER CASES EU, IN ANY SYLLABLE OF A WORD EXCEPT THE
LAST, IS OPEN.

Chapter XXX.
OPEN EU, œ

EU-, -EU-, HEU-, -HEU-, -OEU-, OEI-, -U-.

  In the last syllable of a word, eu is open:
 I.When it is written:
  1.-eu-.In the following terminations:
   a.-euble:
   meuble, etc.
   b.-euf, -oeuf:
   neuf, boeuf, but boeufs (plural) with closed eu and
   silent f, bø ; oeuf, but oeufs (plural) with closed
   eu and silent f, ø.
   c.-eugle.In the following word:
   aveugle.
   d.-euil, -ueil, -euille, -ueille, oeil:
   fauteuil, accueil, feuille, cueille, oeil, etc.
   e.-eul, -eule:
   seul, aïeule, etc.
EXCEPTIONS (ø):
meule, veule.
   f.-eune:
   déjeune, jeune.
   g.-eur, -eure, -eurre, -oeur:

meilleur, meilleure, beurre, coeur, etc.
2.heu-, -heu-:
heure, malheur, etc.
3.-u-.In words borrowed from the English:
club, tub, etc.

> NOTE: All such words may also be
> pronounced with u, **y**:
> *klyb, tyb.*

Chapter XXXI.
OU, *u*

AOÛ-, HOU-, HOUL-, OU-, -OU-, -OÛ-, -OUE-, -OUL-, -OW-;
-AOUL, -OU(S), -OU(X), -OUBS, -OUD, -OUDS, -OUE, -OUE(S),
-OUENT, -OUES, -OUL, -OÛL, -OULD, -OULS, -OUP(S), -OUS,
-OUT, -OUT(S), -OÛT(S), -OUX, AOÛT, HOUE, HOUX.

I.When it is the last sound of a word, <u>ou</u> is written:
  1.-aoul, -ou, -oubs, -oud, -ouds, -oue, -ouent, -oues,
  -oûl, -ould, -ouls, -oup, -ous, -out, -oût, -oux:
  saoul, sou, Doubs, elle coud, tu mouds, je joue,
  ils louent, tu joues, soûl, Sainte-Menehould,
  pouls, loup, dessous, tout, goût, Chateauroux, etc.
II.When it is not the last sound of a word, <u>ou</u> is written:
  1.hou-, houe-, houl-, ou-, -ou-, -oû-, -oue-, -ow-:
  hourra, houement, houlque, outrage, mouton,
  coûter, dévouement, clown,*klun*, etc.
  2.aoû-. In the following word only:
  aoûteron.
  Note 1.The following words are pronounced as one sound
only:
houe, houx.
  Note 2.In the following word the pronunciation of **t** is
optional:
août, *u or ut.*

> NOTE: For the spelling <u>ou</u> repre-
> senting the semi-vowel *w*, see
> page 155.

Chapter XXXII.
I, *i*

HI-, HY-, -HI-, -HY-, I-, -I-, -Î-, -Ï-, -IE-, -IS-, -Y-;
-I, -I(S), -I-, -IC(S), -ID(S), -IE, -IE(S), -ÏE, -IENT,
-IES, -ÏES, -IL(S), -IS, -ÏS, -IT, -IT(S), -ÎT, -ÏT, -IX,
-IZ, -Y, -Y(S), -YS, -YE(S).

I.When it is the last sound of a word, **i** is written:
1.-hi, -i, -ï, -ie, -ïe, -ient, -ies, -ïes, -is, -ïs,
-it, -ït, -ît, -iz, -y, -ye, -ys.
trahi, ceci, Sinaï, je prie, Isaïe, ils prient,
que tu ries, elles sont haïes, tu fis, je haïs
(preterit), il fit, il haït (preterit), qu'il
dît, riz, Annecy, abbaye, pays, etc.

> NOTE: In the following common
> words in -it, -ît, t is pro-
> nounced:
> accessit, aconit, affidavit,
> Christ, but Jésus-Christ with s
> and t silent, ʒeʒykri ; granit,
> huit (see page 152);introït,
> prétérit, transit.

2.-ic.In the following word only:
cric.

> NOTE: In other words, c is pro-
> nounced and has the sound of k:
> alambic, sic, etc.

3.-id.In the two following words:
muid, nid.

> Note 1.In other words d is pro-
> nounced:
> Cid, crid, David.
> Note 2.In Madrid the pronuncia-
> tion of d is optional.

4.-il.In the following words only:
baril, chenil, courtil, coutil, douzil, fenil, fournil
fusil, gentil, gril, nombril, outil, persil, sourcil.

> Note 1.In other words, l is pro-
> nounced:
> Brésil, cil, fil, Nil, etc.
> Note 2.In fils (Eng. son; sons),
> l is not pronounced, but s is
> sounded, fis.

5.-is.
a.In all verb forms:
tu dis, je vis, etc.
b.In the following words:
Alexis, **avis**, bis (color) but bis (encore) with s
sounded, (bis); brebis, colis, coloris, commis,
compromis, concis, croquis, depuis, devis, Etats-
Unis, exquis, gris, hormis, logis, louis, malap-
pris, marquis, mépris, paradis, permis, pis,
précis, promis, puis, radis, Saint-Denis, souris,
tapis, vernis, vis-à-vis.
6.-ix.In the three following words only:
crucifix, perdrix, prix.

174

NOTE: In the following common
words x=ks:
Cadix, Félix, phénix, préfix,
Vercingétorix.

II.When it is not the last sound of a word, i is written:
1.hi-, hy-, -hi-, i-, -i-, -i-, -î-, -ie-, -y-:
hiver, hygiène, trahison, idéal, discipline,
naïf, abîme, licenciement, analyse, etc.

NOTE: ie placed before a double
mm is pronounced with yod and
anterior a, *ja:*
sciemment. *sjamã*, etc.

2.-is-.In the following words only:
Fismes, Vismes.

NOTE: For the spelling i repre-
senting yod, see p.155.

Chapter XXXIII.
U, *y*

HU-, -HU-, U-, -U-, -Û-, -Ü-, -EÛ-; EU(S), EUE(S), EUS,
EUT, EÛT, -HU, -HUE, -HUES, -HUT(S), -U, -U(S), -Û, -Û(S),
-UE, -UE(S), -UE(S), -UES, -US, -UT, -UT(S), -ÛT, -ÛT(S),
-UX.

I.When it is the last sound of the word, u is written:
-hu, -hue, -hues, -hut, -u, -û, -ü, -ue, -ûe, -ue, -ues,
-ûes, -us, -ut, -ût, -ux:
tohu-bohu, hue, tu hues, chahut, absolu, dû, Esaü,
je tue, dûe, aiguë, tu le tues, dûes, dessus, il
vécut, attribut, qu'il fût, affût, afflux, etc.
II.When it is not the last sound of a word u is written:
hu-, -hu-, u-, -u-, -û-:
huguenot, inhumain, unanime, aucune, flûte, vous
fûtes, etc.
IMPORTANT REMARK.In the following forms of the verb
avoir only, eu is pronounced u, *y*:
j'eus, tu eus, il eut, nous eûmes, vous eûtes, ils eurent
qu'il eût; eu, eue, eus, eues, past participle.

NOTE: For the spelling u repre-
senting the semi-vowel *ɥ*, see
p.155.

Chapter XXV.
AN, *ã*

-AEN-, AM, -AM-, AN-, -AN-, EM-, -EM-, -EMP-, EN-, -ANG-,

-AEN, -AM, -AMP, -AMP(S), -AN, -AN(S), -ANC(S), -AND,
ANDT, -AND(S), -ANG(S), -ANS, -ANT, -ANT(S), -AON, -AON(S),
-EAN, -EMPS, -EMPT(S), -EN, -END, -END(S), -ENDS, -ENG(S),
-ENS, -ENT, -ENT(S).

I. When it is the last sound of a word, the sound an, $\tilde{a}$,
is written:
1.-aen, -amp, -an, -anc, -and, -ang, -ans, -ant, -ean,
-emps, -empt, -end, -ends, -eng:
Caen, Fécamp, camp, océan, banc, quand, allemand,
rang, dans, maintenant, enfant, Jean, temps,
longtemps, exempt, il apprend, tu vends, hareng,
etc.
2.-am. In the following words only:
Adam, dam.

> NOTE: In all other words in -am,
> the vowel is not nasalized and m
> is sounded:
> Cham, islam, macadam, etc.

3.-aon. In the following words:
faon, Laon, paon, taon.

> NOTE: In the following words,
> aon is pronounced in two sylla-
> bles, anterior a+on:
> phara-on, Lyca-on

4.-en. In the following word only:
Rouen, $rw\tilde{a}$

> Note 1. In the following common
> words en is not nasalized, e is
> pronounced like open e and n is
> sounded:
> abdomen, albumen, amen, Beetho-
> ven, cyclamen, eden, gluten,
> hymen, lichen, pollen, Reis-
> choffen, specimen.
> Note 2. Preceded by i, en is al-
> ways pronounced like in, $\tilde{e}$.
> bien, sien, etc.
> Note 3. In all other common words,
> en is pronounced like in, $\tilde{e}$.
> Agen, européen, examen, etc.

5.-ens:
dépens, encens, j'assens, suspens, tu mens, tu
sens, etc.

> NOTE: In the following words s
> is sounded:
> cens, sens and its derivatives
> (contresens, non-sens).
> EXCEPTIONS:

a.($\tilde{\varepsilon}$).In verb forms:

je viens, tu maintiens, etc.

b.($\widetilde{\varepsilon s}$):

Rubens, *rybɛ̃:s*

6.-ent:

a̲g̲e̲n̲t̲, bonnement, il consent, orient, etc.

<u>EXCEPTIONS:</u>

a.($\tilde{\varepsilon}$).In verb forms, third person singular, if preceded by i̲, ent is pronounced i̲n̲, $\tilde{\varepsilon}$:

il tient, il vient, etc.

b.(θ).When e̲n̲t̲ is the mark of third person plural of verb, it represents a mute e:

ils parlent, *ilparl* , etc.

II.When it is not the last sound of a word, the sound a̲n̲, $\tilde{a}$, is written:

1.-aën-.In the following proper name:

Saint-Saëns, *sɛ̃sã:s* .

2.am-, -am-.Before b̲ and p̲:

ambassadeur, ambition, lampe, etc.

<u>NOTE:</u> Before m̲, n̲, or a vowel, a̲m̲ is not nasalized. It is pronounced like anterior a̲, and m̲ is sounded with the next syllable:

amener, *amne*, ammoniaque, *amɔnjak* , amnistie, *amnisti* , flammèche, *flamɛʃ* , ramification, *ramifikasjɔ̃*

3.an-.Before any consonant except n:

ancêtre, ange, danser, etc.

<u>NOTE:</u> Before a vowel or another n̲, a̲n̲ is not nasalized, and it is pronounced like anterior a̲; n is then sounded with the next syllable:

anecdote, *a-nɛk-dɔt* , année, *a-ne* , sanitaire, *sa-ni-tɛ:r* , etc.

4.em-, -em-.Before b̲, p̲ and m̲:

embrasser, emmener, empereur, décembre, remporter,etc.

<u>EXCEPTIONS:</u>

a.(a).In adverbs in -emment; as well as in f̲e̲m̲m̲e̲, m̲o̲e̲l̲l̲e̲, p̲o̲ê̲l̲e̲, s̲o̲l̲e̲n̲n̲e̲l̲ and their derivatives, e is pronounced like anterior a̲; m̲m̲ is then pronounced m̲ and sounded with the next syllable:

femmelette, *famlɛt* , intelligemment, *ɛ̃-tɛl-li-ʒa-mã*,
patiemment, *pa-sjã-mã* , etc.
b. *(ɛm)*.Before me at the end of a
word, em (except in femme mentioned above) is pronounced like
open e and mm is sounded m:
dilemme, *dilɛm*, gemme, *qʒɛm*,
etc.

5. en-, -en-.Before any consonant except another n:
ascenseur, cens, contresens, enfer, non-sens,
pentecôte, science, etc.

EXCEPTIONS: (ɛ̃).In words of Latin or foreign origin, and their
derivatives, en is pronounced
in, ɛ̃. The most common of these
words are:
agenda, appendice, benjamin,
benzine, pensum, Pensylvanie,
Stendahl.
NOTE: Before a vowel or another
n, en usually is not nasalized,
e is pronounced like an open e.
n is sounded:
doyenne, *dwajɛn*; enigme, *enigm*
ennéade, *eneãd*; ennemi, *enmi*;
énorme, *enɔrm*; etc.
BUT in the following words and
their derivatives, en is nasalized and pronounced an, ã, while
n sounds also with the next syllable:
enamourer, *ã-na-mu-re* ,
enivrant, *ã-ni-vrã* , ennoblir,
ã-no-bli:r , ennui, *ã-nɥi* ,
enorgueillir, *ã-nɔr-gœ-ji:r* .

6. -ang-.In the following word:
sangsue.

7. -emp-.In forms of the following verb:
exempter, j'exempte, etc.

BUT exemption has sounded p.

GENERAL NOTE.Em at the end of a word is not nasalized,
and it is pronounced like an open e plus m, *ɛm* :
Bethléem, hem! Jerusalem, etc.

Chapter XXXIV.
ON, ɔ̃, õ

OM-, -OM-, ON-, -ON-, -ONT-, UN-; -OM, -OM(S), -OMB,

-OMB(S), -OMPS, -OMPT, -ON, -ON(S), -ONC(S), -OND, -OND(S),
-ONDS, -ONG(S), -ONS, -ONT, -ONT(S).

I.When it is the last sound of a word, the sound on, $\tilde{o}$,
is written:
    1.-om, -omb, -omps, -ompt, -on, -ond, -onds, -ong,
-ons, -ont.
    Riom, nom, Christophe Colomb, plomb, je romps,
prompt, Didon, il répond, profond, tu confonds,
long, nous allons, ils font, pont, etc.
    2.-onc.In the three following words only:
ajon , jonc, tronc.

> NOTE: In the following word, c
> is often pronounced like k:
> donc (see p. 147).

II.When it is not the last sound of a word, the sound on,
$\tilde{o}$, is written:
    1.om-, -om-:
    a.Before b or p:
    accompagner, nombre, ombre, etc.
    b.In the following words:
    comte and its derivatives; Domrémy.
    2.-omp-.In the following words and their derivatives:
compte, dompte, prompte.
    3.-on, -on-.Before any consonant except n:
bonté, monde, oncle, etc.
    4.-ong-.In the following word:
longtemps.
    5.-ont-.In words derived from mont:
mont-de-piété, Montmartre, Montmorency, Mont-
parnasse, etc.
    6.un-, -un-.In unusual words from Latin and in the fol-
lowing common words:
de profundis, $depr\jmath f\tilde{o}dis$, punch, $p\tilde{o}{:}\int$,
secundo, $s\vartheta g\tilde{o}do$, etc.

Chapter XXXVI.
IN, $\tilde{\varepsilon}$

AIN-, -AIN-, -EIM-, -EIN-, EN-, -EN-, IM-, -IM-, IN-, -IN-,
-YM-, -YN-; -AIM(S), -AIN, -AIN(S), -AINC, -AINCS, -AINS,
-AINT, -AINT(S), -EIN, -EIN(S), -EING(S), -EINS, -EIN(S),
-EINT, -EINT(S), -EN, -EN(S), -(I)ENS, -(I)ENT, -IN(S),
-INCT(S), -ING(S), -INGT(S), -INS, -INT, -INT(S), $\hat{I}$NT, -YM.

I.When it is the last sound of a word, the sound in, $\tilde{\varepsilon}$,
is written:
    1.-aim, -ain, -ainc, -aincs, -ains, -aint, -ein,

eing, -eins, -eint, -(i)en, -(i)ens, -(i)ent, -in,
-ing, -ingt, -ins, -int, -înt, -ym:
faim, Ain, américain, il vainc, tu convaincs,
je plains, il craint, saint, hein, plein, seing,
je peins, dessein, il teint, teint, sien, main-
tien, je viens, il tient, Berlin, vin, poing,
vingt, j'appartins, elle vint, qu'il vînt, qu'il
tînt, thym, etc.

2.-en:
Agen, européen, examen, moyen, etc.

       EXCEPTIONS:
       a.(ã).In the following word:
       Rouen,
       b.(εn).In the following words, en
       is not nasalized and it is pro-
       nounced open e plus n:
        abdomen, albumen, amen, Beethoven,
        ven, cyclamen, eden, gluten,
        hymen, lichen, pollen, Reis-
        choffen, spécimen.

3.-inct.In the two following words only:
instinct, succinct.

       Note 1.In words derived from the
       two above, ct is pronounced:
        instinctivement, succincte, etc.
       Note 2.In the following word and
       its derivatives, ct is pro-
       nounced:
        distinct, distinction, etc.

II.When it is not the last sound of a word, the sound in,
ɛ̃, is written:

1.ain-, -ain.Before any consonant:
ainsi, craindre, plaintivement, etc.

       NOTE: Before a vowel, ain is not
       nasalized; it is pronounced like
       open e, and n is sounded:
        aine, Bazaine, douzaine, Maine,
        vingtaine, etc.

2.-eim-:
Reims,

3.-ein-:
ceinture, peindre, teinte, etc.

       NOTE: Before a vowel ein is not
       nasalized; it is pronounced like
       open e, and n is sounded:
        peine, Seine, etc.

4.en-, -en-:
a.en-.In the two following words only:
endécagone, endécasyllabe.

b.-en-.Generally in scientific, rare or unusual words of Latin or Italian origin, and their derivatives, as well as in the following more common words:
agenda, appendice, benjamin, benzine, pensum, Pensylvanie, Stendahl.

5.im-, -im-.Before b or p:
imbécile, impossible, simple, timbre, etc.

> NOTE: Before a vowel or another m, im is not nasalized and m is sounded with the next syllable:
> image, immobile, limite, etc.
> In the three following words, and their derivatives, i may or may not retain its nasal quality:
> immangeable, $\tilde{\varepsilon}$-$m\tilde{a}$-ζabl or $m\tilde{a}$-ζabl; immanquable, $\tilde{\varepsilon}$-$m\tilde{a}$-$kabl$ or i-$m\tilde{a}$-$kabl$; immesurable $\tilde{\varepsilon}$-$m\vartheta$-zy-$rabl$ or i-$m\vartheta$-zy-$rabl$.

6.in-, -in-, -în-.Before any consonant except n:
incapable, nous maintînmes, prince, etc.

> NOTE: Before a vowel or mute h or another n, in is not nasalized and n is sounded with the next syllable:
> binocle, inhumain, innocence, inutile, sinistre, etc.

7.-ym-, -yn-.Before any consonant:
larynx, lymphatique, lyncher, nymphe, etc.

GENERAL NOTE.Im at the end of a word is not nasalized and m is sounded:
interim, Joachim, $\zeta oakim$; olim, etc.

Chapter XXXVII.
UN, $\tilde{œ}$

HUM-, -UN-; -EUN, -EUNG, HUN(S), -UM(S), -UN, -UN(S), -UNT(S).

I.When it is the last sound of the word, the sound un, $\tilde{œ}$, is written:
1.-eun, -eung, hun, un, -un, -unt:
à jeun, Jean de Meung, Hun, un, Verdun, emprunt, etc.
2.-um.In the following word only:
parfum.

> NOTE: In all other words in -um, u is pronounced like open o, and

m is sounded:
album, maximum, opium, etc.

II. When it is not the last sound of the word, the sound un, $\tilde{œ}$, is written:

1. hum-:
humble.

NOTE: hum before a vowel is not nasalized, and m is sounded with the next syllable:
humanité, humilité, humour, etc.

2. -un-:
défunte, emprunte and its derivatives; pétunsé.

Note 1. Un before a vowel is not nasalized and n is sounded with the next syllable:
brunette, unanime, union, etc.

Note 2. In scientific and unusual words of Latin origin, un placed before a consonant is pronounced on, $\tilde{ɔ}$:
uncial, etc.

and also in the following more common words:
punch, $p\tilde{ɔ}:ʃ$, secundo, $səg\tilde{ɔ}do$.

Chapter XXXVIII.
SEMI-VOWEL OU, u

HOU(+vowel), O(+e), O(+ê), OU(+vowel), (q)U(+a), (g)U(+a),
O(+i), O(+ids), O(-id)(s), O(+ie), O(+ie)(s), O(-ies),
O(+igt)(s), O(+in), O(+in)(s), O(+ing)(s), O(+ins),
O(+int)(s), O(+is), O(+it), O(+it)(s), O(+ix), O(+y),
-OO(ing).

The sound u is written as follows:

I. hou(+vowel):
houache, houette, etc.

II. o(+e), o(+ê). In the following words and their derivatives, e is sounded like anterior a:
moelle, $mual$; poêle, $pual$; etc.

NOTE: In all other words oè is pronounced in two syllables, open o, $ɔ$, and open e, $ɛ$:
po-ète, $po-ɛt$; tro-ène, $tro-ɛn$, etc.

III. o(+i), o(+id), o(+ids), o(+ie), o(+ies), o(+igt),
o(+in), o(+ing), o(+ins), o(+int), o(+is), o(+it), o(+ix):
oiseau, moitié, roi, froid, poids, que je voie,

que tu t'asseoies, doigt, loin, lointain, coing,
moins, point, que tu sois, qu'il soit, exploit,
choix, etc.

> EXCEPTIONS: In the following
> words and their derivatives, oi
> is pronounced like open o, ɔ:
> encoɼgnure, ᾶkɔɲɥːr, moɼgnon,
> mɔɲᴣ, oignon, ɔɲᴣ.

IV.o(y):
croyant, incroyable, loyal, loyauté, etc.

> EXCEPTIONS (ɔ):
> In the following words o retains
> its quality of open o:
> boyard, bɔ-jaːr , oyant, ɔ-jᾶ .

V.-oo(+ing):In the following word borrowed from the English:
schampooing,

VI.ou(+vowel):
louis, ouest, oui, etc.

> EXCEPTIONS (u):
> a.When preceded by two consonants
> forming a co-called inseparable
> group belonging to the same syl-
> lable, ou plus a vowel is pro-
> nounced in two syllables. The
> groups of inseparable consonants
> are:
> bl, br, cl, cr, dr, fl, fr, gl,
> gr, pl, pr, tr, vr:
> brouette, bru-ɛt ; éblouisse-
> ment, e-blu-is-mᾶ; trouer,
> tru-e , etc.
> b.In the first and second person
> plural of the imperfect indica-
> tive and present subjunctive, ou
> plus a vowel is pronounced in
> two syllables:
> vous nou-iez, vu-nu-jɵ , que
> nous allou-ions, kɵ-nu-a-lu-
> jᴣ , etc.

VII.(q)u(+a), (g)u(+a).In scientific or unusual words of
which the majority are of Latin origin. The most usual are:
adéquat, aquarelle, aquarium, équateur, équation,
in-quarto, loquace, quadrangulaire, quadruple,
quartette, quatuor, quaternaire, square, Guadeloupe,
jaguar, lingual, Nicaragua, Paraguay.

> NOTE: In all other usual words
> qua is pronounced ka; and ɡua,
> ga:

qualité, quantité, quatre,
légua, navigua, etc.

VIII.-hu, -o(+a):In the following words:
   :acahuête, *ka-ka-wɛt*, joaillier, *ʒwa-jе*, Roanne,
   rwan

Chapter XXXIX.
SEMI-VOWEL U, ɥ

HU(+i), U(+vowel), (q)U(+e or i), (g)U(+i).

The sound ɥ is written as follows:

I.hu(+i):
aujourd'hui, huile, huitaine, etc.

II.-U(+any vowel), -u(+any vowel)-:
affectueux, cuisine, duel, ennuyeux, juin, nuance,
nuit, puits, ruelle, vertueux, etc.

        EXCEPTIONS (*y*):
        a.When preceded by two consonants
        forming a so-called inseparable
        group belonging to the same syl-
        lable, u+any vowel (except i) is
        pronounced in two syllables. The
        groups of inseparable consonants
        are:

        bl, br, cl, cr, dr, fl, fr, gl,
        gr, pl, pr, tr, vr.
        cru-auté, cru-elle, monstru-
        eux, obstru-èrent, etc.
        b.In the first and second person
        plural of the imperfect indica-
        tive and present subjunctive, u
        plus a vowel is pronounced in two
        syllables:
        que nous pollu-ions, que vous
        tu-iez, etc.

III.(g)u(+i,+e,+in), (q)u(+i,+e,+in):Generally in scientific and unusual words of Latin origin; also in the following
more common words, and their derivatives:
aiguille, aiguiser, ambiguité, arguer, inextinguible,
linguiste, obséquieux, quiet, quintuple.

        NOTE: In all other common words,
        qu before a vowel is pronounced
        k; gu before a vowel is pro-
        nounced g:
        acquis, *a-ki*, alangui, *a-lã-gi*,
        convainquit, *kɔ̃vẽki*, gui, *gi*,
        marquis, *mar-ki*, qui, *ki*, etc.

184

Chapter XL.

THE SOUND YOD, j

HI(+vowel)-, -HI(+vowel)-, HY(+vowel)-, -I(+vowel), -Ï(between vowels)-, -(vowel+)ILL-, -(I+)LL-, -LH-, Y(+vowel)-,
-Y(+vowel, -(vowel+)ILLE(S), -(I+)LLE(S), -(vowel+)IL(S).

I.When it is the last sound of a word, the sound yod is
written:
  1.-il, -ille, preceded by a vowel.In this case i does
not combine with the preceding vowel which thus retains its own timbre:
    appareil, Auteuil, détail, soleil, travail; gre-
nouille, merveille, tu travailles, etc.
  2.-lle, preceded by i:
    Bastille, bille, famille, etc.
                  EXCEPTIONS (il):
                  a.In the following words and
                  their derivatives, -lle is pro-
                  nounced like l:
                    il distille, Lille, mille,
                    Millet, pupille, tranquille,
                    ville.
                  b.In scientific and rare words:
                    Achille, bacille, etc.
                  NOTE: In the following word, -lle
                  may be pronounced l or j:
                    scintille, $s\tilde{e}til$ or $s\tilde{e}tij$.
  3.-(a)ye, -(e)ye, in subjunctive forms. In such cases,
y first combines with the preceding vowel to make it
sound like open e; next, it is sounded vod:
    que je paye, $k\partial\mathfrak{z}\partial p\varepsilon j$; qu'il égaye, $kileg\varepsilon j$;
    que tu essayes, $k\partial$-ty-ε-$s\varepsilon j$; que je m'asseye, $k\partial\mathfrak{z}$-
ma-$s\varepsilon j$; que tu grasseyes, $k\partial tygras\varepsilon j$; etc.
II.In the middle of a word, the sound yod is written:
  1.-hi(+vowel)-, -i(+vowel)-:
    cahier, bien, etc.
  2.-ï-, between two vowels of which the second is not
mute e:
    aïeul, a-$j\oe l$; faïence, fa-$j\tilde{a}{:}s$; païen, pa-$j\tilde{\varepsilon}$; etc.
                  NOTE: When mute e follows i, i
                  retains the characteristics of a
                  vowel, the dieresis preventing
                  it from combining with the pre-
                  ceding vowel:
                    haïe, a-i; Isaïe, i-$\mathfrak{z}a$-i;
                    etc.
  3.-ill-,preceded by a vowel.In such cases, i does not
combine with the preceding vowel which thus retains

its own timbre.

ba-illi, *ba-ji*; groseillier, *gro-ze-je* travailler, *tra-va-je* ; ve-iller, *ve-je* ; etc.
5.-ll-, preceded by i:
billet, fillette, etc.

> EXCEPTIONS (*il*):
> a.In the following words and
> their derivatives ll is pro-
> nounced like l:
> Lille, mille, Millet, pupille,
> tranquille, ville, etc.
> b.In rare or scientific words ll
> is pronounced like double l:
> bacillaire, instiller, etc.

6.-y-, between vowels.In such cases, first, y combines
with the preceding vowel in the following way:
ay= open e, ε ; ey= open e, ε; oy= ou semi-vowel
plus anterior a, wa; uy=u semi-vowel plus i, ɥi;
and next it has the sound of yod, *j* , in the same syllable with the following vowel:
balayer, *ba-lε-je* ; ennuyer, *ã-nɥi-je* ; nous
croyons, *nu-krwa-jõ* ; voyager, *vwa-ja-ʒe* ; etc.

> EXCEPTIONS.In the following com-
> mon words y does not combine
> with the preceding vowel, but
> has only the sound of yod in
> the same syllable with the next
> vowel:
> Ba-yard, *ba-ja:r* ; bo-yard,
> *bo-ja:r* ; bru-yamment, *brɥi-*
> *ja-mã* ; bru-yant, *brɥi-jã* ;
> bru-yère, *brɥi-je:r*; gru-yère,
> *grɥi-jε:r*; ma-yonnaise, *ma-*
> *jo-nε:z* ; o-yant, *o-jã* .

4.-lh-,in a few names of towns in the south of France:
Milhau (often written Millau), *mi-jo* ; Nolhac,
no-jak ; Pardalhac, *par-da-jak*,etc.
III.At the beginning of a word:
1.hi(+vowel)-, hy(+vowel)-:
hier, hyène, etc.
2.y(+vowel):
yacht, yole, etc.

Chapter XLI.
THE SOUND AND LETTER P , *p*

P-, -P-, -PE-, -PP-, -PPE-; -P(S), -PE, -PE(S), -PES, -PPE,
-PPE(S), -PPES.

I.At the beginning or in the middle of a word the sound p is written:

p-, -p-, pe-, -pp-, -ppe-:
partir, psaume, psychologie, psychée, opération, équipement, appartement, Assomption, concept, contempteur, Neptune, rapt, transept, laps, jappement, etc.

SILENT P
The letter p is silent in the following words and their derivatives:
baptême, cheptel, compte, dompte, exempt, but exemption; il rompt, je romps, prompt, promptitude, tu romps, sculpter, sept, septième, septièmement, but septante, septembre, septentrion, temps.
And in nouns composed with champ:
Champlever, Champmêlé, etc.

II.At the end of a word the sound p is written:
1.-pe, -pes, -ppe, -ppes:
type, tu tapes, Dieppe, enveloppe, tu développes, etc.
2.-p:
cap, croup, Gap, hop! houp! etc.

SILENT P
The letter p is silent in the following words:
beaucoup, camp, cep (de vigne), champ, coup, drap, Dupanloup, Fécamp, galop, Longchamp, loup, sirop, trop.

Chapter XLII.
THE SOUND AND LETTER B, b

B-, -B-, -BB-, -BE-, -BH-; -B, -B(S), -BBE, -BBES, -BE, -BE(S), -BES.

I.At the beginning or in the middle of a word the sound b is written
b-, -b-, -bb-, -be-, -bh-:
beau, abolir, table, abbé, bombement, abhorrer. etc.
II.At the end of a word the sound b is written:
1.-bbe, -bbes, -be, -bes:
je gobbe, tu gobbes, je dérobe, globe, tu dérobes, etc.
2.-b:
club. Jacob, etc.

SILENT B
The letter b is silent in the following words:
aplomb, plomb, surplomb, Christophe Colomb,

Dou~~b~~s, Lefe~~b~~vre.

Chapter XLIII.
THE SOUND AND LETTER T, *t*

T-, -T-, -TE-, TH-, -TH-, -TT-, -TTE-; -T, -T(S), -TE,
-TE(S), -TES, -THE(S), -TTE, -TTE(S), -TTES; D (in liaison)

I.At the beginning or in the middle of a word the sound
t is written:
  t-, -t-, -te-, th-, -th-, -tt-, -tte-:
    timbre, fatigue, lentement, thé, mythologie,
  flatteur, nettement, etc.
    SILENT **T**
    The letter t is silent:
      a.In words containing the prefixes mont- and pont:
      Mon~~t~~martre, Pon~~t~~château, Mon~~t~~parnasse, Mon~~t~~-
      réal, Mon~~t~~pellier, etc.
                 NOTE: However, if the letter t
                 is followed by a vowel or if
                 mont represents the combination
                 of mon (Eng. my), plus the t of
                 the following syllable, the let-
                 ter t is sounded:
                 Montauban, Montrésor, Montreuil,
                 Pontoise.
      b.In the following words and their derivatives:
      as~~t~~~~h~~me, *asm*; is~~t~~~~h~~me, *ism*.
PRONUNCIATION OF THE LETTER T WHEN FOLLOWED BY I+A VOWEL:
    1.When t(i) is preceded by s or x it is pronounced t:
    bestial, hostie, mixtion, question, Sébastien,
    vestiaire, etc.
    2.In the following terminations t=s:
    a.-tiade, -tiaire, -tial, -tiale, -tiaux, -tiane,
    -tiate, -tiel, -tielle, -tience, -tieux, -tieuse,
    -tio, -tium, -tius:
    Miltiade, pénitentiaire, initial, initiale,
    initiaux, nicotiane, Spartiate, confidentiel,
    patience, ambitieux, tertio, patio, consortium,
    Helvétius, etc.
    b.-tia:
    initiative, initiation, insatiable, opuntia, etc.
                EXCEPTIONS.t=t in the following
               words and their derivatives:
               centiare, *sãtja:r* ; châtiable,
               ʃatjabl ; éléphantiasis, *ele-*
               fãtjazis ; galimatias, *ga-*
               li-ma-tja; tiare, *tja:r* .

c.-tie:
aristocratie, idiotie, suprématie.

> EXCEPTIONS: <u>t=t</u>:
> 1.If preceded by a written consonant:
> dynastie, *dinasti*; hostie, *ɔsti* ; garantie, *garãti* ; ortie, *ɔrti*; partie, *parti*; apprentie, *aprãti* ; etc.
> However in the two following words, although preceded by a written consonant, <u>tie= *si*</u> :
> ineptie, *inɛpsi* ; inertie, *inɛrsi* .
> 2.In verb forms:
> elle est assujétie, *asyʒeti;* elle est rebâtie, *rəbati;* elle s'est appesantie, *apəzãti;* il l'a abrutie, *abryti;* il l'a pressentie, *presãti;* etc.
> However in the four following verbs <u>t=s</u>:
> elle différentie, *diferãsi* ; il balbutie, *balbysi* ; il transsubstantie, *trãsybstãsi* ; j'initie, *inisi*; etc.
> 3.In the following words, although preceded by a vowel:
> chrestomathie, *krestomati* ; Claretie, *klarti* .

d.-tien:
capétien, Le Titien.

> ONLY EXCEPTIONS: <u>t=t</u>:
> chrétien, *kretjɛ̃*; entretien, le tien, maintien, Sébastien.

e.-tiens, -tient:
impatient, quotient, etc.

> EXCEPTIONS: <u>t=t</u>:
> In all the forms of the verb tenir:
> il tient, *iltjɛ̃* ; je tiens, *ʒətjɛ̃*; etc.

f.-tier. In the following verbs only:
balbutier, différentier, initier, transsubstantier, throughout their conjugation.

> NOTE: In all other words in -tier, <u>t=t</u>:
> cafetier, *kaftje*; châtier, *ʃatje* ; papetier, *paptje* .

g.-tiole:
gratiole, pétiole and their derivatives.

> EXCEPTIONS: t=t:
> In the following words, and
> their derivatives:
> bestiole, *bɛstjɔl*; étiole,
> *etjɔl* .

h.-tion-, -tion:
action, actionner, constitutionnellement,
fraction, fractionnel, etc.

> EXCEPTIONS: t=t:
> In the termination -tions, of
> verb forms only:
> nous éditions, *nuzeditjɔ̃* but
> les éditions, *edisjɔ̃* ; nous
> portions, *nuportjɔ̃*but les por-
> tions, *leporsjɑ̃*

i.In the following words: t=s:
a fortiori, amphictyon, propitiateur and its derivatives; satiété.

II.At the end of a word the sound t is written:
  -te, -tes, -the, -tte, -ttes:
bête, tu habites, Marthe, labyrinthe, chatte, tu
luttes, etc.

> SILENT T
> The letter t is usually silent at the end of a word:
> avocat̸, Bossuet̸, debut̸, delicat̸, dent̸, doigt̸,
> effet̸, et̸, forêt̸, fret̸, Hérault̸, influent̸, in-
> quiet̸, jouet̸, maintenant̸, Rembrandt̸, salut̸,
> tribut̸, vingt̸, etc.
>
> and in verb forms:
> elle allait̸, elle est̸, but est (east) *ɛst*;
> il boit̸, il rompt̸, il sent̸, il veut̸, etc.

> > EXCEPTIONS: t is pronounced in
> > the following common words:
> > abject, abrupt, accessit, aco-
> > nit, affidavit, Apt, Brest,
> > brut, Bucarest, cet, Christ but
> > Jésus-Christ̸; chut, compact,
> > concept, contact, direct, dis-
> > tinct, but succinct̸, instinct̸;
> > district, dot, entre le zist et
> > le zest; Ernest, est (east) but
> > est̸ (verb); fat, granit, huit,
> > incorrect but aspect̸, respect̸,
> > suspect̸; indirect, infect, in-
> > tact, introït, Japhet, Josaphat,
> > Lot, mat, net, ouest, prétérit,
> > rapt, sept, soit, (meaning: so

be it, agreed) but qu'il soi~~t~~;
stri~~ct~~, ta~~ct~~, transe~~pt~~, transi~~t~~,
verdi~~ct~~.
Note 1.In the two following
words, the pronunciation of t is
optional:
aoû~~t~~ or aoû<u>t</u>; bu~~t~~ or bu<u>t</u>.
Note 2.In the following word the
pronunciation of ct is optional:
exa~~ct~~ or exa<u>ct</u>.
Note 3.In liaison d is sounded t:
quand il viendra, second enfant,
grand homme, il prend une
fourrure.

Chapter XLIV.
THE SOUND AND LETTER D, *d*

D-, -D-, -DD-, -DE-, -DH-; -D, -D(S), -DS, -DE, DE(S),
-DES.

I.At the beginning or in the middle of a word the sound
<u>d</u> is written:
   d-, -d-, -dd-, -de-, -dh-:
   aider, dame, addition, avidement, adhérer, etc.
II.At the end of a word the sound <u>d</u> is written:
   1.**-de, -des:**
   j'aide, avide, tu vides, etc.
   2.**-d**, in the following endings:
   -ad, -ed, -ud:
   Alfred, Bagdad, Caïd, Cid, David, Port-Saïd, sud,
   Valladolid, etc.
      SILENT D
   1.The letter <u>d</u>, and the spelling <u>ds</u> are silent when
   they are the mark of the first, second and third
   persons singular of the present indicative of verbs
   of the third conjugation.
      il mou~~d~~, je per~~ds~~, tu confon~~ds~~, etc.
   2.The letter <u>d</u> is silent in the following endings:
   **-ai~~d~~, -an~~d~~, -ar~~d~~, -au~~ld~~, -au~~d~~, -ie~~d~~, -o~~d~~, -oeu~~d~~,
   -oi~~d~~, -on~~d~~, -or~~d~~, -ou~~ld~~, -our~~d~~:**
   lai~~d~~, marchan~~d~~, billar~~d~~, La Rochefoucaul~~d~~,
   chau~~d~~, pie~~d~~, Gouno~~d~~, noeu~~d~~, froi~~d~~, blon~~d~~,
   abor~~d~~. nor~~d~~. Sainte Menehou~~ld~~. *sẽtmənəu* or
   sẽtmənu; lour~~d~~.

         ONLY EXCEPTION:
         George San<u>d</u>
         NOTE: With the following com-

pound words, liaison (with <u>d</u>) or
linking (with <u>r</u>) is optional:
nor<u>d</u>-est, nor<u>d</u>-ouest.
    <u>D</u> is silent in the following words in <u>-id</u>:
    cri~~d~~, mui~~d~~, ni~~d~~.
<u>NOTE</u>.In <u>Madrid</u> the pronunciation of <u>d</u> is optional.
Madri~~d~~, or Madri<u>d</u>.

Chapter XLV.
THE SOUND AND LETTER **K**, *k*

C-, -C-, -CC-, -CCH-, CH-, -CH-, -CK-, -QUE-, K-, -K-,
KH-, Q-, X-, -Q-. QU-, -QU-; -C, -C(S), -CH. -CH(S), -CK,
-CK(S), -K, -Q, -Q(S), -QUE, -QUE(S), -QUES, -C(in liaison)
-CT(in liaison), G(in liaison).

I.At the beginning or in the middle of a word the sound
<u>k</u> is written:
    1.<u>c</u>-, <u>-c</u>-, before <u>a</u>, <u>o</u>, <u>u</u>, or any consonant:
    académie, codifié, curé, clavecin, acné, acrobate,
    cravate, etc.
                        EXCEPTION:
                        <u>c=g</u> in the following word and
                        its derivatives:
                        second, *səgɔ̃*.
    2.<u>-cc</u>-:
    acclamer, baccalauréat, raccommoder, etc.
                        NOTE: <u>cc</u> before <u>e</u> or <u>i=ks</u>:
                        accent, accident, etc.
    3.<u>ch</u>-, <u>-ch</u>-.
    a.Before any consonant:
    achromatique, chloroforme, chrétien, Christ,
    chrysanthème, ichtyologie, etc.
    b.In most scientific or unusual words and their de-
    rivatives.The most common are:
    archaïque, archange, archéologue, archiépisco-
    pat, but archevêque with *ʃ*; Bacchus, catéchu-
    mène, but catéchisme with *ʃ*; Cham, chaos,
    choeur, chorus, écho, eucharistie, lichen, ma-
    chiavel, but machiavélique with *ʃ*; Michel-Ange,
    but Michel with *ʃ*; orchidée, psychologie.
                        Note 1.In the following word, <u>ch</u>
                        is pronounced either *ʃ* or <u>k</u>:
                        pachyderme.
                        Note 2.In common words except
                        those mentioned above, <u>ch=ʃ</u>:
                        acheter, chacun, chose, etc.
    4.-cch-:

ecchymose, saccharine.

5.-ck-, -cqu-, k-, -k-, kh-:
nickel, jockey, Mecklembourgeois, becquée, képi,
kilo, balkanique, khédive, etc.

6.q(+ua)-, -q(+u):In scientific or unusual words from
Latin.The most usual are:
adéquat, aquarelle, aquarium, équateur, équation,
in-quarto, obséquieux, quadrangulaire, quadruple,
quartette, quatuor, quaternaire, quiet, quintuple,
square.

7.qu-, -qu-.In all the common words not mention in 6:
marquis, qualité, quantité, quatre, qui, quiconque,
etc.

8.-que-:
manquement.

9.x-.In the two following words:
Xérès, *keres*; Ximénès, *kimenes*.

II.At the end of a word the sound k is written:
-c, -ch, -ck, -cq, -cque, -k, -q, -que, -ques:
avec, Forbach, Melchisédech, Roch, bock, Ourcq,
La Mecque, Danemark, coq, casque, tu critiques,
etc.

SILENT K:
The letter c, usually sounded k, is silent in the
following words:
accroc, ajonc, banc, blanc, broc, caoutchouc,
clerc, cric, but alambic, chic, etc; croc,
escroc, estomac, flanc, franc, jonc, il vainc,
lacs (net) but lac(s) (Eng. lake), hamac, sac,
etc; marc (grounds of coffee)but Marc (proper
name); porc (meat) but porc (living animal);
Saint-Brieuc, tabac, tronc.

Note 1.In the following expressions only, the letter c is
sounded in liaison, and is pronounced k:
franc-alleu, franc-archer,
franc-étrier.
In other words in which final c
is silent, liaison never takes
place.
Note 2.In the following expression only, ct is sounded in
liaison, and is pronounced k:
respect humain.
In other words in which final ct
is silent, liaison never takes
place.
Note 3.In the following expres-

sions only, g is sounded in
liaison and is pronounced k:
sang impur, suer sang et eau.

Chapter XLVI.
THE SOUND AND LETTER G , *g*

-C-, G-, -G-, GH-, -GH-, GU-, -GU-, -GUE-; -C(S), -G(S),
-GUE, -GUE(S), -GUES.

I.At the beginning or in the middle of a word the sound
g is written:
  1.-c-.In the following word and its derivatives:
  second,
  2.g-, -g-.
  a.Before a, o, u, l, m, or r:
    garçon, glace, gorille, gangrène, grande, gymna-
    se, gutturale, flegme, bigote, Victor-Hugo, etc.
                    NOTE: gn=g+n: that is to say,
                    two consonant sounds, in scien-
                    tific or unusual words. The
                    most common are:
                      agnat, agnus, diagnostic, gnome,
                      inexpugnable, magnétisme, magni-
                      ficat, magnolia, recognition,
                      stagnant, Wagner.
                    In all other common words with gn,
                    g melts with n to make a single
                    sound, ɲ:
                      magnifique, répugnant, signer,
                      etc.
        SILENT G
        The letter g is silent:
        1.In words compounded with long before a consonant:
          Longchamp, longtemps, etc.
        2.In the following words:
          amygdale, doigt, Magdeleine, sangsue, vingt.
      b.Before e in a few words of German or Scandinavian
      origin:
      Bergen, Gessler, Hegel, etc.
    3.gh-, -ghi-:
    ghetto, Enghien.
    4.gu-, -gu-.Before any vowel:
    guêpe, guide, vigueur, etc.
                    Note 1.gu=two sounds: *g+y*:
                    In the following common words and
                    their derivatives:
                      aiguille, aiguiser, ambiguité,

arguer, inextinguible,
linguiste.
Note 2.gu=two sounds: $g+w$:
In the following words and their
derivatives:
Guadalquivir, Guadeloupe,
jaguar, lingual, Nicaragua,
Paraguay.

5.-gue-:
vaguement.

II.At the end of a word the sound g is written:
-g, -gue, -gues:
Dantzig, zigzag, bague, Copenhague, tu distingues,
etc.

SILENT G
The letter g is silent after a nasal vowel or in
words ending in -berg and -bourg:
Bourg, Cherbourg, coing, Estaing, faubourg,
gong, Gutemberg, hareng, long, Luxembourg,
Meung, Nuremberg, poing, rang, sang, seing,
Strasbourg, Wurtemberg, etc.

Note 1.In the following words
the pronunciation of g is optional:
joug or joug; iceberg or iceberg
Note 2.c=g or k in the following
word:
zinc, $z\tilde{\varepsilon}{:}k$ or $z\tilde{\varepsilon}{:}g$.
Note 3.In legs s is silent and
the pronunciation of g is optional:
$l\varepsilon$ or $l\varepsilon g$.
Note 4.In the following expressions only, g is pronounced in
liaison and is sounded k:
suer sang et eau, sang impur.

Chapter XLVII.
THE SOUND AND LETTER F, f

F-, -F-, -FF-, -FFE-, PH-, -PH-; -F, -F(S), -FE, -FE(S),
-FES, -FF-, -FFE, -FFE(S), -FFES, -PHE, -PHE(S), -PHES.

I.At the beginning or in the middle of a word the sound
f is written:
f-, -f-, -ff-, -ffe-, ph-, -ph-:
faire, infidèle, offense, attiffement, étouffement,
philosophe, morphine, etc.

II.At the end of a word the sound f is written:
 -f, -fe, -fes, -ff, -ffe, -ffes, -phe, -phes:
  infinitif, girafe, tu agrafes, Falstaff, je griffe,
  étoffe, tu chauffes, philosophe, tu triomphes, etc.
   SILENT F
   The letter f is silent in the following words:
   boeufs but boeuf; cerf, cerf-volant, chef-
   d'oeuvre but chef, chef-lieu; clef, nerf but
   in the following expression f is pronounced:
   avoir du nerf; oeufs but oeuf.

Chapter XLVIII.
THE SOUND AND LETTER V, v

V-, -V-, -VE-; W-, -VE, -VE(S), -VES, -F(in liaison).

 I.At the beginning or in the middle of a word the sound
v is written:
  1.v-, -v-, -ve-:
  vendredi, avant, avenir, etc.
  2.w-, -w-.In words of German, Flemish or English origin, and their derivatives:
  Wagner, Wagram, Weimar, Wissembourg, Wurtem-
  bourgeois, Brunswick, Wallon, Waterloo, Watteau,
  wagon, wallace, warrant.
                    EXCEPTIONS (w):
                    tramway, $tramw\varepsilon$, whist, $wist$.
 II.At the end of a word the sound v is written:
  -ve, -ves:
  cave, tu laves, etc.
                    NOTE: In liaison in the two fol-
                    lowing expressions only, f=v:
                    neuf ans, $n\alpha v\tilde{a}$, neuf heures,
                    $n\alpha v\alpha:r$.

Chapter XLIX.
THE SOUND AND LETTER S, s

C-, -C-, ç-, -ç-, -C-, -CE-, S-, -S-, SC-, -SC-, -SS-,
-SSE-, -T(I)-, -X-; -CE, -CE(S), -CES, -S, -SCE, -SCE(S),
-SCES, -SSE, -SSE(S), -SSES, -Z, -TZ.

 I.At the beginning or in the middle of a word the sound
s is written:
  1.c-, -c-.Before e, i, oe:
  cette, ciel, coecum, acide. monceau, ici, etc.
  2.ç-, -ç-.Before a, o, u:

aperçu, ça, garçon, etc.
3.-ce-:
lancement.
4.s-:
sage, scrupule, sucrer, etc.
5.-s-:
a.Before or after a consonant:
absent, absolu, destrier, verser, Montespan
Nestor, de Maistre, etc.

> EXCEPTIONS.s z, in the following
> words:
> Alsace, Arsace, balsamine,
> subside.

SILENT S:
The letter s is silent in the following words:
Aigne, A$nières, Avegnes, Cosme, Delisle,
Desbordes, Descartes, Despréaux, Duchesne,
Duquesne, Fismes, Isle-Adam, Leconte de Lisle,
Nesles, Presles, Prévost, Suresnes, Vismes,
desquels, -elles; lesquels, -elles; Vosges.

b.Preceded by a nasal vowel and followed by any vowel
or semi-vowel:
bonsoir, consul, tension, transi, etc.

> EXCEPTIONS.s z in words derived
> from transi:
> transit, intransigeant, etc.
> However, in the following words
> s=s:
> transept, transi, Transylvanie.

c.Between two ordinary vowels in many scientific or
unusual words, and their derivatives. The most common
of these words are:
antisémite, antiseptique, antiseptie, anti-
social, aseptie, aseptique, asymétrie, cosinus,
désuet, dysenterie, entresol, Lesage, Lesueur,
monosyllabe, parasol, présalé, préséance, pré-
supposer, primesautier, resalir, resaluer, re-
sécher, résection, resonger, soubresaut, tourne-
sol, vivisection, vraisemblable, etc.
6.sc-, -sc-, -sce-, -ss-, -sse-:
science, sceptique, disciple, acquiescement,
dessert, assez, bassement, etc.
7.-t(+1)-:
See t(+1)-, pp. 187, 188, 189.
8.-x-:In the following words only:
Auxerre, Bruxelles, Saulxure, Xaintonge, written
also Saintonge.
II.At the end of a word the sound s is written:

1. -ce, -ces, -sce, -sces, -ss, -sse, -sses, -x:
   Alice, face, tu divorces, acquiesce, tu t'immisces,
   express, basse, tu lasses, dix, etc.
2. -s. In the following common words classified according
   to termination:
   a. -aëns. In the following word only:
   Saint-Saëns.
   b. -as:
   alcarazas, as, Barabbas, Carabas, Cujas, Damas,
   d'Assas, Jonas, Mathias, Ménélas, Midas, pan-
   créas, Stanislas, vasistas.
   c. -ès:
   Agnès, aloès, cacatoès, Cérès, Damoclès, ès,
   Méphistophélès, palmarès, pataquès, Périclès,
   Xérès.
   d. -is, -ïs:
   Adonis, bis (encore) but bis (color); cassis,
   Clovis, de profundis, fils (Eng. son and sons)
   but fils (wires); gratis, ibis, iris, jadis, lis
   but the pronunciation of s in fleur de lis is optional; maïs, Médicis, Memphis, métis, myosotis,
   oasis, orchis, Senlis, tennis, Thémis, tamaris,
   Tunis, vis (screw) but je vis; volubilis.
   e. -eims:
   Reims.
   f. -ens ($s\tilde{a}{:}s$) and ($\tilde{\varepsilon}{:}s$):
   cens, $s\tilde{a}{:}s$; contresens, $k\tilde{o}tr\partial s\tilde{a}{:}s$; non-sens,
   $n\tilde{o}s\tilde{a}{:}s$; Rubens, $ryb\tilde{\varepsilon}{:}s$; sens, $s\tilde{a}{:}s$.
   g. -os:
   albatros, albinos, Burgos, Calvados, Carlos,
   intra-muros, mérinos, os (singular) but os
   (plural); rhinocéros, $rinoseros$ or $rinoseros$,
   tétanos.

   > NOTE: In proper names derived
   > from the Greek, the letter s is
   > pronounced and o may be either
   > closed or open:
   > Argos, Eros, etc.

   h. -aps:
   laps, relaps.
   i. -eps:
   biceps, forceps, reps.
   j. -ars:
   Mars.
   k. -us:
   Agnus, Angélus, autobus, chorus, Crésus, eucalyptus, hiatus, lapsus, lotus, Marius, motus,
   omnibus, prospectus, sinus, syllabus, terminus,
   typhus, Vénus, virus.

> NOTE: In the following word, the letter s may be silent or may be sounded s or z:
>
> obus, *ɔby*, *ɔbys*, *ɔby:z*.

1.-ous:

tous (pronoun) but tous (adjective).

> NOTE: In the following word the pronunciation of s is optional:
>
> moeurs, *mœrs* or moeurs,
> *mœ:r*.

SILENT S

The letter s is silent:

a. When it is the mark of the plural:
cent histoires, ces allées, ces cuisines, ces enfants, ces fenêtres, des femmes, des filles, des hommes, des jardins, douze livres, huit pierres, les miens, les murs, les tables, les verres, les vitres, mes cahiers, mes crayons, ses amis, tes soeurs, vos frères, etc.

b. When it is the termination of a verb:
je bois, je dis, j'écris, j'entends, je fais, je hais, prendrais, je travaillais, nous faisons, nous parlions, tu romps, tu valus, vous faites, etc.

> NOTE: The letter s of the plural forms and of verb terminations may be pronounced in liaison under certain circumstances, then it is sounded z.

c. And in all the common words which are not included in special lists for sounded s:
ailleurs, alors, Angers, Anglais, brebis, chaos, corps, dans, fonds, fonts, gars, hors, Lourdes, nous, pays, pouls, procès, puits, Pyrénées, remords, suspens, tapis, temps, etc.

3.-z, -tz. In the following words:
Alvarez, batz, Coblentz, Cortez, Fez, Metz, quartz, ranz, ruolz, Suez, Velasquez.

> NOTE: In Saint-Jean-de-Luz, the letter z may be pronounced s or z:
>
> *lys* or *ly:z* .

Chapter L.
THE SOUND AND LETTER Z, *z*

-S-, -SE-, Z-, -Z-; -S, -SE, -SE(S), -SES, -Z, -ZE, -ZE(S),

-ZES; S(in liaison), X(in liaison).

I.At the beginning or in the middle of a word the sound
z is written:
   1.z-, -z-:
   zèle, azur, etc.
   2.-s-:
   a.Between two vowels:
   aisance, basé, liaison, etc.
> EXCEPTIONS s=s:
> 1.When the first vowel is a na-
> sal:
> nous dansons, panser, penser,
> etc.
> However, in the following words
> formed with trans-, and in their
> derivatives, s=z:
> transaction, transalpin, tran-
> satlantique, transiger, transit,
> transitaire, transitif, tran-
> sitoire.
> But in the four following words
> s=s:
> transept, transi, transir,
> Transylvanie.
> 2.In many scientific or unusual
> words, and their derivatives.The
> most common of these words are:
> antisémite, antiseptique, anti-
> septie, antisocial, aseptie,
> aseptique, asymétrie, cosinus,
> désuet, dysenterie, entresol,
> Lesage, Lesueur, monosyllabe,
> parasol, présalé, préséance,
> présupposer, primesautier,
> resalir, resaluer, resécher,
> résection, resonger, soubre-
> saut, tournesol, vivisection,
> vraisemblable, etc.
   b.Between a consonant and a vowel in the following
   words, and in their derivatives:
   Alsace, Arsace, balsamine, subside.
   3.-se-:
   embrasement.
   4.x-, -x-:In the following words and their derivatives:
   a.Xavier, deuxième, dixième, sixième, etc.
   b.In liaison:
   deux enfants, dix-huit, six hommes, etc.
II.At the end of the word the sound z is written:

1.-se, -ses, -ze, -zes:
Anglaise, tu jalouses, douze, tu gazes, etc.
2.-z:
Berlioz, fez, gaz, Rodez, etc.

Note 1.z=s in the following
words:
Alvarez, batz, Coblentz, Cortez,
Fez, Metz, quartz, ranz, ruolz,
Suez, Velasquez.
Note 2.In Saint-Jean-de-Luz the
letter z may be pronounced z or
s:
lys or *ly:z* .
Note 3.The letters s and x=z in
liaison:
deux enfants, deux ou trois,
dix élèves, dix héroines,
doux ami, etc.

SILENT Z
The letter z is silent in words ending in -ez except those just mentioned:
assez, chez, nez, vous parlez, etc.
and in the following word also:
riz.

Chapter LI.
THE SPELLING AND SOUND CH, ʃ

CH-, -CH-, -CHE-, SCH-, SH-; -CHE, -CHE(S), -CHES.

I.At the beginning or in the middle of a word, the sound
ʃ is written:
ch-, -ch-, -che-, sch-, sh-:
Michel but Michel-Ange with k; chacun, achat.
acheter, schéma, schampooing, trachée but trachéal,
trachéen, etc., with k; chic, choc, choir, chute,
etc.

Note 1.ch=k before any consonant:
chloroforme, chrétien, Christ,
chromatique, chrysanthème,
Chrysostome.
Note 2.ch=k in most scientific
or unusual words and their derivatives. The most common are:
archaïque, archange, archéo-
logue, archiépiscopat but arche-
vêque with ʃ ; Bacchus, catéchu-
mène but catéchisme with ʃ;

Cham, chaos, choeur, chorus,
écho, eucharistie, lichen,
machiavel but machiavélique
with $\int$; Michel-Ange but Michel
with $\int$; orchidée, psychologie.
Note 3.In the following word ch
is pronounced $\int$ or k:
pachyderme.

II.At the end of a word the sound $\int$ is written:
-ch, -che, -ches, -sch, -sh:
sandwich, Autriche, que tu saches, haschisch,
kirsh, etc.

NOTE:ch=k.In the following words:
aurochs, Mélchisédech, Moloch,
Munich, Saint-Roch, Zurich.

SILENT CH
The letters ch are silent in the following word:
almanach.

Chapter LII.
THE SOUND $\mathcal{Z}$

G-, -G-, GE-, -GE-, J-, -J-; -GE, -GE(S), -GES, -JE.

I.At the beginning or in the middle of a word the sound
$\mathcal{Z}$ is written:
g-, -g-, ge-, -ge-, -(g)g-, j-, -j-:
1.g-, -g-.Before e, i, y:
gendre, girafe, agiter, gynécée, dégingandé, etc.
2.ge-, -ge-.Before a, o, u or a consonant:
geai, geôle, geôlier, mangeons, gageure, engage-
ment, jugement, etc.
3.j-, -j-:
juge, majeure, etc.
4.-(g)g- (g$\mathcal{Z}$):
suggestion, $syg\mathcal{Z}estj\eth$, etc.
II.At the end of a word the sound $\mathcal{Z}$ is written:
-ge, -ges, -je:
loge, je siège, tu protèges, ai-je, etc.

Chapter LIII.
THE SOUND AND LETTER M , m

M-, -M-, -ME-, -MM-; -M, -M(S), -ME, -ME(S), -MES, -MME,
-MME(S), -MMES.

I.At the beginning or in the middle of a word the sound

m is written:

<u>m</u>-, -<u>m</u>-, -<u>m</u>e-, -<u>mm</u>-:
  mari, demoiselle, sixièmement, hommage, immense,
  etc.

> ### SILENT M
> The letter <u>m</u> is silent in the following words:
> automne but automnal; damner and its derivatives.

>> <u>Note 1</u>.Before <u>b</u> and <u>p</u>, <u>m</u> is
>> merely the mark of the nasaliza-
>> tion of the preceding vowel:
>> accompagner, camp, aplomb,
>> imbécile, etc.
>> <u>Note 2</u>.<u>mm</u> is pronounced as one
>> or a double consonant (p. 144)
>> and the preceding vowel is not
>> nasalized:
>> ho-mmage, i-mmense, etc.
>> EXCEPTIONS:However, in the fol-
>> lowing words, and their deriva-
>> tives, the first <u>m</u> nasalizes the
>> preceding vowel:
>> em-magasiner, *ãmagazine*; em-
>> mailloter, *ãmajote* ; em-man-
>> cher, *ãmãʃe* ; em-mener,
>> *ãmne* ; em-murer, *ãmyre* .
>> <u>NOTE</u>: In the following words,
>> and their derivatives, <u>i</u> may or
>> may not retain its nasal quality:
>> immangeable, *ɛ̃mãʒabl* or *imã-*
>> *ʒabl* ; immanquable, *ɛ̃mãkabl* or
>> *imãkabl* ; immesurable, *ɛ̃məzy-*
>> *rabl* or *iməsyrabl* .

II.At the end of a word the sound <u>m</u> is written:
  1.-<u>m</u>e, -<u>m</u>es, -<u>mm</u>e, -<u>mm</u>es:
  j'acclame, dame, tu réclames, comme, dilemme, tu
  nommes, etc.
  2.-<u>m</u>:
  album, Amsterdam, intérim, Jerusalem, muséum,
  Potsdam, Stockholm, Wagram, etc.

> ### SILENT M
> The letter <u>m</u> is silent in the following words, and
> their derivatives. It is merely the mark of the na-
> salization of the preceding vowel, and consequently
> is not sounded:
> Adam, dam, daim, dom, essaim, étaim, faim,
> nom, parfum, Riom.

Chapter LIV.
THE SOUND AND LETTER N, *n*

N-, -N-, -NE-, -NN-; -N, -N(S), -NE, -NE(S), -NES, -NNE, -NNE(S), -NNES.

I.At the beginning or in the middle of a word the sound n is written: n-, -n-, -ne-, -nn-:
  non, faner, crânement, donner, honnête, etc.

> Note 1.Before a consonant other than n, n is the mark of the nasalization of the preceding vowel, and consequently is not sounded:
> défunte, honte, mince, ondulation, tante, etc.
>
> Note 2.nn is sounded as one or a double consonant and the preceding vowel is not nasalized:
> do-n*n*er, paysa-n*n*e, etc.
>
> EXCEPTIONS: However in the following words and their derivatives, n, although placed before another n, is the mark of the nasalization of the preceding vowel, and the second n is sounded:
> en-nui, *ã-nчi;* en-noblir, *ã-no-bli:r;* etc.
>
> To these exceptions should be added the following words and their derivatives in which a single n, first nasalizes the preceding vowel, then sounds as an initial consonant, with the following vowel:
> enamourer, *ãnamure* ; enivrant, *ãnivrã* ; enorgueillir, *ãnorgœji:r* .
>
> Note 2.n placed after g is pronounced separately in scientific words, as well as in the following more common words and their derivatives:
> agnat, agnus, diagnostic, gnome, inexpugnable, magnificat, magnétisme, magnolia, recognition, stagnant, Wagner.

II.At the end of a word the sound n is written:

1.**-ne**, **-nes**, **-nn**, **-nne**, **-nnes**:
que je prenne, Seine, âne, tu mènes, djinn,
bonne, que tu donnes, etc.
2.**-n,**After a consonant:
Béarn, Tarn, etc.

SILENT N
The letter n placed after a vowel, is usually the
mark of nasalization of the preceding vowel and
consequently is not sounded:
examen, an, rien, quelqu'un, bon, etc.

EXCEPTIONS.In the following common words n is pronounced:
abdomen, albumen, amen, Beetho-
ven, cyclamen, eden, gluten,
hymen, lichen, Lohengrin, Men-
delssohn, pollen, Reischoffen,
specimen, clown,

Chapter LV.
THE SOUND AND SPELLING GN, *gn* or *ɲ*

GN-, -GN-, -GNE-; -GNE, -GNE(S), -GNES.

I.At the beginning or in the middle of a word the sound
ɲ is written:
gn-, -gn-, -gne-:
gnangnan, gnognote, agneau, Agnès, magnifique,
signification, ignorance, ignominie, incognito,
répugnant, éloignement, etc.

EXCEPTIONS:gn=two sounds, g+n, in
scientific or unusual words, of
which the most common are:
agnat, agnus, diagnostic, gnome,
inexpugnable, magnificat, magné-
tisme, magnolia, recognition,
stagnant, Wagner.

II.At the end of a word the sound *ɲ* is written:
-gne, -gnes:
signe, il daigne. tu peignes, etc.

Chapter LVI.
THE SOUND AND LETTER L. *l*

L-, -L-, -LE-, -LL-, -LLE-; -L(S), -LE, -LE(S), -LENT,
-LES, -LL, -ELLE, -ELLE(S), -ELLES, -LS.

I.At the beginning or in the middle of a word the sound

l is written:
   1.l-, -l-, -le-:
   là, talent, tabler, blond, parler, bêlement, etc.
    SILENT L
    The letter l is silent in the following words:
     Bel̸fort, cul̸ blanc and all other derivatives of
     cul̸; houl̸que, Ménil̸montant.
   2.-ll-:
   a.Preceded by any vowel except i:
   aller, ballon, belladone, bulletin, mollesse,
   etc.
   b.Preceded by i.In words derived from scientific or
   unusual words and from the following more common
   words:
    distille, distiller; Lille, Lillois, mille, mil-
    lionnaire; Millet; pupille, pupillaire; tran-
    quille, tranquillement; ville, village; etc.
              Note 1.ill=j:
              In all other common words:
               billard, cédiller, fillette,
               etc.
              Note 2.(i)ll=ll:
              In scientific or unusual words,
              and their derivatives, the two
              l's are pronounced double l
              (p. 144):
              illégal, illicite, illusion,
              désillusion, illustration, etc.
II.At the end of a word the sound l is written:
   -l, -le, -les, -ll, -lle, -lles:
   Brésil, cil, fil, Nil, je file, seule, tu parles,
   (Guillaume) Tell, j'appelle, tu t'appelles, etc.
              NOTE: When preceded by i, l or
              ll combines with it, thus pro-
              ducing the sound of yod:
              bille, cédille, de Noailles,
              fille, je réveille, travail.
              However, in scientific or un-
              usual words as well as in the
              following words, -ille=i+l:
              distille, Lille, mille, Millet,
              pupille, tranquille, ville.
    SILENT L
    The letter l is silent in the following words:
    aul̸x (plural of ail); baril̸, chenil̸, courtil̸,
    coutil̸, douzil̸, faul̸x, fenil̸, fil̸s (son; sons);
    fournil̸, fusil̸, gentil̸ but gentille with yod,
     ʒɑ̃tij ; gentil̸shommes but gentilhomme with
    yod, ʒɑ̃tijom; gril̸; Héraul̸t and in all other

words with -au~~l~~t; La Rochefoucau~~ld~~ and in all
other words with -au~~l~~d; nombri~~l~~, outi~~l~~, persi~~l~~,
pou~~l~~s, Sainte-Menehou~~l~~d, saou~~l~~ or soû~~l~~, sou~~l~~,
sourci~~l~~ but ci<u>l</u>.

Chapter LVII.
THE SOUND AND LETTER R , *r*

R-, -R-, -RE-, RH-, -RH-, -RR-, -RRE-, -RRH-; -R, -R(S),
-RC(S), -RD, -RD(S), -RDS, -RE, -RE(S), -RENT, -RES,
-RF(S), -RG, -RG(S), -RPS, -RRE, -RRE(S), -RRENT, -RRES,
-RRHE(S), -RS, -RT, -RT(S).

I.At the beginning or in the middle of a word the sound
<u>r</u> is written:
<u>r</u>-, -<u>r</u>-, -<u>re</u>-, <u>rh</u>-, -<u>rh</u>-, -<u>rr</u>-, -<u>rre</u>-, -<u>rrh</u>-:
rare, arabe, perte, rhubarbe, rarement, enrhumé,
terrain, errement, catharrhal, etc.

II.At the end of a word the sound <u>r</u> is written:
1.-<u>rd</u>, -<u>rds</u>, -<u>re</u>, -<u>res</u>, -<u>rg</u>, -<u>rps</u>, -<u>rre</u>, -<u>rres</u>, -<u>rrhe</u>,
-<u>rs</u>, -<u>rt</u>.
il perd, d'abord, tu perds, j'admire, cigare,
pauvre, tu admires, bourg, Cherbourg, corps,
beurre, j'abhorre, tu te terres, catharrhe, ailleurs, alors, tu cours, Albert, il sort, expert,
etc.

SILENT R
The letters <u>rs</u> are silent in the following words:
Ange~~rs~~, Coulommie~~rs~~, Poitie~~rs~~, Louvie~~rs~~, vo-
lontie~~rs~~, Messieu~~rs~~, *mesjø* ; but sieur~~s~~, *sjœːr*

2.-<u>r</u>:
ai<u>r</u>, Arthu<u>r</u>, Césa<u>r</u>, dormi<u>r</u>, marty<u>r</u>, mento<u>r</u>, ame<u>r</u>,
me<u>r</u>, sieu<u>r</u> but Monsieu~~r~~, *məsjø* ; soeu<u>r</u>, etc.

SILENT R
The letter <u>r</u>, when preceded by <u>e</u> without written accent, is usually silent:
aime~~r~~, bouche~~r~~, Alge~~r~~, Gerardme~~r~~, épicie~~r~~,
boulange~~r~~, pommie~~r~~, etc.

> EXCEPTIONS: However, the letter
> <u>r</u> is pronounced in the following
> common words:
> ame<u>r</u>, cance<u>r</u>, enfe<u>r</u>, éthe<u>r</u>, fe<u>r</u>,
> fie<u>r</u> (adjective) but fie~~r~~ (verb)
> hie<u>r</u>, hive<u>r</u>, me<u>r</u>, revolve<u>r</u>, te<u>r</u>,
> ve<u>r</u>.

3.-<u>rc</u>:
cler~~c~~, mar~~c~~ (coffee grounds) but Marc; por~~c~~ (meat)
but por<u>c</u> (living animal)

4.-**rf**.In the following words:
cerf but serf; cerf-volant, nerf.

> NOTE: In the following expres-
> sion, **f** is pronounced:
> avoir du nerf.

Chapter LVIII.
A FEW COMMON WORDS OFTEN MISPRONOUNCED

	Incorrect Pronunciation	Correct Pronunciation
Alexandre	alɛgzã:dr	alɛksã:dr
appartement	apartmã	apartəmã
appeler	apele, apɛle	aple
auxiliaire	ogziljɛ:r	oksiljɛ:r
besoin	bezwɛ̃	bəzwɛ̃
capitaine	kaptɛn	kapitɛn
déjeuner	deʒne	deʒœne
développe	develop	devlop
élever	elɛve	elve
ennui	ãɥi	ãnɥi
ennuyeux	ãɥijø	ãnɥijø
enveloppe	ãvelop	ãvlop
Eugène	jyʒɛn	øʒɛn
Eugénie	jyʒeni	øʒeni
genre	ʒã:dr	ʒã:r
inutile	ɛ̃ytil, ɛ̃nytil	inytil
justement	ʒystmã	ʒystəmã
leçon	lɛsɔ̃	ləsɔ̃
magasin	magzɛ̃	magazɛ̃
magnifique	magnifik	maɲifik
ordinaire	ordnɛ:r	ordinɛ:r
réchauffer	rəʃoʃe	rəʃoʃe
Victor-Hugo	viktor hygo	victorygo
vingt-et-unième	vɛ̃teœ̃njɛm	vɛ̃teyɲjɛm
voyage	voadʒ	vwajá:ʒ

INDEX OF SPELLINGS

With the exception of regular forms for the plural of nouns, pronouns, and adjectives, and for the third person plural of verbs, this index contains the different spellings of the sounds discussed in Part III.

INDEX OF WORDS USED AS EXAMPLES

In this index will be found the words given as examples
to illustrate rules or explanations. The definitive edition will include in addition, all those used in the reading lessons as well as the phonetic transcription of every
word.

datte, 162
de, 119, 120, 121, 123, 125,
   127
débarras, 161
debout, 120, 127
début, 189
décagone, 164, 166
de ce, 125
décembre, 176
déclame (elle), 159, 161
dedans, 120
défunte, 181, 203
dégingandé, 201
dehors, 145, 146
déjeune, 171
de le, 125
délicat, 161, 189
délicatesse, 85
Delisle, 196
demande, 125
demande (il ne), 121
dame, 125
démêler, 143
demoiselle, 202
démontre, 87
de ne, 125
dent, 189
de profundis, 177, 197
dépens, 175
depuis, 120, 126, 173
dérape, (il), 159
dernier, 128, 129
dérobe (je), 186
dérobes (tu), 186
des, 15, 128, 130, 168, 198
désaxe, 122
Desbordes, 196
Descartes, 196
descendre, 169
de se, 124, 125
désillusion, 205
désosse, 164, 166
désossement, 165
Despréaux, 196
desquels, -elles, 196
dessein, 179
dessert, 196
dessiner, 169
dessous, 172

dessus, 174
destrier, 196
désuet, 196, 199
détail, 161, 183, 184
détester, 143
Deutéronome, 171
deux, 2, 132, 150, 200
deux à deux, 131
deux cents, 128, 154
   deux cent un, 154
   deux cent deux, 154
   deux cent trois, 154
deuxième, 146, 171, 199
deux ou trois, 131
devant, 119, 129
développer, 86
développes (tu), 186
devers, 121
devin, 125
devis, 173
dévotion, 165
dévouement, 172
dextrier, 147
diable, 122, 159, 161
diagnostic, 193, 203, 204
Diane, 162
diapason, 160
Didon, 178
Dieppe, 186
différentie (elle), 188
différentier, 188
difficile, 14
dilemme, 177, 202
direct, 170, 189
dis (je), 173, 198
disciple, 196
discipline, 14, 174
discipliner
disent (ils), 117
dis-le, 126
dispos, 163
distille, 184, 205
distiller, 145, 205
distinct, 179, 189
distinction, 179
distingues (tu), 194
district, 189
dît (qu'il), 173
divers, 136

instiller, 185
instinct, 179, 189
instinctivement, 179
intact, 189
intelligence, 145
intelligemment, 163, 177
intérim, 180, 202
intra-muros, 163, 197
intransigeant, 196
introït, 173, 189
inutile, 40, 180
iras (tu), 161
iris, 197
Isaac, 159
Isabelle, 87
Isaïe, 173, 184
islam, 175
Isle-Adam, 196
Ismaël, 170
isthme, 187

Jacob, 160, 186
Jacques, 159
jadis, 197
jaguar, 182
jalouses (tu), 200
jamais, 135
Japhet, 189
jappement, 186
jardin, 198
Jason, 160
je, 119, 123, 126
Jean, 137, 174
Jeanne, 163
je le, 124
je me, 124
je ne, 124, 125
Jérusalem, 177, 202
Jésus-Christ, 173, 189
je te, 123, 125, 125, 126
je te le, 126
tiens (je), 142
jeudi, 171
jeûn (à), 180
jeune, 170, 171
jeûne (fasting), 170
Joachim, 180
joaillier, 183
jockey, 192

joie, 159, 161
jolie, 145
Jonas, 197
jonc, 178, 192
Josaphat, 189
joue (je), 172
jouer, 134, 155
joues (tu), 172
jouet, 132, 169, 189
joug, 194
jouons (nous), 134
journalisme, 142
Judas, 158
judaïsme, 142
juge, 3, 201
jugeaient (ils), 85
jugement, 201
juin, 183

képi, 192
khédive, 192
kilo, 192
kirsch, 201

la (music), 158, 160
la, 14, 22, 205
labyrinthe, 189
lace (elle), 159, 161
lacs, 158, 192
laid, 168, 190
laide, 170
lait, 2, 53
lampe, 175
lancement, 196
Laon, 167, 175
Laonnois, 167
laps, 186, 197
lapsus, 197
La Rochefoucauld, 163, 190,
    206
larynx, 147, 180
las, 158
lasse, 149, 162
lasses (tu), 197
Laure, 164, 166
Laurence, 165
laves (tu), 195
le, 2, 14, 32, 119, 120,
    121, 123, 125, 126, 144

INDEX OF SUBJECTS TREATED

Distributed by

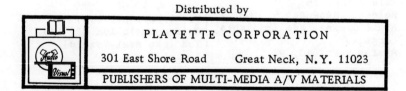

PLAYETTE CORPORATION

301 East Shore Road   Great Neck, N.Y. 11023

PUBLISHERS OF MULTI-MEDIA A/V MATERIALS